Advance Praise for L[...]

"In *Leading Men* Jackson Katz draws from an[d ...] [...] work about *women* and the presidency, but his goal is to push presidential studies toward a more explicit engagement with feminist ideas about *men* and the presidency. Katz's book manages to be both intellectually exhilarating and highly accessible even as it greatly advances our understanding of presidential politics. It should be widely read by students, scholars, pundits, and political junkies."
—Dr. Caroline Heldman, Chair, Department of Politics, Occidental College, coeditor of *Rethinking Madam President: Are We Ready for a Woman in the White House?*

"For years, scholar and activist Jackson Katz has been providing crucial insights into the relationship between cultural representations of manhood and the actual social and economic circumstances of men's lives. In *Leading Men*, Katz brings his formidable critical skills to bear on modern American politics and the US presidency, offering a fresh and fascinating new take on men's voting patterns and the cultural politics of manhood. Whether he's looking at how candidates go to extremes to position themselves as tough on crime and strong on defense, or at how Republican political operatives have mastered the art of winning white working-class men's votes by attacking the masculinity of their Democratic opponents, Katz makes a powerful case that presidential elections in the modern era have been fundamentally shaped by competing visions of American manhood. This is first-rate social and political commentary, a valuable resource for political activists, political junkies, and armchair pundits alike."
—Sut Jhally, PhD, Professor of Communication, UMass-Amherst, Founder-Director, Media Education Foundation

Praise for The Macho Paradox

"This profound and vitally important book illuminates the roots of men's violence against women and makes it clear that men must get involved in stopping it... Jackson Katz is a true revolutionary and a national treasure."
—Jean Kilbourne, author of *Can't Buy My Love: How Advertising Changes the Way We Think and Feel*

"Men need to read this book. Not only because it will make the world safer for women, but because it will free men to be their true selves."
—Eve Ensler, author of the *Vagina Monologues*

"Jackson Katz is one of the most important voices of our generation."
—Rosalind Wiseman, author of *Queen Bees and Wannabes*

"Jackson Katz is an American hero! With integrity and courage, he has taken his message—that the epidemic of violence against women is a men's issue—into athletic tarms, the military, and frat houses across the country. His book explains carefully and convincingly why—and how—men can become part of the solution and work with women to build a world in which everyone is safer."
—Michael Kimmel, author of *Manhood in America*, spokesperson, National Organization for Men Against Sexism (NOMAS)

"If only men would read Katz's book, it could serve as a potent form of male consciousness-raising."
—*Publishers Weekly*

"This book leaves no man behind when it comes to taking violence against women personally... After reading this book you can see how important it is to be a stand-up guy and not a standby guy, no matter what race or culture you come from."
—Alfred L. McMichael, 14th Sergeant Major of the Marine Corps

"A candid look at the cultural factors that lend themselves to tolerance of abuse and violence against women."
—*Booklist*

"These pages will empower both men and women to end the scourge of male violence and abuse. Katz knows how to cut to the core of the issues, demonstrating undeniably that stopping the degradation of women should be every man's priority."
—Lundy Bancroft, author of *Why Does He Do That?: Inside the Minds of Angry and Controlling Men*

LEADING MEN

PRESIDENTIAL CAMPAIGNS ☆ AND THE ☆ POLITICS OF MANHOOD

JACKSON KATZ

Interlink Books

An imprint of Interlink Publishing Group, Inc.
Northampton, Massachusetts

First published in 2013 by

INTERLINK BOOKS
An imprint of Interlink Publishing Group, Inc.
46 Crosby Street, Northampton, Massachusetts 01060
www.interlinkbooks.com

Library of Congress Cataloging-in-Publication Data available
ISBN 978-1-56656-903-3 (pbk)

Printed and bound in the United States of America

To request our catalog, please call us toll free at 1-800-238-LINK, visit our website
at www.interlinkbooks.com, or write to
Interlink Publishing
46 Crosby Street, Northampton, MA 01060
e-mail: info@interlinkbooks.com

Table of Contents

Acknowledgments

I come from a family of poor immigrants who set out for this country over a century ago seeking a better life for themselves and their progeny. I want especially to acknowledge the sacrifices of my late grandparents Esther and Willy Tambor, and Aaron and Esther Katz, who had precious little formal schooling, but who believed in education as a path to a better life for their children and grandchildren. I am forever indebted to them for the opportunities their struggles provided me.

This book has its roots in an illustrated slide lecture I produced in 1992 entitled "Fighter Pilots and Draft Dodgers: images of presidential masculinity, 1972–1992." I want to thank everyone who contributed to that project over the years and who gave me the opportunity to test my ideas in front of audiences that ranged from friends in the living rooms of various apartments to college and high school faculties and students, to activists in grassroots community groups and women's organizations.

Special thanks to colleagues and friends at the UCLA Graduate School of Education and Information Studies, especially Doug Kellner for his brilliant scholarship, mentorship, and flexibility in allowing me the latitude to pursue my vision; Rhonda Hammer, for her encouragement and advice; and Jeff Share, who guided me through.

I am indebted to several friends and colleagues who read and rendered critical judgment and feedback on either a specific section or the entire manuscript. In the former category I want to thank Leah Aldridge, Paul Basken, Tom Gardner, and Byron Hurt. In the latter, special shout-outs to Caroline Heldman for her cutting-edge scholarship in political science and general feminist fearlessness, and Jeremy Earp, my close friend and longstanding collaborator, who along with all of his other unquantifiable contributions to my thinking and work also provided a clever assist with the title.

A special place in my heart, and in these acknowledgments, goes to my old friend Mark Mlawer, who went way beyond the call of duty and provided not only deeply insightful suggestions that helped strengthen my arguments but also first-rate editing at every stage of the process.

Although the finished product is significantly better because of their efforts than anything I could have accomplished alone, I would be remiss if I did not succumb to convention and accept all responsibility for the contents. Whether you have a minor quibble with anything I've written or are massively offended, please take it up with me—or better yet, take a long walk.

I want to thank my publisher Michel Moushabeck for embracing the manuscript with open arms and seeing it through to publication, and my editor John Fiscella, whose insightful and judicious editing measurably improved the final product. Many thanks to Robin Kurka for expertly organizing and typing the endnotes and references, as well as for regularly taking on and executing many other crucial tasks.

Over the course of writing this book I've gotten by with a little (and a lot) of help from my friends. I want especially to thank Miriam Zoll, Michael Shashoua, Gail Dines, David Levy, Rob Okun, Adi Bemak, Daryl Fort, John Badalament, Sut Jhally, Sandy Holstein, Jeff O'Brien, Zeus Leonardo, Brian Lampman, and my nephew Dan Miller for their friendship, support, political conversation and camaraderie.

I am grateful to members of my family who have encouraged this project along the way, especially my mother, Frieda Miller, my mother-in-law Jan Bue, and my son Judah, whose love inspires me and whose political insights continually amuse and amaze me. Finally, I'd like to express my gratitude and love for my wife Shelley Eriksen, who has provided the foundation for my work, has long supported my life's mission, and has been a crucial sounding board for my ideas at various stages of this project.

Introduction

For a brief moment during the 2008 presidential campaign, conservative strategists were dumbfounded. They couldn't figure out how to criticize candidate Barack Obama. They worried that if they attacked the first African American presidential nominee from a major party, they would open themselves up to accusations of racism. Conservative columnists and pundits wondered aloud about the propriety of challenging Obama's background, his affiliations, his credentials. As Rush Limbaugh put it, "You can't criticize the little black man-child. You just can't do it, 'cause it's just not right. It's not fair. He's such a victim."[1]

The conservatives soon found a way out of their dilemma. Mindful of their need to secure a large majority of white male voters in order to win—and led once again by the shock troops of right-wing talk radio—conservative Republicans settled on the same strategy they had employed so successfully in presidential elections for nearly forty years: they attacked the Democratic candidate's manhood. They ridiculed Obama. They called him a lightweight and a wimp. They warned that electing him would weaken America. Limbaugh summed up the line of attack on the senator from Illinois: "He can't take a punch, he's weak, and he whines," he said. "I'm sure some women find that attractive because they would look at him as a little boy and would want to protect him…But it embarrasses me as a man."[2]

The Right has long taken for granted what the Left has only recently begun to figure out: that presidential politics are the site of an ongoing cultural struggle over the meaning of American manhood. As the center stage of that debate, presidential campaigns function as symbolic contests over competing definitions of "real manhood," and thus over what kind of man can, and should, be in charge. This is not exactly a new debate; from the time of the

Founding Fathers, Americans have been arguing about the manly qualities necessary in the man who would lead the nation. But since the early 1970s, when Richard Nixon figured out how to get working-class white men to vote for the party of the rich by appealing not to their economic interests but to their cultural values, contests for the presidency have arguably been about the interlocking and contentious forces of racial, gender, and national identity as much as anything else. And like no other single person, the man—or one day the woman—who occupies the office of President of the United States literally embodies those forces, and the struggles around them.

The president wields enormous material *and* symbolic power—including the power, in a sense, to personify not only "America," but American manhood. As a result, how the president is regarded *as a man* has a lot to do with his political success or failure—especially when politics is dominated by a media culture that emphasizes storytelling and personal narratives to make sense of the workings of larger economic and political forces, and which is governed by the values of entertainment. This does not mean that image is everything and issues don't matter. Voters make judgments about a (male) candidate's manhood based on both his personal attributes *and* his positions on certain key issues. For example, if he comes down on the "right" side of an issue, he's considered more masculine: "tough on crime," "tough on immigration," "strong on national security." If he comes down on the "left" side, he's likely to face criticism that his position represents personal weakness: he's "soft on crime," "weak-kneed on immigration," "naïve on matters of national security." There is little room in all of this for the nuances of either personality or policy.

Style and public presentation do matter; Ronald Reagan's chief strategist Richard Wirthlin acknowledged that Reagan's political success had something to do with how Reagan walked and talked, how he "came across as a man."[3] But Reagan's popularity with white men wasn't just about surface impressions; it had to do with the perception that he was a man of principle. Wirthlin observed, "…in a world so full of ambiguities…having a leader who is able to articulate clearly and strongly, right and wrong, in direct terms, I think would garner extra support (among men). I don't think a strong leader paints in pastel colors." The social conservative Gary Bauer, who worked in Reagan's White House, opined that moral clarity resonates with "Joe Six-Pack" because it represents a kind of manliness. "A man takes a stand, toes the line, doesn't budge even if it gets hot or tough, and it is seen by some of those kinds of voters who may not always be comfortable with politics and moral issues. It is something they can identify with, in contrast to a more feminist or more feminine approach."[4] George W. Bush's media consultant Mark McKinnon summed up what Republican strategists have banked on since the Reagan years: "In presidential elections people don't vote on issues, they vote on attributes, and the single most important one is strong leadership."[5]

Strong leadership, in turn, has a particularly gendered meaning. When applied to the US presidency it is nearly synonymous with the personal qualities associated with dominant masculinity. In other words, voting for strong leadership means voting for a strong man. Right-wing political operatives understand this implicitly. Among the many advantages this insight confers is that voters—especially white men—make visceral assessments about candidates *as men* before deciding whether or not to support them for president. In fact, "independent" voters who claim to be less motivated by partisanship or ideology might be even more susceptible to this gendered logic, because people who say things like "I vote the person, not the party" are more likely to make electoral choices based on perceptions of personal characteristics rather than political programs. This has given conservatives an enormous advantage in elections over the past forty years, because GOP campaign strategists are masters at presenting their (male) candidates as bold, decisive leaders—and painting their opponents as vacillating poseurs. They know that presidential elections in the age of media spectacle are won and lost largely in the realm of myth, symbolism, and identity, where *feelings* about a candidate's intangible qualities of character, stature, and gravitas carry much greater weight than *facts* about where they stand on issues or whose economic interests they actually represent. Elizabeth Wilner in 2004 put it this way in the *Washington Post*: "Republicans today understand that presidential races are about character and personality, whereas the Democrats' instinct is to try and beat their opponent into submission with sheaves of policy papers."[6] As Andy Stern, former head of the Service Employees International Union, said, "Democrats somehow think that presidential elections are like *College Bowl* or *Jeopardy*. We nominate the person who gets all the answers right. And Republicans understand it's *American Idol*."[7] A less charitable way to put this is to say that

INTRODUCTION

presidential elections are a slightly more sophisticated version of the classic high school stand-off between adolescent males: jocks versus nerds.

In this book I introduce a new way to think about what voters are voting for—or against—every four years when they cast their ballots. It's the masculinity, stupid. Each election cycle, voters are asked to choose not only which policies they favor or which direction they want to see the country headed, but what kind of man they want to see speaking to the nation on television from the Oval Office—and leading the nation as commander in chief of its armed forces. Presidential elections are obviously struggles over issues, like the size and role of the federal government in the management of the economy and national security. But when examined closely through the lens of gender, presidential elections can also be seen as quadrennial competitions not only between divergent political ideologies, but between two (or three) distinct versions of masculinity. Every four years, voters are literally participating in a kind of referendum on the meaning of American manhood.

Like almost everything else in American politics, this contest of meanings has a racial dimension. Since 1980, the Republican Party has regularly received less than 10 percent of the African American vote in presidential elections. There is a very slight gender gap in African Americans' voting patterns; nonetheless only about one in ten African American men support Republican presidential candidates. This dramatic statistic suggests the idea—which the main argument in this book reinforces—that it is not "masculinity" which candidate image handlers were packaging and selling until the 2008 elections, but distinctive versions of *white* masculinity. If not, one would expect men of color to respond in a similar fashion as white men to candidates who perform the type of presidential masculinity that emphasizes "regular guy" qualities, such as knowledge of and interest in blue-collar sports, ease of rapport with the uniformed military, and the willingness to take on our adversaries, as well as to support candidates who will get "tough" on crime, make the "hard" choices on budgetary priorities, etc. But they do not, because for the majority of men of color—not only African American men but other men of color as well—issues of racial identity and solidarity seem to trump issues of "masculinity" when it comes to voting preferences. The implication for the study of presidential masculinity is clear: the entire enterprise needs to incorporate a racialized understanding of gender, not to mention a gendered understanding of race. Political communication researchers, journalists, and others need to look closely at the complexities of multicultural masculinities, especially as they relate to presidential manhood. In other words, it is not enough simply to say that "men" since the late 1960s have favored more conservative candidates; one must say *white men*, and offer explanations at the intersections of race and gender (and sexual orientation). The election in 2008 of Barack Obama adds another fascinating layer to this area of inquiry: both how he was able to navigate successfully the complex terrain of race and gender—especially against a white male "war hero"—and how his performance as a black man in the office of president is creating a new archetype of presidential masculinity.

During the 2008 Democratic primary season, many critics bemoaned the infusion of identity politics into the presidential race, as if the presence of an African American man and a (white) woman introduced "race and gender" into a heretofore untainted process. What was left largely unsaid is that race and gender have *always* been critical factors in presidential politics, with one crucial qualification: the *race* was always white, and the *gender* was always men. Until 2008, presidential races had always been in part about white masculinity. A major historical barrier was broken that year, when instead of two versions of white masculinity vying for cultural ascendance, the contest featured one version of white masculinity (Republican John McCain) versus one version of black masculinity (Democrat Barack Obama). But it was still a race between men. Barack Obama was not only the first African American *person* to run as the nominee from a major party; he was the first African American *man*. Even without Hillary Clinton on the ticket, gender was a critical factor in the general election of 2008—as in every previous election. Gender is a central factor even in races *between* men.

Unfortunately, few political commentators or theorists describe contemporary presidential elections in this way. Most don't even mention gender as a central factor—unless a woman is running. The "manhood question" remains hidden in plain sight. Take Drew Westen's work on the role of emotion in politics. Westen's book, *The Political Brain: The Role of Emotion in Deciding the Fate of the Nation*, garnered a considerable amount of attention from Democratic Party operatives and positive reviews in mainstream media during the 2008 election season. The book seeks to explain "how the mind works, how the brain works, and what this means for why candidates win and lose elections."[8] Using the latest research in cognitive neuroscience and psychology, Westen argues that three things determine how people vote: their feelings toward the parties and their principles, their feelings toward the candidates, and their feelings toward the candidates' policy positions. Westen's central thesis is that emotions and not rational judgments largely form the basis of people's political decision making, and that Democrats and progressives have failed utterly in recent decades to package their ideas in a way that resonates emotionally with a majority of voters—even those who generally agree with their policy positions. As Westen writes,

> Republicans have a keen eye for markets, and they have a near-monopoly in the marketplace of emotions. They have kept government off our backs, torn down that wall, saved the flag, left no child behind, protected life, kept our marriages sacred, restored integrity to the Oval Office, spread Democracy to the Middle East, and fought an unrelenting war on terror. The Democrats, in contrast, have continued to place their stock in the marketplace of ideas. And in so doing, they have been trading in the wrong futures.[9]

His argument that liberals and the Left need to develop a heightened awareness of the importance of emotional intelligence to political success in a media culture is a welcome shot across the bow to Democratic Party strategists who after all these years persist in thinking that campaigns are won by people and parties with "the best ideas," the best debating skills, or the most impressive grasp of the issues. How many presidential elections have Democrats lost with candidates whose erudition and knowledge about policy far exceeds that of their Republican counterparts? Westen's focus on emotions that are activated by certain political narratives is especially necessary in a political culture that is dominated by mass media coverage, in which the conventions of entertainment and spectacle profoundly influence what gets talked about on television—and how.

But Westen barely even discusses the gendered aspects of emotions, or the way cultural constructs of what is considered "masculine" or "feminine" help to structure how people respond to various messages. He recognizes gender as a politically organizing principle; he discusses issues of particular concern to women voters, and he goes so far as to say that from infancy, women are more attuned to the emotional signals around them than are men. But it is revealing that in a 420-page book, he barely mentions men *as men*, or offers even a hint that he understands that campaigns *between* men might have a gender component worth theorizing. Instead, he attributes to other factors in campaign events that are centrally about (white) masculinity. For example, in a discussion about Michael Dukakis's (in)famous answer to a question about the death penalty in a 1988 debate with George H. W. Bush, Westen maintained that Dukakis answered the wrong question. The moderator, Bernard Shaw, asked Dukakis if he would favor the death penalty if his wife were raped and murdered. Dukakis answered that he would not, as "there are better and more effective ways to deal with violent crime." Political pundits and academic observers widely believe that at that moment, Dukakis's chances for victory in November were finished. Westen explains that voters wanted to hear that he understood this was a "moral" question, and Dukakis's answer spoke in the language of rational utility. This is a perfectly reasonable, if partial, explanation.

A better explanation is that Shaw's question posed a challenge to Dukakis. The diminutive, cerebral governor was given a chance to prove his masculine bona fides with an expression of controlled violent anger, something that would signal to voters—especially white men—that in spite of his technocratic approach to political problems, at heart he was a fighter. ("Bernie, I would want to kill that man myself, but the question here is whether the death penalty is sound social policy. I don't believe it is a deterrent—and research confirms this. And what if we convicted the wrong guy?") Instead, Dukakis failed to rise to the occasion. It is altogether possible that Michael Dukakis recognized the racial subtext of the question, especially in a campaign where his opponent's chief strategist, Lee Atwater, had been shamelessly exploiting white fear of black men in racially coded appeals about crime and punishment. It might very well be that Dukakis is not the kind of man who would want to exact bloody revenge with his own hands. He might not even fantasize about such things, but would rather see justice served in the context of due process in the criminal justice system. This is honorable and perhaps even praiseworthy; he should be respected for refusing to compromise his core values for the sake of political expediency. But it is just as reasonable to suggest that as a result of his calm, unemotional presentation of a principled stance, millions of American voters—men and women—deemed him insufficiently "manly" to be entrusted with the presidency in a dangerous world, where the Soviet Union was still our archrival and bad men at home and abroad meant to do us harm, and where they desired a president who (they felt) would not hesitate to stand up, protect, and defend them. Dukakis's answer did not even show that same impulse with respect to his own wife! Dukakis didn't blow a seventeen-point lead and lose the election to George H. W. Bush because, as he later said, he allowed the Bush campaign to define him. He lost because millions of white men were convinced that he wasn't man enough for the job. The day after that CNN debate, Dukakis's favorability rating fell from 49 percent to 42 percent. Bush beat Dukakis among white men by 27 percentage points—the same percentage that Ronald Reagan beat Jimmy Carter by eight years earlier.

It can be quite deflating to think that with so much at stake, modern campaigns for the presidency mimic some of the characteristic features of the classic high school popularity contest, with all of the attendant name-calling and frenzied attention to superficial personality traits. In fact, one measure of the decline of our democracy in the age of media spectacle is that voters routinely tell pollsters that they vote for politicians "who understand people like me" rather than ones whose ideology and governing philosophy seem best to align with their material interests, like access to meaningful employment, health care, and quality education for their children. During the presidency of George W. Bush it became fashionable among liberals and progressives to decry the naiveté of voters who professed to support the candidate "I would most want to have a beer with."

It is easy to dismiss such sentiments, but those populist metrics actually speak to something deeper at work in American society. As television and other forms of mass media have come to dominate political discourse, and as entertainment values have triumphed over coverage focused on issues, voters have been asked to ratify the rule of political elites based less on rational assessments of their bread and butter interests and more on questions of cultural affinity and group identity. An entire cottage industry has arisen on the left that seeks to explain the seemingly contradictory phenomenon of working-class (white) people supporting the party of tax cuts for the wealthy, even at a time when public education and other services to poor and working families are being routinely downsized and cut from state and federal budgets. Thomas Frank makes the case in *What's The Matter With Kansas?* (2004) that the GOP uses "wedge issues" like abortion and gay rights to harvest the votes of working people, but once in office Republican politicians push for economic policies that benefit the rich as working and middle-class people continue to fall behind. Rick Perlstein shows in *Nixonland* (2008) how Richard Nixon used cultural appeals based in patriotism and American values to peel working-class white male voters away from the Democrats. But Westen (referenced above), Frank, and Perlstein all neglect to discuss or even mention the potential implications of shifting beliefs and identities about masculinity, and how this has affected white men's gendered voting habits.

The urgency of this conversation is arguably more pronounced in the late twentieth and early twenty-first centuries, when on top of ongoing economic anxieties that have accompanied levels of income inequality not seen since the Gilded Age, modern multicultural women's movements have repeatedly challenged unquestioned male authority in both the public sphere and the private realm of family relations, and upended traditional notions of manhood and leadership. At the same time, the gay rights revolution has disrupted the heterosexual monopoly on overt human sexual identity and expression. If, as the political scientist Georgia Duerst-Lahti says, "executive political power is the most manly of all areas," how could popular ideas and expectations about the presidency—and the *man* who occupies that symbolically potent position—not be affected by the dramatic cultural transformations catalyzed by these profound changes in the gender and sexual order?

Moreover, few of the books, articles, op-ed columns, and blog postings that do discuss issues related to masculinity and politics offer much analysis of media culture and its relationship to gender and presidential politics. This is stunning, because in the contemporary era most people experience presidential campaigns through the televisual performance of candidates and the rhetoric about them generated on cable TV and talk radio, and increasingly on the Internet and social media. As the *billions* of dollars spent on political ads during presidential campaigns make clear, US presidential politics is first and foremost a media spectacle. With scant exceptions, what has been sorely missing from the copious output of presidential scholarship and journalistic commentary on the presidency is an explanatory framework for how cultural ideas about (white) masculinity have, especially in the television era, played a powerful subtextual role in presidential campaigns and electoral outcomes.

This book explores some of the political developments, news events, campaign strategies, and other factors that have been part of the cultural conversation about manhood and the presidency over the past few decades, with special attention to how this has all played out in media culture. Feminist media scholars have long focused on the role of media culture in the shaping of cultural norms of femininity, and the relation between the representation of women in the symbolic realm versus their progress (or lack thereof) in the material world of familial, economic, and political power. The interplay of these complex gender dynamics is the subject of the 2012 documentary film *Miss Representation,* which explores how women's leadership in politics and business is undermined by the rampant objectification of women in entertainment media.

Building on feminist scholarship about the representation of women, men's studies scholars and queer theorists have taken up the subject of media representations of masculinity, and what these suggest about various developments in men's lives and identities. This emergent focus on men and media has been part of an outpouring of research and critical inquiry—and to some extent popular discussion—over the past two decades into various aspects of multicultural masculinities.

For anyone who is interested in the American presidency, this move to "pull back the curtain" on cultural performances of manhood raises a number of critical questions about media and politics in the twenty-first century: to what extent are voters' electoral choices shaped by the televisual performance of candidates and politicians? Which (white) masculine styles or archetypes have been politically successful over the past fifty years, and why? Does the election of Barack Obama change that, and if so, how? How does paid political advertising on television—by far the biggest expenditure of funds in presidential campaigns—shape voters' perceptions of the relative "manliness" of candidates? What are the similarities and differences between how women and men ascertain whether male political figures measure up to the "masculine ideal" that is circulating in media culture at a given historical moment? What types of gendered language about leadership do journalists and other media commentators use, and how do those language choices affect who is seen as a credible—or electable—candidate? What role does right-wing talk radio play in policing the boundaries of what are considered acceptable "masculine" traits expected in a commander in chief? How do new digital media formats, including YouTube, either reinforce or subvert traditional constructions of presidential masculinity? And finally, how can aspiring women political leaders demonstrate that they are "presidential timber" when the office of the presidency has been throughout American history a key symbolic marker of (white) masculine power and privilege?

It has been clear for some time that the modern electoral fortunes of the Republican Party have been made possible by the party's skill at playing a sophisticated game of identity politics with white male voters. It's hard to argue with the Right's recent track record; they keep doing it because it works. Exhibit A is the Republican Party's success at winning the votes of blue collar and middle-class white men, and not just in the post-civil rights South. Although the Democratic Party is responsible for most of the political gains for working men and women over the past century, the last Democrat to win the white male vote was Jimmy Carter, in the post-Watergate election of 1976. In 2000 George W. Bush beat Al Gore among white men by 27 points; four years later he beat John Kerry with the same group by 25 points.

The *white* part of this equation is well-chronicled and was quite predictable: when he signed the Civil Rights Act in 1964, Lyndon Johnson, a white Southerner, lamented that due to white backlash against the civil rights movement, the Democratic Party would lose the South for many years to come. What has been less well understood is the *male* backlash against the cultural upheavals catalyzed, although not wholly created, by feminism. In retrospect, someone in the 1970s could just as well have predicted that because of their embrace of equal rights and opportunity for women, the Democrats would lose the men's vote for a generation. There are many complicating factors in this analysis, like the progressive gender politics of some (now endangered) moderate Republicans and the conservative gender politics of many Blue Dog Democrats. But white male backlash against challenges to their power—in the family, the workplace, and in the psychological and symbolic realm—is as good an explanation as any for the persistent gender gap in voting patterns since 1980.

The Democrats' reputation as the "party of women" hurts them with (white) male voters. But it's not simply that many white men are alienated from the Democratic Party, which they see as the primary political home for a cultural movement—feminism—that they think has undervalued and derided men and advocated primarily for the rights and needs of women and children. Since the early 1970s, conservative propagandists in media have also waged a campaign to paint liberal Democratic men—and liberal men in general—as neutered, passive, less-than-fully masculine. This strategy has been highly effective in part because of a kind of self-fulfilling prophecy. Conservatives attack liberalism as an ideology of permissiveness and wrong-headed compassion at home and appeasement abroad. But instead of forcefully countering that false and misleading caricature, many liberals have retreated into a defensive stance and sought to either deny or minimize their commitment to progressive principles, including many that have contributed mightily to the success of this country (the eight-hour day, public education, Social Security, Medicare, etc.). Conservatives then point to the timidity of Democrats as evidence of their emasculation: if they can't stand up for their own beliefs, they won't stand up for you.

While conservatives relentlessly ridicule the manhood of (male) liberals, it doesn't work the same way in reverse. Liberals who critique the masculine projections of conservatives are likely to accuse them of being "reckless" or too eager to use force. In other words, they're *too manly*. This is one place where the clueless elitism of some liberals creates real communication problems: many of them seem not to get that many male voters consider it a compliment for a man to be accused of being "too manly." It merely reinforces what relentless conservative propaganda over the past generation has led so many men to believe: Democrats are wimps, and "real men" should vote Republican.

Conservative attacks on liberals also resonate because a key pillar of traditional manhood rests on the continued power of an aspect of misogyny—the devaluation of anything deemed "feminine." Thus "manhood" consists of a negation: a man is not-a-woman. A real man is not feminine. So when the Right actively tries to feminize left-of-center men by saying they "apologize for America" or they're "soft on crime" or "soft on terrorism," they send an implicit message to other men that they'd better move to the right, or they, too, will be unmanned. Men receive this message both consciously and unconsciously. The author of *The Wimp Factor*, Stephen Ducat, argues that until this gender subtext is debated openly and widely, "men's fear of the feminine will continue to be central among the various motives that drive electoral campaigns."[10]

The deliberate feminization of Democratic men, which is almost always on display in the conservative media, pays added dividends for conservatives, because when liberal Democrats are subjected to what amounts to juvenile name-calling and verbal bullying over the public airwaves, men who take "conservative" positions come off looking strong and manly by contrast. This applies in relation to domestic issues like the economy, but is especially true when it comes to foreign policy. Sarah Palin understands this instinctively, which is one reason she is idolized by otherwise chauvinistic conservative men. They realize, for example, that when she criticized President Obama's antiterrorism approach by saying "We need a commander in chief, not a professor standing at the lectern," she was not just attacking his policy approach, she was attacking his manhood—and implicitly praising theirs. (Palin, like others on the Right, had to shift gears on this particular aspect of Obama-bashing after he ordered the killings of Osama bin Laden and Anwar al Awlaki—in Palin's world, decidedly unprofessorial acts of leadership).

For conservatives, the political calculus of exploiting cultural anxieties about manhood is simple. Because media narratives help shape political identities, to the extent that right-wing politicians and opinion makers in the political media complex can succeed in painting Democratic presidential candidates (or presidents) as "soft," "weak and indecisive," or insufficiently bellicose in their projection of masculine authority, the less likely white men are to support them—and white women too. This dynamic is true for domestic issues like street crime, but is especially pronounced on issues of foreign policy. Since the days of class conflict and confrontation stoked by the US war in Vietnam and dissent against it at home, conservatives have effectively impugned the manhood of liberal and moderate Democratic men on issues related to the military budget and national security, especially when it comes to ritualized performances of American manhood on the international stage. Consider how much chatter on talk radio, cable TV, and the blogosphere was sparked by Obama's diplomatic gesture of bowing to Hu Jintao when the Chinese premier visited the US in 2009. What began, presumably, as Obama's attempt to demonstrate respect for cultural differences—especially after the disastrous bravado and arrogant unilateralism of the George W. Bush administration damaged the reputation of the US around the world—became an opportunity for right-wing accusations that his eagerness to "kow tow" to dictators communicated timidity and weakness—his and his country's. Even worse, they alleged, this was further evidence of his supposedly liberal—and therefore wimpy—tendency to "apologize for America." Not coincidentally, former Massachusetts governor and Republican presidential candidate Mitt Romney titled his 2010 political memoir *No Apology: the Case for American Greatness*, a transparent attempt to question Obama's patriotism and simultaneously outman him, in order to bolster his own manhood credentials with GOP voters.

GOP operatives understand instinctively what former President Bill Clinton meant when he said that when people are insecure, they'd rather have somebody who is strong and wrong than someone who's weak and right. What Clinton neglected to add is that American voters—especially white men— have been insecure for most of the past half-century. In particular what has been happening to working-class men for the last thirty years is unprecedented since the Great Depression, as real wages have stagnated and their standard of living has declined. This, in turn, has prompted a kind of identity crisis: if I'm always struggling just to provide the basics for my family, then what kind of a man am I? In the absence of a strong labor movement that in past decades gave voice to these concerns and supplied the political muscle to advance the interests of working families, many white men have turned to the Right— culturally and politically. In a time of economic uncertainty that is also a time of rapid gender and sexual transformation, millions of white male voters—not all of them conservatives and reactionaries—seem drawn to (male) candidates who can project old-fashioned masculine authority, impose order on the chaos, and make the world right again, like the reassuring patriarchs of Frank Capra movies or old-school football coaches. This longing for a reassertion of old-fashioned white male authority can be seen in a variety of cultural venues outside of politics: in the revival of an explicitly male-dominant and antifeminist conservative Christianity since the Second Wave of the women's movement in the 1970s; in the continuing popularity of John Wayne, who in polls remained one of the most popular leading male actors more than thirty years after his death in 1978; on right-wing talk radio and cable TV, where bombastic hosts like Rush Limbaugh and Bill O'Reilly perform a cartoonish (white) masculinity replete with simplistic analyses of complex social problems, and dismiss and ridicule liberals or anyone else who fails to see the wisdom of their propagandistic pronouncements; even in Hollywood films, where hypermasculine twentieth-century comic book superheroes like Superman and the X-Men have found expansive new audiences in their continuing quest to save the world from alien invasions, and from nihilist forces on earth.

In this jacked-up cultural climate, it's no wonder that so many books by Republican presidential candidates unabashedly trumpet their manly virtues: *Why Courage Matters* (John McCain), *The Courage to Stand* (Tim Pawlenty), or *Time to Get Tough*, by the erstwhile candidate Donald Trump. By the same logic, it makes sense that Karl Rove, the preeminent GOP presidential strategist of recent decades, titled his political memoir *Courage and Consequences*. These men understand that voters—especially but not exclusively white male voters—are concerned less about who knows the most or has the best grasp on policy than about whom they admire and identify with as a leader and as a man. As the social conservative Gary Bauer said, "…what Americans do is take the measure of the candidate. They may not always be able to put into words why they identify with one and don't with another…for a variety of reasons the Republicans have been putting up manly men and the Democrats have been putting up people who fall quite short from that."[11]

Amazingly, conservatives have long held a near-monopoly on this insight, at least in mainstream journalism and politics. But it's not as if no one on the Left has been paying attention to the centrality of gender. In his 1996 book *Moral Politics*, the cognitive scientist George Lakoff argued that political differences between conservatives and liberals are linked to ideologies of the family: conservatives adhere to a "Strict Father" model, while liberals believe in a "Nurturant Parent" approach. Over the past couple of decades, feminist activists and academics have focused on women as candidates and voters, and chronicled some of the changes in US politics occasioned by women's increasing political activity and electoral participation. Books such as *Rethinking*

Madam President: Are We Ready for a Woman in the White House? edited by Lori Cox Han and Caroline Heldman, explored structural obstacles in the political process, as well as cultural stereotypes that have held women back.

More recently, scholars and journalists have turned their attention to the gendered aspects of *men's* candidacies and voting patterns. The feminist writer Susan Faludi has been particularly prescient and prolific on this front, publishing numerous op-eds about the politics of presidential masculinity and also a book, *The Terror Dream: Fear and Fantasy in Post 9-11 America,* which explores the role of men's *and* women's paternalistic rescue fantasies and how they play out in American politics. By now it is common to read in mainstream journalism about the problem the Democratic Party has had for several decades in attracting white working-class male voters. David Paul Kuhn's book *The Neglected Voter: White Men and the Democratic Dilemma* puts the onus of responsibility for this on the Democrats themselves, and their inability to see that in their rush to embrace multiculturalism and feminism, they failed to stay connected to the voters who were once central to the old New Deal coalition: white working-class men.

But some Democratic political strategists still seem not to recognize the gendered nature of the terrain on which they toil. The prominent Democratic consultant Robert Shrum, who has run dozens of successful senatorial campaigns but has advised eight losing presidential ones, published a lengthy memoir entitled *No Excuses: Concessions of a Serial Campaigner* in which he explicitly mentioned masculinity only once. Shrum notwithstanding, some Democratic operatives get the basic idea that presidential campaigns can usefully be understood as contests about manhood. They understand that part of their job is to push Democratic candidates, many of whom in recent elections have seemed to recoil from engaging in this sort of ignoble competition, to give as well as they get.

The celebrated political consultant James Carville always seems to be doling out advice to Democrats to come on strong. In 2003 he wrote a book entitled *Had Enough?: A Handbook for Fighting Back,* where he was pictured on the cover with a black eye. In *Foxes in the Henhouse,* Steve Jarding and Dave "Mudcat" Saunders gave the Democrats advice about how to take back the issue of patriotism and national defense:

LEADING MEN

If the Republicans or their talking heads say Democrats are unpatriotic, the Democrats need to tell them them's fightin' words. And we don't mean slap-across-the-face fightin' words. We mean black-eye, broken-nose, knock-teeth-out, kick-the-hell-out-of-somebody fightin' words."[12]

Countless liberal and progressive activists and commentators over the past several decades have urged Democratic presidential candidates and sitting presidents to "grow a spine" or "take on" the big banks and corporate lobbyists, such as *Washington Post* columnist E. J. Dionne, who argued in his book *Stand Up, Fight Back: Republican Toughs, Democratic Wimps, and the Politics of Revenge* that Democrats are so fearful of looking soft that they abandon their strongest arguments and make whatever claims are in fashion at any given time. But Dionne, like most mainstream political analysts, failed to identify this problem as centrally about gender. It is rare to hear and read analyses from liberal and progressive pundits that demonstrates their understanding of the direct impact that anxieties about masculinity have on electoral outcomes, as millions of working and middle-class white men hesitate to vote for Democratic male candidates who might better represent their class interests but who have rhetorically been feminized in media discourse.

New York Times columnist Maureen Dowd is a notable exception—and she is sometimes dismissed by conventional political sophisticates for "psychoanalyzing" candidates and emphasizing superficial things like the cultural politics of gender and personality. But whatever one thinks of her generally liberal politics and her sometimes harsh judgments about people's character, she is without a doubt the most attuned person in the mainstream media to the masculinity drama at the heart of American politics. For example, from the start of Obama's first presidential run, Dowd fashioned an ongoing narrative about Barack Obama's manhood and how it played out in political rhetoric and discourse. The narrative keeps changing, especially when the focus turns from domestic to foreign affairs. In the fall of 2011 when public pressure was building for Obama to introduce a bold jobs bill, she wrote testily in the *New York Times*: "People are longing for a president who can understand their pain, mix it up and get action—not one who averts his gaze, avoids conflict, delegates to Congress, wastes time hunting for common ground, cedes the moon to opponents and fails to get anywhere."[13] In an early 2012 column entitled "Who's Tough

Enough?" she noted that Vice President Joe Biden was "talking up Obama's spine, aiming to show that all traces of Obambi are gone."[14] Dowd praised the president's "amazing missions accomplished," contrasted with his predecessor Bush's "unnecessary missions mangled."

The majority of this book is focused on presidential masculinity and analyzes a cultural and political system that to date has produced only male presidents. But all of this has enormous implications for women, both as presidential candidates and perhaps even more importantly as citizens. For a generation, feminist scholars have been studying the complex cultural barriers to women's political leadership. Some of this scholarship is especially revealing not only of the extent to which the presidency has always been a masculine institution, but of some of the mechanisms through which this is achieved. Thus throughout this book I draw on the work of feminist scholars and journalists, and their work on gender and electoral politics. For example, in a later section I outline some of the rhetorical practices in media commentary about politics, especially the gendered binary definitions by which men in politics are often judged as successes or failures: strong/weak; tough on crime/soft on crime; experienced/naïve on foreign policy, etc.; and how those track with traditional sexist binaries (men/rational, woman/emotional). Feminist political scientists have also examined such topics as how women candidates are affected by the use of "masculine" words like "attack," "strong," "compete," and "control" to describe strong leaders. Can women demonstrate those traits without evoking the negative judgment of being an aggressively dominating woman? What are some of the special challenges faced by women candidates for public office, such as cultural barriers to the acceptance of women's executive-level leadership, and the role of national security in shaping public expectations about the qualities (supposedly) necessary in a president? How much have things changed for women in politics over the past forty years?

It is important to note that while there has been a gender gap in presidential voting since 1980, in every presidential election which Republicans have won since 1980, a majority of white women (although not women as a whole) have also voted for the GOP candidate. This raises questions about white women's voting behavior, and how it might be affected by the kinds of mediated constructions of presidential masculinities that are the focus of this book. For example, do (white) women admire (white) male politicians for the same reasons (white) men do, or do they find different qualities attractive? Do issues play a greater or lesser role in women's assessment of candidates? What is the relationship between a politician's stance on "issues"—including so-called "women's issues"—and his constructed image in media culture? Since violence plays an important role in shaping cultural definitions of masculinity, to what extent do white women voters respond positively to male presidential candidates whose public personae emphasize toughness and the willingness to use violent force against our adversaries, versus male politicians who are perceived to be more pacifistic?

For that matter, to what extent do men—and women—respond positively to *women* candidates who display traditionally "masculine" characteristics in questions of foreign policy and the use of force? This question was raised by the groundbreaking candidacy in 2008 of Hillary Clinton, which brought into clear focus some of the ways the American presidency functions symbolically as a bastion of masculine power. Clinton came closer than any woman who previously sought to integrate this historically all-male club, but some of the obstacles she encountered were predictable, and they will be faced by women candidates in future elections. Because the president symbolically personifies not only "America" but American manhood, having a woman occupy that position would, by definition, disrupt the entire symbolic architecture on which the presidency rests. The critical question of when a woman will be elected president is not a question of when a woman will appear who possesses the necessary skills or experience to be a competent chief executive of the country. Over the past couple of generations (and before) there have been many prominent women whose executive talents clearly outshined those of some men who have been elected to the position. The question is when will the country be ready to elevate a woman to the symbolic status of being the public face of a country that has long understood itself as the most potent masculine force in the world, if not in human history? And what are the necessary personal qualities of a woman candidate for that position? The first woman to be elected president will be one who has mastered the complexities and nuances of the symbolism that she is redefining, and figured out a way to gain the support of a critical mass of both women and men in that project. Of course, issues and interests matter, but the symbolic realm is the true Rubik's Cube of women's quest for the US presidency.

PRESIDENTIAL CAMPAIGNS SINCE 1980

The cultural conversation about manhood and the presidency that is the subject of this book is a product both of recent changes in American society catalyzed by modern multicultural women's movements *and* the increasing centrality of mass media to American politics. These historical processes have been steadily building since 1960, when television first played a decisive role in presidential campaigns. The impact of media in politics, and the influence of entertainment values, accelerated with the 1980 election of the former Hollywood actor Ronald Reagan. In the late twentieth and early twenty-first centuries, the presidency itself has become a kind of cultural flashpoint about the state of manhood in the US, as media-driven constructions of presidential masculinity have played an increasingly prominent role in contemporary US culture and politics.

Presidential elections are about many things, to be sure. For example, it has long been received wisdom in mainstream political science as well as in the political punditocracy that elections are nearly always about the state of the economy as an election year looms, a position famously expressed by James Carville's exhortation to Bill Clinton in 1992: "It's the Economy, Stupid!" But it's not enough simply to say that elections are about the economy; it is more accurate to say they are influenced greatly by how voters understand their place in the economy, and the complex relationship between government, labor, and the private sector. In other words, what's more important than "the economy" in voters' minds is how they connect their personal experiences to larger economic and political processes and developments, and how the stories that circulate in and outside of media help to shape people's perceptions about these subjects. But regardless of the limitations of strict economistic explanations for voter behavior, the one notable exception to the argument for the primacy of economics was historically that when the country was at war, issues of "national security" trumped all others. Gender matters whether elections are about "economy-first" or "national security." But for purposes of brevity and clarity, this book focuses mainly on election years since 1980 in which foreign policy issues took center stage.

There are many ways to analyze electoral outcomes, so it is necessary to proceed with caution when offering any theory or framework that attempts to explain how elections turned out the way they did, or why. But my purpose is not to catalog the myriad forces at work in presidential politics. Rather, it is to examine how presidential elections serve as a vehicle for cultural conversations and clashes over changing ideas about masculinity. If US presidential elections are always about masculinity in one form or another, or if, as the political scientist Georgia Duerst-Lahti points out, traditions that dominate the presidency make presidential elections "masculine space," it follows that some of the key gendered themes, issues, and events that shape those elections merit closer scrutiny.

I have highlighted national security because questions about presidential masculinity rise to the surface of political debate and commentary most quickly when violence is involved. The salience of this frame of reference was driven home by commentary about Barack Obama after he ordered the killing of Osama bin Laden in the spring of 2011. Many liberal and progressive pundits applauded the president and expressed hope that he had retired once and for all the idea that Democrats couldn't be strong commanders in chief. On the other side, right-wing propagandists like Rush Limbaugh sought to minimize Obama's role and therefore blunt any manhood chops he might have earned. Some erstwhile right-wing critics of the president did find cause to praise him, such as Rudy Giuliani, the former mayor of New York and former Republican candidate for president, who said that he admired "the courage of the president to make a decision like this." Whatever their political leanings, virtually everyone across the political spectrum seems to intuitively understand that debates over national security centrally involve cultural questions about national identity and manhood that get played out around the particular strengths and weaknesses of the (man) in charge.

The main body of the book is organized into a series of narratives about key elections in recent decades. After a brief historical summary that makes reference to the masculine projections of Teddy Roosevelt in the early twentieth century, the analysis turns for background to the crucial election of 1972, which featured issues and political developments that have affected presidential politics to the present moment. I then examine the landslide victory in 1980 of Republican Ronald Reagan over the incumbent Democrat Jimmy Carter. The size and scope of Reagan's victory, as well as the electoral triumph of the conservative movement that it represented, make 1980 a watershed year in American politics. In addition, Reagan was a former

Hollywood actor, corporate TV pitchman, and television series host of *Death Valley Days* who was marketed by his astute media consultants as the political embodiment of cowboy masculinity, an icon of western, rugged individualism, and an old-fashioned champion of law and order. With his telegenic media presence and carefully stage-managed public persona, Reagan not only starred in a real-life version of a movie along the lines of John-Wayne-goes-to-Washington, but also created a powerful template of presidential masculinity that influences US politics to this day.

The next election analyzed is the 1988 race between the incumbent vice president, George H. W. Bush, and Massachusetts governor Michael Dukakis. The 1988 campaign featured the debut in presidential politics of GOP political consultant Lee Atwater, whose tactic of attacking the masculinity of Democratic candidates has been widely adopted by Republicans over the past two decades. The 1992 election was not defined by issues of war and peace. But Arkansas Governor Bill Clinton's election and presidency were pivotal in the history of the cultural politics of presidential masculinity, in part because of Clinton's attempts to remasculinize the Democratic Party and also because of the emergence of Hillary Clinton as a feminist cultural icon and lightning rod—and future presidential contender. The next race analyzed is the 2004 race between President George W. Bush and Senator John F. Kerry, in which the struggle to perform a kind of heroic masculinity reached cartoonish proportions, followed by the 2008 race between Senators John McCain and Barack Obama, in which the historic pattern of struggles between competing versions of white masculinity was supplanted by a contest between one version of white and another of black masculinity. The final chapter offers some analysis about the role that presidential masculinity played in the election of 2012.

Several key themes and emphases are woven into the narrative as it progresses chronologically: how the American president functions as national alpha male, and thus serves as the focal point of an ongoing cultural conversation about manhood; the presidency as a contest between competing versions of manhood; violence and the symbolic power of the presidency; how entertainment media contribute to cultural definitions of masculine leadership; the role of sports metaphors in framing presidential politics and campaign coverage as masculine competitions; and implications for women candidates of the masculine nature of cultural meanings ascribed to the presidency. Because the narrative is organized chronologically, I have tried to introduce each theme in the context of an election year in which it emerged as a major force. For example, I discuss the influence of Rush Limbaugh and conservative talk radio beginning with the election and presidency of Bill Clinton in the early 1990s. However, talk radio has been a factor right up to the present, and hence discussion of its role in shaping cultural definitions of manhood resurfaces regularly throughout the book. So it is with each of the major themes. I end the book with some speculation about the implications of my analysis for the future of presidential politics.

INTRODUCTION

Chapter 1
It's the Masculinity, Stupid

In the US constitutional system, the president wields enormous *material* power: (he) sets budgetary and legislative priorities for the federal government, appoints Supreme Court justices, and commands the armed forces. But the president also possesses enormous *symbolic* power, in part because he is under the glare of worldwide media 24/7. On top of that, the US presidency is a political office that also serves a multitude of ceremonial and ritualistic functions, both formal and informal. For example, the president is the "mourner in chief" when tragedy strikes or beloved Americans die: President Reagan delivered a moving and memorable speech after the Shuttle Challenger exploded in 1986. All eyes were on George W. Bush after 9/11. More recently, President Obama's speech in the wake of the Tucson shooting of Congresswoman Gabrielle Giffords and others in early January, 2011 reinforced this quasi-clerical role and helped to improve his job approval rating. The president and (his) wife and children literally comprise the "First Family." Their home, the White House, is regarded as the nation's home, and so forth. Presidential historian Forrest McDonald makes the classical case for the special role of the American chief executive:

> ...in addition to the powers and responsibilities vested in the presidential office by the Constitution and those acquired over the years, the office inherently had the ceremonial, ritualistic, and symbolic duties of a king-surrogate. Whether as warrior-leader, father of his people, or protector, the president is during his tenure the living embodiment of the nation.[1]

In a culture that has been male-dominated since its inception, it only makes sense that the "living embodiment of the nation" would be a man. In fact, up until January 20, 2009, every single US president had been a white man; 42 of 43 had been Protestant Christians. To the extent that a single person can at once contain characteristics of the dominant gender, race, class, religion, and sexual orientation, while he literally and figuratively serves as a stand-in for the entire nation in its dealings with other nations, the president is as close to the masculine ideal as possible. His manhood is central to his cultural iconic status, which is why it is has proven so difficult for a woman to occupy that symbolic space.

The man who is the American president plays an important function in the gender order that transcends his purely political duties. How he performs his manhood—and how his identity *as a man* is described and debated through the filters of a 24/7 media culture—both reflects and simultaneously helps to produce and reinforce masculine norms. In one sense he is analogous to a national alpha male; the leader of the pack against whom other men measure their status. The historian Andrew Bacevich describes the modern president as "Pope, pop star, scold, scapegoat, crisis manager, commander in chief, agenda setter, moral philosopher, interpreter of the nation's charisma, object of veneration, and the butt of jokes... all these rolled into one."[2]

In sociological terms he embodies what R. W. Connell (1987) identified as the hegemonic (dominant) masculinity in our society. Hegemonic masculinity is a conceptual tool that refers to the idealized and dominant form of masculinity in a given cultural context. In our culture, it is white, middle and upper class, and heterosexual, and is further characterized as aggressive and competitive. Not surprisingly, the qualities considered "presidential"—with the notable exception of Barack Obama's blackness—track closely with those associated with hegemonic masculinity.

Feminist scholars have looked at the question of what it means for someone to be considered "presidential," or in old school language, to be of "presidential timber," because of the implicit exclusion of women from that men-only club. "Presidential," it appears, means "manly"—or to be specific, a certain kind of manly. Thus, when they elect presidents voters are not just selecting the country's chief executive; they're making a statement about manhood: specifically, what kind of manhood is most exalted and should be in charge. When elections are understood in this way, all sorts of questions arise: which masculine characteristics must a man running for office possess, or at the very least be able to perform, before he passes the threshold for presidential consideration? What role do race, ethnicity, religion, and sexual orientation play in this process? Does it matter if a man acts differently in private than the image he is able to project on camera? At what points do the differences between a man's private and public selves become a political liability? To what extent are the qualities expected of a president expected of all dominant men? To what extent are they now and will be in future elections expected of women? Is it possible for a man to achieve and then successfully wield political power if he does not conform to certain masculine conventions of "strength" and stoicism that can effectively be conveyed by televisual performance? Is it possible for a woman to achieve and then successfully wield political power if *she* does not conform to certain "masculine" conventions of strength and stoicism that are similarly performative?

The answers to these questions have consequences beyond the political realm, because the presidency itself can be understood as a kind of teaching platform, with the president as a kind of pedagogue in chief. He literally teaches—by example—what one highly influential version of dominant masculinity looks like. The cultural theorist Henry Giroux, in a critique of the Hollywood movie *Fight Club,* argues that certain Hollywood films play a role as teaching machines that purposely attempt to influence how and what knowledge and identities can be produced within a limited range of social relations. The presidency *as it is constructed in media culture* plays a similar function, especially insofar as it defines the masculine ideal, and thus serves to model for boys and men the most socially acceptable and validated qualities of manhood at a given cultural moment. Like masculinity itself, this masculine ideal is not static, but instead is ever-changing and subject to ongoing historical evolutions, retrenchments, and assorted other pressures. Because masculinity is unstable, and because new tests in the form of unanticipated events and issues are always occurring, presidents need constantly to prove their manhood, just like other men. Moreover, in a culture awash in media spectacle, they must perform their manhood on the public stage. Hence one of the critical functions of the White House Office of Communications is to manage the president's masculine image and sell it to the public. Fortunately for them, they have lots of props and symbolic back-drops to work with: Air Force One, the Oval Office, the Secret Service, etc.

CHAPTER 1: IT'S THE MASCULINITY, STUPID

How the president, his party, and his policies are portrayed and described outside of the political-media complex of cable TV, talk radio, and the blogosphere also contributes to how people regard him as a man. For example, late-night comedians routinely use presidents and presidential candidates as fodder for jokes and impersonations. In part, the jokes and comedy routines that work do so because politicians embody some of the many contradictions in contemporary American identity, including those related to gender. By poking fun at them, the best comedians tap into deep-seated anxieties in male (and female) audience members/voters and offer comic relief. There are numerous example of comedians doing routines and delivering punchlines that have contributed to the construction of presidential masculinities, from Dana Carvey's emasculating sketches of George H. W. Bush in the late 1980s, to late-night comedians' jokes about Bill Clinton as a henpecked husband (before the Monica Lewinsky scandal, when the jokes switched to playful jabs at his "player" status), to editorial cartoons throughout his two terms of George W. Bush as a swaggering cowboy. In a 24/7 media environment, the pedagogical impact of the presidency is felt far and wide.

Cultural chatter about presidents helps to define the masculine ideal, but it also helps to determine which qualities in men are not worthy of respect and emulation. One characteristic of many recent Democratic presidential candidates that conservative Republicans on cable TV and talk radio have mocked ceaselessly is the proclivity to ponder the complexity of problems and not rush to judgments or make rash decisions. To many populist conservatives, this tendency is regarded as evidence of a man's "indecisiveness," and hence inability to serve as commander in chief. Presumably this cultural belief about authoritative manhood continues to resonate with many Americans; recall that George W. Bush, who often told audiences that "I don't do nuance," was reelected in 2004 with more votes than any president in history. Another way that male presidential candidates are mocked is for showing vulnerability—such as tearing up—outside of the ritually approved occasions. One of the most famous examples of this was the criticism heaped on Ed Muskie, the then-frontrunner for the 1972 Democratic presidential nomination, when what appeared to be tears streamed down his face on a snowy New Hampshire day as he was responding to negative reports in the media about his wife's behavior. Muskie later claimed they were not tears but melted snowflakes, but the damage had been done to his reputation as calm and self-assured. To this day, the Muskie "crying" episode serves as a cautionary tale for politicians: don't show even the slightest hint of vulnerability—or expect negative consequences.

Until now, the role of the presidency in establishing or maintaining norms of masculinity has not been widely appreciated or discussed. But this role is not itself a product of the era of mass media. In fact, in the late eighteenth century, the founders of the American republic were quite clear about the idea that the presidency was a masculine institution. They were also explicit about their desire to have a great and heroic man in that position who could model "independent manhood." As Mark Kann wrote in *The Republic of Men*:

> His [the president's] public exhibition of manly prowess heightened the other men's awareness of their own masculine shortcomings and encouraged them to strive for male maturity. His manly language and masterful deeds provided criteria by which most men could measure, judge and rate one another. His public persona as a self-disciplined man who transcended personal prejudices, parochial loyalties, and factional politics fostered a sense of fraternal solidarity and national pride that bound men together.[3]

Michael Kimmel's cultural history *Manhood in America* (1996) demonstrates that through the centuries, common-sense ideas about what is considered "manly" have been continuously negotiated and are subject to a multitude of economic, social, and political pressures. Throughout US history, presidential masculinity has both reflected and helped to produce broader cultural shifts in the notion of what it means to be a man. Kimmel takes up this subject in several historical contexts, such as his brief discussion of the election of 1840, whose rhetoric Kimmel describes as "a political masterpiece of gendered speech."[4] This campaign, which pitted the "self-made man of the people," William Henry Harrison, against the incumbent Martin Van Buren, featured blistering attacks by Harrison's Whig party on Van Buren's aristocratic and European tastes and his effete manhood. The strategy paid off for Harrison, as Van Buren was defeated. But according to Kimmel, the strategy set a dubious precedent: "Since 1840 the president's manhood has always been a question, his manly resolve, firmness, courage, and power equated with the capacity of violence, military virtues, and a plain-living style that avoided refinement and civility."[5] Notably, Kimmel's study was published four years before the aristocrat George W. Bush reached the White House after successfully presenting himself as a "regular guy," and almost a decade before he won reelection against John Kerry, whose war hero status failed to insulate him from the same sort of attack that Van Buren sustained, even down to the similarity between the attacks by Van Buren's populist opponents, who asserted that his "French cooks" furnished the president's table in "massive gold plate and French sterling silver." Kerry's detractors, such as conservative talk radio icon Rush Limbaugh, derisively referred to the senator from Massachusetts as "Looks French" Kerry.[6]

If, since the nation's founding, the president was supposed to embody qualities expected of successful men, the act of choosing a president is part of a cultural process whereby voters help to define those qualities. Think of politicians running for president as analogous to actors auditioning for a part. The voters have the role of casting director. They're looking for a particular set of qualities, and they ultimately select the leading (man) they think is right for the part. How they decide who is "right" for the part is the core subject of this book, especially how cultural definitions of manhood shape voters' choices. Of course, one unavoidable reality in a culture where the presidency is a media spectacle is that presidential candidates' physical characteristics such as height, weight, and presence or absence of hair are all factors that are central to their electability. It is not simply that "the tallest guy wins," as many armchair pundits like to point out. It is that our culture's definition of manhood is inevitably shaped by surface impressions. Taller, conventional-looking, more athletically fit men are closer to the masculine ideal than other types of men. This fundamentally impacts our politics because it explicitly excludes women, who literally can't "measure up" to cultural definitions of strength that equate it with masculine physical characteristics. It also confers an unfair advantage to men with certain body types, while discriminating against other types of men. This process has been exacerbated due to the disproportionate impact media have on transmitting political information—and images. Neil Postman argued over a quarter-century ago in *Amusing Ourselves to Death: Public Discourse in the Age of Show Business* that television has fundamentally altered how we assess presidential potential. Because television is a "conversation in images," he wrote, "it is implausible to imagine that anyone like our twenty-seventh president, the multi-chinned, three-hundred pound William Howard Taft, could be put forward as a presidential candidate in today's world."[7] There are obvious twenty-first century analogues. The issue of his obesity has dogged New Jersey Governor Chris Christie from the moment his Republican supporters started talking about him as presidential material. Fat jokes are hardly passé in contemporary political discourse; HBO's Bill Maher repeatedly makes fun of Christie's weight and has compared Christie's lack of discipline around food to disgraced Congressman Anthony Weiner's inability to control his appetite for sexual exhibitionism on the Internet. And just as Christie's girth might present a serious political obstacle on the national stage, it is similarly unlikely that a very short man could be elected president. In 2011, before Indiana Republican Governor Mitch Daniels took himself out of the running for the 2012 GOP presidential nomination, numerous commentators sheepishly mentioned his height as a political liability. One political expert on the radio said euphemistically that one strike against Daniels was that he was "not tall"—something that was so self-evidently detrimental that the expert saw no reason to explain why it would be a political liability.

If, as the saying goes, Washington is Hollywood for ugly people, the analogy between politicians and movie stars extends further to how a president—like a movie star—channels the hopes, dreams, and dark and light projections of millions of people. They are a vessel through which critical cultural narratives and tensions play out, including those around gender. As modern feminism has shaken the old order and catalyzed dramatic changes in what is expected of both women and men, the office of the president has become either a source of stability and continuity with the old patriarchal ideal (for the right), or the vehicle for a new, more egalitarian and less authoritarian manhood (for the left). One reason the country is so divided politically is that it is still playing out these larger cultural struggles sparked by feminism, gay liberation, and other transformative social movements of the 1960s and 1970s, and the reaction to them in subsequent decades.

The philosopher Douglas Kellner could have been talking about presidential narratives of manhood when he wrote

...successful presidencies presented good movies that were effective and entertaining in selling the presidency to the public. Failed presidencies, by

CHAPTER 1: IT'S THE MASCULINITY, STUPID

contrast, can be characterized as bad movies, which fashioned a negative image that bombed with the public and left behind disparaging or indifferent impressions and reviews.[8]

The movie analogy would have resonated with the late Michael Deaver, Ronald Reagan's longtime confidant and advisor. Deaver said that

> the Reagan Revolution succeeded not because Reagan told the people what they wanted to hear, but what *he* wanted to hear—and for most of America it was the same thing....the perception of what was done often mattered as much as what was actually done. These may be harsh thoughts, and not what the scholars and intellectuals and other wizards want to believe. But in the television age, image is sometimes as useful as substance. Not as important, but as useful.[9]

Just as the skillful deployment of political imagery affects presidents' political effectiveness, the degree to which presidents are politically successful has an effect on the extent of their cultural influence as masculine exemplars. Compare, for example, the enduring hagiography surrounding Reagan, the cowboy hero who in the words of Margaret Thatcher "won the Cold War without firing a shot," to the much more disparaging commentary that emerged about another faux cowboy, George W. Bush, whose failures of leadership in the Iraq War led to historically low public approval ratings. To this day Reagan, who left office moderately popular but whose historical reputation has been enhanced by a concerted campaign of mythification by conservatives, is revered by millions of Americans as the pinnacle of twentieth-century white American manhood, while Bush, who wore cowboy hats and mimicked such Reaganesque theatrics as brush-clearing photo-ops on his ranch, is still regularly described as bungling and incompetent, his attempts at masculine imagemaking mocked by late night comedians as an overgrown boy playing dress-up.

THE NATIONAL ALPHA MALE IN A DANGEROUS WORLD

The playwright Arthur Miller wrote that the ultimate foundation of political power is "the leader's willingness to resort to violence should the need arise."[10]

This is a specific application of a much broader gendered cultural norm. With limited exceptions, a man must be willing to use violence to protect himself and his family in order to be considered a "real man." Thus issues of war and peace, terrorism, and threats to American lives and interests bring into sharp relief the salience of traditional masculine qualities (fearlessness, toughness, decisiveness) respected and expected in a national leader. Miller pointed out that

> one need only scan the list of what are normally called the 'great presidents' to realize they were all leaders in war: Washington, Jackson, Lincoln, Theodore Roosevelt, Franklin Roosevelt, Truman. To be sure war was not all they did but without it a dimension of their dominance would never have shown itself.

Miller argued further that "as war leader, a president rises to the stature of tragic figure touched by the arcane, the superhuman, entrusted as he is with not only the lives of our sons and daughters but the purity of the ideals which justify their sacrifice."[11]

Throughout this book, I analyze three major clusters of political and campaign issues over the past forty years that have violence at their core: the Cold War, the rise of domestic (violent) crime as a political issue in the 1960s and 1970s, and the emergence of terrorism as a political issue in the 1990s, especially after September 11, 2001. Politics and violence are enmeshed in countless other ways on both ideological and practical levels. The German military theorist Carl von Clausewitz famously wrote that war is a continuation of politics by other means. The great sociologist Max Weber defined the state as the institution that holds a monopoly on the legitimate use of violence. More recently, in his book *Bomb Power: The Modern Presidency and the National Security State*, Garry Wills argues that the expansion of executive power since World War II derives from the president's responsibility for, and authority to use, nuclear weapons. Even the word "campaign" has etymological roots in warfare; it derives in part from "camp," meaning field, as old armies used to spend winters in quarters and then take to the open field to seek battle in summer. It was first used to refer to politics in American English in 1809.[12]

Because of the great symbolic power of the presidency, the president has come to reflect US national masculinity and is judged by whether he lives up to that standard. One of the chief responsibilities of the US president is to respond to threats of violence against Americans, both domestically and internationally. In other words, the electorate invests in the president both the *constitutional* authority to protect Americans and American interests, and the *symbolic* authority to define the appropriate masculine response to the threat of violence. In the Weberian sense, the person who leads the state is the person we authorize to enact *our* violence, or violence done in our name. In classical sociological theory, of which Weber is a founding figure, discourse about violence was degendered. But most violence is perpetrated by men. Whether committed by states, non-state actors, or in the case of domestic street crime, violence is gendered masculine. In fact, the president is the (man) we choose to protect and defend us not against "violence" in some abstract sense, but against violent *men*, either as agents of states, as actors affiliated with "non-state entities" such as al-Qaeda, or for that matter as gang members or loner criminals. As George W. Bush boasted in a 2004 campaign swing in West Virginia, "The founders would be happy to see a nation which stands strong in the face of violent men."[13]

How is the "manliness" of presidential candidates measured in terms of their response (or perceived stance toward) the problem of "national security," both real and imagined, and how do images and rhetoric contribute to popular perceptions about this? Which types of men can persuasively demonstrate their capacity to defend the country? What role do the class and family background of a candidate play? Does a male presidential candidate without a military record need to "prove" his manhood on another stage? What stage? Business, Hollywood, sports? How can some men with proven records of military heroism (e.g., John Kerry) be judged not "man enough" for high public office, while others who avoided military service (e.g., Dick Cheney) escape similar judgments? What is the role of partisan conservative media coverage and commentary in this process—in the tabloid press, on *Fox News*, talk radio?

This does not mean to suggest that US foreign policy (or the foreign policy of other democracies) is driven primarily by the individual personalities and character of leaders. The president himself, while a critically important person, can be seen as merely the most visible representative of a constellation of powerful interests. The presidency is not so much about individual men (and eventually, women) as it is about the central role of the president in pursuing policies that are presumed to advance the "national interest" as defined by influential political and business elites.

But to the extent that those elites require the consent of the population to enact policies—especially those that relate to when and with whom we go to war—perceptions about the manhood of presidents matter. They affect the political space within which leaders have to operate. Arthur Miller suggested that Lyndon Johnson's monumental decision not to run for re-election in 1968 despite his accomplishments in civil rights and other areas was due to the fact that he had been, in a sense, unmanned. Using theatrical language to make his point, Miller wrote:

> Events had stripped (Johnson) of his star's credibility, the power to domi-
> nate the stage, and he had devolved into a rather ordinary player smaller
> than his costume, his rank and his elevated throne merely emphasizing his
> failed ordinariness. In other words, his failure in Vietnam had stripped him
> of the dangerousness of the star-leader.[14]

In theory (if not always in practice) the more "manhood capital" a president possesses the less he needs to project strength through military means. Ronald Reagan arguably was able to negotiate arms deals with the Soviet Union in the 1980s precisely because the voices on the right who opposed *any* negotiations with the Soviets couldn't gain any traction by mocking his manhood. When Howard Phillips of the Conservative Caucus accused Reagan of being a "useful idiot for Soviet propaganda," it fell flat, just as it did when then-Congressman Newt Gingrich complained about the "impotence and incompetence" of Reagan's policy in Afghanistan.[15] Perhaps even more consequentially, for decades Democratic presidential candidates and members of Congress—especially liberal Democrats—have faced pressure to counter charges that they're "soft on defense" by promising to maintain and periodically increase enormously bloated military budgets. Failure to do so would result in devastating attack ads and ridicule in the corporate media.

CHAPTER 1: IT'S THE MASCULINITY, STUPID

Since at least 1972, when the Democratic presidential nominee was the liberal Senator George McGovern, a former World War II fighter pilot who opposed the Vietnam War, polls have consistently shown that a majority of voters believe the Republican Party is more trustworthy on "national security."[16] One way to interpret this belief is that, for whatever reasons of substance or style, the GOP is perceived to be the party that is "tougher" on communism/terrorism, which translates to mean more willing to increase military spending and resort to military force to project strength and defend US interests around the world. Because violence is seen as a masculine prerogative,[17] the Republican Party attracts a greater percentage of votes from men, who are more likely than women to prioritize "foreign policy" as an issue that determines their vote for president.

This book examines an era when electronic media—especially television and the Internet—have come to dominate political discourse. But contemporary debates about the qualities necessary to be an effective US president in a dangerous world have numerous historical antecedents. For example, historians have noted that the presidency of Theodore Roosevelt at the turn of the twentieth century helped usher in a new archetype of presidential masculinity, one that continues to have great resonance in the early twenty-first century. Roosevelt was a sickly, frail boy, born to the genteel privileges of East Coast aristocracy. After a trip to the rugged west as a young man, he reinvented himself as a robust outdoorsman and self-conscious champion of manly pursuits. As a politician one of his signature phrases, which he took from a West African proverb, was to "speak softly and carry a big stick." Roosevelt's embrace of a "muscular" foreign policy and a robust place for US military might in the world has proven especially attractive to contemporary neoconservatives, who are attracted to his articulation of "national greatness conservatism"; the 2008 Republican presidential nominee John McCain repeatedly told reporters that he was a lifelong admirer.

Since the end of World War II, when the US emerged as the leading economic and military power in the world, cultural attitudes toward presidential masculinity have been shaped by the idea that in a world in which totalitarian states and assorted collections of bad men want to do us harm, the president of the United States—as "leader of the free world"—needs to "stand tall" on the global stage, exhibit toughness, and at times even ruthlessness. But this focus on the president as the man who will protect us comes at a significant cost. As the political scientist and feminist theorist Cynthia Enloe writes:

> American political culture during the last century increasingly imagined the job description for the presidency as prioritizing just one part of its myriad complex responsibilities: commander in chief of the uniformed armed services. This imagining is a serious political distortion. It amounts to the militarization of what is constitutionally designed to be a multidimensional civilian post. Imagining that "commander in chief" is the *essence* of the US presidency is a profoundly gendered distortion...[18]

Because the president is elected to the position of commander in chief of the armed forces, his decisions about where and when to use military force are, at least in theory, supposed to be made in the best interests of the American people. But there is a gender dynamic at work. Stephen Ducat references a Gallup survey on men's and women's differing rationales for the use of US military force. The survey showed that men were substantially more concerned with "US credibility" as a reason to justify military action. Men have:

> ...a particular identification with the American nation state not shared (to the same degree) by women, one that is personified as an individual warrior whose honor (read "phallic manhood") is on the line in any potential conflict. This interpretation is consistent with the findings of my own research on the nature of men's psychological investment in the outcome of a war. In other words, a military intervention in which one's country might assert manly dominance over another is an opportunity to achieve (or fail to achieve) a vicarious sense of personal worthiness and efficacy, which in phallic terms is expressed as potency.[19]

Because men's *identities* are thusly involved in their political beliefs, they are more likely than women to be invested in candidates who in their physical person, military credentials, or campaign rhetoric seem willing or eager to use military force to "defeat our enemies." This also helps explain the social psychology underlying conservative hostility to multilateral organizations

CHAPTER 1: IT'S THE MASCULINITY, STUPID

such as the United Nations, who are often characterized by conservative commentators as attempting to "tie our hands" in military engagements where nothing less than our national masculinity is at stake.

A CONTEST OF MEANINGS ABOUT MANHOOD

Just as presidential campaigns are fertile ground for competition between various cultural and political ideologies, they are also fertile ground for an ongoing contest about the meanings of American manhood. If presidents are the national "alpha male," then presidential elections are where that "alphaness" gets defined and refined. To put it another way, presidential elections can be seen as struggles between competing versions of the national masculine ideal. They are in essence quadrennial referenda on what sort of "masculine" qualities a majority of the voting public identifies with, admires, and expects in the person who seeks to ascend to the position of highest status man.

For the past several decades, a routine practice in political journalism has been to compare and contrast various aspects of presidential candidates' personality, ideology, and style. Everything from the candidates' temperament, to the importance of religious faith in their lives, to their taste in movies and music are put forth as data for voters to use in making their choice. But most of these analyses fail to recognize that what's really being debated are competing versions of American manhood. This crucial fact is overlooked because few people understand that gender is a central factor in contests between men. If a woman were running against a man, certain differences between the candidates would likely be attributed to gender differences—even when they shouldn't be. But when two men run against each other, their gender is routinely rendered invisible.

Sometimes the manhood factor is obscured by a focus on class or race. For example, a *Newsweek* cover in the spring of 2008 showed some leaves of arugula set off against a full beer mug, with the headline, "Obama's Bubba Gap." Notwithstanding the visual and the headline, the article barely mentioned gender. A few weeks later the conservative *Weekly Standard* ran a piece entitled "It's Not Race, It's Arugula," in which Noemie Emery discussed the political analyst Michael Barone's breakdown of the white vote in the Democratic primary struggle between Barack Obama and Hillary Clinton. Barone identified two types of white voters: the Academicians and the

Jacksonians. Obama was doing well with the former and not the latter. Emery also referenced the political reporter Ronald Brownstein's idea of a split in the Democratic Party going back to 1968 between those he described as "warriors" and "priests." In both cases, Emery argued that the key division among Democratic whites was based not in racial ideology but in class. The academicians/priests represented an educated, affluent elite, while the Jacksonians/warriors represented blue-collar workers. Emery argued that Obama was having trouble with middle-and lower-class whites not because they were bigoted or put off by his racial otherness but because he is an intellectual and represents the interests of cultural elites. Throughout her piece, Emery used the issues of foreign policy and patriotism to demonstrate the divide since the late 1960s between the national Democratic Party and white rural voters in Appalachia and elsewhere. She described the Democrats as the "party of peace" that has an "aversion to war." When they "lost their warrior edge they started losing the White House" because they put up candidates "who seemed both weak and too wordy in foreign affairs." The Reagan Democrats were drawn to Reagan's "muscular" foreign policy, etc. The heart of her argument was that Democratic presidential nominees over the past forty years have been perceived as unmanly—and hence unpresidential—by many rural whites. But not once in the article did Emery use the words "manhood" or "masculinity," or suggest that the class divide among white Democrats had explicitly gendered undertones.[20]

Presidential races are a proxy for broader cultural trends, transformations, and backlashes, and in that sense they bring into stark relief the various sides of the ongoing struggle over who gets to define what it means to be a man. For example, Ronald Reagan's landslide victory over Jimmy Carter in 1980 was more than a referendum on the incumbent administration's policies or priorities. It also signaled a refutation of the 1970s "new man," whom Carter, fairly or not, had come to symbolize. Although politically Carter was moderate-to-conservative, his personal style and image was folksy and soft-spoken, as befitting a man who promised, in the first post-Watergate, post-Vietnam election, to bring back honesty and humility to the exercise of American power at home and abroad. But if the real-world results under the rule of a kinder, gentler, more thoughtful and reflective man were stagflation, malaise, and Iranian students humiliating the United States on TV every day for well over a year, then maybe the "new masculinity" itself had proven it wasn't up to the job. By electing Ronald Reagan, voters were in effect saying that restoring America's economic, spiritual, and military vitality required a return to the older and time-tested manly virtues of self-reliance, traditional values, and military muscle—all embodied in an aging actor/father figure/action hero. It's worth remembering that in 1981, *Time Magazine* named Ronald Reagan "*Man* of the year." "*Person* of the year," and the inclusive gender politics that linguistic shift implied, was still almost two decades in the future.

If Reagan's election marked a major turning point in the cultural politics of masculinity, other presidential races offer their own unique lens on the contested meanings of manhood. Georgia Duerst-Lahti sees the 2000 election as a competition between "expertise masculinity" and "dominance masculinity," with the smart and technologically savvy Al Gore in the former position, versus the ex-Major League Baseball owner and all-around regular guy George W. Bush in the latter. The comedian Bill Maher phrased it more metaphorically: "IQ versus barbeque." It was also, of course, a contest between two members of the political aristocracy, although Bush successfully performed his role as a down-home man of the people, while Gore's haughty speaking style raised questions about his sincerity. Nonetheless, it is important to remember that Gore actually won the popular vote by more than a half-million votes.

Bush-Kerry in 2004 presented its own set of masculine dualisms: the "Decider" who disdained deliberation versus the cerebral statesman who appreciated the nuances and complexities of policy and politics. The stakes were high; the country was at war. Would voters choose a leader who goes with his gut, or one who reads and reflects deeply? Missouri Republican Representative Roy Blunt was blunter than most when he said, just months after 9/11, that "my personal view is that complexity in a leader is not a helpful thing, and certainly not a helpful thing in a crisis."[21] Whether or not he was merely being a good partisan, or making a virtue of necessity, is a matter of opinion. First Lady Laura Bush summed up her husband's masculinity: "George is not an overly introspective person. He has good instincts, and he goes with them. He doesn't need to evaluate and reevaluate a decision. He doesn't try to overthink. He likes action." And he was reelected. After four years of being led by a man who shunned introspection and instead "liked action," a majority of the electorate endorsed that type of masculinity over the kind represented by Kerry, a man who by all accounts would have brought a considerable amount of intellectual curiosity and personal contemplation to the exercise of his presidential responsibilities. The election returns offered compelling evidence that the masculine archetype popularized in Hollywood Westerns that played so well to audiences in the second half of the twentieth century had retained its grip on millions in the heartland of America in the twenty-first.

And then voters in 2008 chose a new masculine archetype in the person of a largely untested but self-assured African-American man who rejected rugged individualism, supported gender equality, and promised to seek bipartisan consensus at home and build coalitions abroad. The voters chose to elevate this young progressive version of black masculinity over a more conservative white masculinity embodied in the person of an older white war hero who talked tough on military matters and had a record of opposition to women's rights. In *Newsweek*, Michael Hirsh described these competing notions of manhood—again without using the term "manhood"—in a piece about the contrasts in the two men's views on foreign policy: "John Wayne McCain, as he was known at Annapolis, is the tough-talking ex-flyboy who envisions the United States locked in battle with formidable foes, yet steeled to confront them. Obama is the more cerebral cosmopolitan, at ease with other cultures and calculating America's interests in broad, strategic terms."[22]

The conventional view of presidential campaigns is that they are contests between competing political organizations and the weapons of choice are political ads; the side with the most money usually wins. This certainly held true in the 2008 campaign, when the amounts spent on advertising were truly staggering. According to the Campaign Media Analysis Group, from January 1, 2007, through October 29, 2008, Obama spent $292,766,093 for 535,945 airings; McCain spent $131,724,492 for 269,143 airings during the same period. And that is just what was spent by the campaigns themselves, apart from the expenditures of independent groups that produced and aired their own ads. In 2012, the first presidential election since the US Supreme Court's 2009 *Citizens United* ruling that corporate speech was protected political expression opened the floodgates for business interests to influence elections, estimates of the amount that will be spent for political ads run in the billions.

The importance of political ads has grown in recent years as traditional news organizations like TV stations have scaled back costly investigative reporting and in-depth political coverage. Thus voters are getting less and less information from news sources and more from paid ads whose intent is much more to persuade than to inform. Political ads, like other forms of consumer product advertising, work to create visceral reactions and emotional impressions; accuracy of information is not their primary purpose. This distinction between information presented and emotions stimulated is crucial because as the political communications theorists Maria Elizabeth Grabe and Erik Bucy argue, "For a critical component of the electorate, which is only semiattentive to civic affairs, political decisions may be based more on affective attachments and nonverbal signals expressed by leading politicians on television than careful consideration of issue positions."[23] In a male-dominant culture, among those "affective attachments," presumably, are attachments to the idea of the president as father and protector of the nation.

Presidential campaign ads create visceral reactions in part by telling stories about America at a given moment in history, and by telling stories about the men (and women) who seek to lead the country. Winning campaigns construct winning narratives, an outcome all the more likely when a candidate's public persona matches the mood of the electorate and literally embodies the dreams or resentments of a voting majority. In election years in which national security and foreign policy concerns are paramount, campaigns might seek to inspire fear in order to bolster their contention that their man (or woman) is the better choice to protect the country. This was especially resonant in 2004, the first presidential election since 9/11, when George W. Bush ran as the plainspoken (transplanted) Texan who would "keep America safe." But political ads don't just exist in their own closed universe. The stories they tell seep into popular consciousness, whether they're accurate or not. Kathleen Hall Jamieson, often described as one of the nation's foremost experts on political advertising, explains that in a crowded media environment, voters are often unaware of where they got information about a candidate: was it from a legitimate news item, or perhaps from a distortion of a candidate or their record that originated in an attack ad? A classic example of this is the "Willie Horton" ads that George H. W. Bush's campaign used so successfully in the 1988 election. Jamieson's research showed that due to seemingly deliberate distortions in the Bush campaign ads, many voters thought that former Massachusetts Governor Michael Dukakis actually presided over a "revolving door" system of justice, where convicted murderers and rapists regularly roamed free on weekend furloughs. This reinforced the right-wing narrative, whose roots dated back to the late 1960s, that Democrats like Dukakis were "soft on crime." In fact, Horton was the rare exception; he was the only convicted felon who violated the terms of the Massachusetts furlough program—a program initiated by Dukakis's Republican predecessor.

The efficacy (and morality) of attack ads has itself been a subject of lively debate in the field of political communication for decades. One school of thought holds that attack ads have a deleterious effect on democracy because they turn voters off, which makes them less likely to participate. Another defends attack ads, claiming they make an invaluable contribution to democratic discourse, primarily because they provide candidates with an unfiltered forum to educate voters about their positions and how they differ from those of their opponents.

But most journalistic and academic analyses of attack ads lack any kind of sustained gender analysis. They analyze the decision to "go negative" in the context of media campaign tactics and strategies, but utterly fail to discuss or even recognize its deeply gendered implications. This is myopic when you consider how important ads are in packaging the masculine image of candidates for public consumption, especially, as Hall Jamieson points out, given the visual capacity of television to reconfigure "reality" in ways that heighten the power of the visceral appeal.

But if the *content* of ads is important, so too is the *process* of attack and counterattack. One way to see presidential campaigns is as staged competitions between two distinct conceptions of American manhood, and ads, especially attack ads, as primary "weapons" in those mediated battles. The "war of the airwaves" is really in many ways a proxy for a one-on-one fight between the two candidates that draws upon long-standing cultural traditions and masculinity rituals that mandate certain courses of action in competition between men. In the American culture of honor, whose historical roots are strongest in the South but not confined to that region, a man is duty-bound to defend himself against not only physical threats but even personal slights; if he fails to defend his reputation he leaves himself and his

CHAPTER 1: IT'S THE MASCULINITY, STUPID

family open to exploitation or violence. Likewise if a presidential candidate is attacked in an ad by his opponent or an independent group, especially if the attack can be read as directly besmirching his honor, he is duty-bound to respond, sometimes with (metaphorical) displays of violence. If he does not respond with indignant fury, like John Kerry failed to do in 2004 after the Swift Boat ads alleged that he was a poseur and faux-warrior who exaggerated his wartime experiences and faked battlefield injuries, it's not just that it leaves the impression that the charges might be true. It also appears as if he has walked away from a fight, which immediately raises doubts about his manhood. In the right-wing media universe of tabloid newspapers, cable TV, and talk radio, where millions of white men go for both news information and political analysis, this is more than enough proof that he is not enough of a fighter to be president. If he can't stand up for himself, how can he stand up for the little guy, for his fellow citizens? How can he go toe-to-toe with America's enemies? Even more to the point: how many men are going to feel comfortable identifying with and supporting the candidacy of a would-be "leader of the free world" who has been symbolically unmanned in this way?

Arguably one of the strongest features of Barack Obama's 2008 presidential campaign, both in the primaries and the general election, was the speed with which he and his surrogates responded to rhetorical attacks from his opponents and in the media. It was not so much that the rapid responses prevented his opponents from defining him as much as they represented a metaphorical message of strength, primarily to white male voters, including independents whose class affinities lean Democratic but who have in recent decades recoiled from identification with Democratic presidential nominees. The message said: *It is okay to identify with this guy—he's tough. He's unflappable even in the face of withering criticism. He won't be pushed around.* Or as Obama's campaign manager David Plouffe wrote about Obama, "He would never shy away from a vigorous fight."

In *Image-Bite Politics: News and the Visual Framing of Elections*, Grabe and Bucy claim that visual modes of communication have largely been overlooked in the great narratives about politics, democracy, and the public sphere, and that "surprisingly little research attention has been paid to the systematic analysis of political visuals." Their study seeks to correct this exclusion by pointing out that

LEADING MEN

Campaigns actively engage in visual framing strategies to promote desired candidate qualities and favored themes and to reinforce policy positions. Journalists routinely apply camera and editing techniques, including varying camera angles, lens movements, shot selections, and story packaging, that place candidates in a more or less favorable visual light. The candidates' nonverbal behavior adds another dimension of visual information, evoking emotions, shaping impressions, and influencing audience attitudes. Indeed, when citizens are evaluating leaders, televised portrayals are remarkably potent.[24]

Grabe and Bucy insist that the entire field of political communication needs to acknowledge how central visual presentation is to twenty-first century politics. But like so many other academic writers and political journalists, they fail to provide anything other than the most cursory examination of the gendered implications of their thesis. How do campaign visuals and conventions of media coverage help to construct the manhood of various presidential candidates? Which masculine archetypes do candidates seek to embody as they present themselves through media to the public? The cowboy? The maverick? The statesman? The no-drama avatar of cool competence? How can male candidates visually reassure white male voters that they're strong enough to be president without coming off as immodest and worse, inauthentic? What are the visual markers of male candidates' populist identification with average Joes? Which kind of clothes should they wear? What kinds of exercise should they be photographed doing? What sort of backdrops work best for photo ops? Where should they vacation? How do women candidates communicate populism differently than men do?

If academics have been slow to get the point, and Republicans have it mastered, at least some Democrats understand the electoral necessity of credibly performing a certain kind of traditional manhood. In 2004 Montana Governor Brian Schweitzer shot his television ads while sitting on horseback and brandishing a gun. Schweitzer told the *Washington Post,* "I spoke to men visually and told them I am like them. Hell, I can be on a horse and talk about health care. Ninety percent of them don't ride horses, and many of them don't shoot a gun, but my ads said visually that I understand Montana. My gender gap disappeared. I think I have just summed up why Democrats lose elections."

CHAPTER 1: IT'S THE MASCULINITY, STUPID

Certain stock visuals establish or reinforce a candidate's manly bona fides. A favored photo op of both Republican and Democratic presidents and presidential candidates is one in which the politician is surrounded by men (and sometimes women) in uniform, especially police officers and members of the military. The conventional explanation for these photo ops is that they present the candidate either as an advocate of law and order, or in a populist light, as a (man) of the people. But more than "law and order" and "populism" is at work here. The photo ops are about presidential masculinity, but this plays out differently for the two major parties.

The manhood of Democratic men has been impugned by Republicans for decades, especially around issues related to crime and national security. So when they are surrounded by men who are masculine in traditional ways, men in law enforcement and the military, their virility quotient increases in a kind of manhood-by-association. The pictures send a message to other traditionally masculine men: *It's okay to support a Democratic candidate, because—as you can plainly see—plenty of real men do. No one is going to accuse those cops or soldiers of going soft. No one's gonna think you're soft, either.* It's a popular marketing strategy that has long been used to sell "feminine" consumer products to men, such as light beer. A recent example is the *Weight Watchers* outreach campaign to men, entitled "Lose Like a Man," that employed male icon and NBA Hall-of-Famer Charles Barkley as a TV pitchman. Of all the images of President Obama that appeared in the 2012 election, perhaps the most beneficial politically are the ones where he is surrounded by smiling and admiring American soldiers at Fort Campbell, Kentucky, after the killing of Osama bin Laden. They visually transmit proof of the troops' respect for him as a hands-on commander in chief, and so stand as a stark rebuke to the right-wing media's attempts to smear him as a cerebral and detached intellectual—and therefore a wimpy man and weak leader.

For Republican presidents and candidates, appearing on camera with the troops is less about proving manhood, and more about trying to obfuscate the class differences and competing loyalties between the wealthy conservatives whose interests drive the party's agenda, and the culturally conservative working-class men whose votes are needed to win elections. What unites these two disparate groups is a consensus view not only of American patriotism but of manhood. Two of the most memorable events in George W. Bush's presidency each involved photo ops where he demonstrated command and control while surrounded by working-class men. The first was when he stood next to the rubble at ground zero in New York City two days after 9/11 with a bullhorn in his hand, surrounded by rugged-looking rescue workers, and boldly asserted that "the people who knocked down these buildings will soon hear from all of us." The second was the celebration of "Mission Accomplished" on board the aircraft carrier USS Abraham Lincoln in 2003, just weeks after the beginning of the war in Iraq. Bush was widely criticized for prematurely celebrating the war's end, but at the time he won praise and a boost in popularity for his bold landing on the carrier in a Navy jet, and for how natural he looked in a military flight suit. While the banner that read "Mission Accomplished" dominates commentary about the event, what is often overlooked is the visually powerful sight of thousands of blue collar sailors heartily cheering their aristocratic but manly commander in chief in a moment of national triumph.

SPORTS METAPHORS AND PRESIDENTIAL DISCOURSE

Gender norms influence not just what we think, but how. Consider the pervasive presence of sports metaphors in contemporary American politics. Metaphors are not merely figures of speech. According to the cognitive scientists and philosophers George Lakoff and Mark Johnson (1980), human thought processes themselves are largely metaphorical. Our brains use them to organize and make sense of the world. According to Lakoff and Johnson:

> Our ordinary conceptual system, in terms of which we both think and act, is fundamentally metaphorical in nature…The concepts that govern our thought are not just matters of the intellect. They also govern our everyday functioning, down to the most mundane details. Our concepts structure what we perceive, how we get around in the world, and how we relate to other people. Our conceptual system thus plays a central role in defining our everyday realities…the way we think, what we experience, and what we do every day is very much a matter of metaphor.[25]

Everyday speech by and about politics and politicians routinely contains sports terminology whose meaning resonates with a large number of voters.

But sports metaphors in politics—whether they're used by politicians, media pundits, or coworkers at the water cooler—do more than provide a shared language for members of the good ol' boys' club. They also help to define key characteristics of manhood, and to identify who measures up—and who does not. Sports metaphors also play an important role in defining what are considered "presidential" qualities. Because they play such an important role in how people think and talk about politics and the presidency, I have included commentary about sports metaphors at various points in this book. For now, I'd like to sketch out some ideas about how to think about their effects.

Metaphors and other sports references define political reality for millions of men—and women. Examples abound. The number one *New York Times* bestseller and one of the most talked-about books from the 2008 election was entitled *Game Change*. One of the best-known cable TV shows on politics is MSNBC's long-running *Hardball with Chris Matthews*. Early in George W. Bush's first term Central Intelligence Agency director George Tenet infamously asserted that the presence of weapons of mass destruction in Iraq was a "slam dunk." United States Supreme Court Chief Justice John Roberts asserted during his confirmation hearings that "Judges are like umpires…They make sure everybody plays by the rules." In 2008, then-presidential candidate Barack Obama stated that "A nuclear Iran would be a game-changing situation not just in the Middle East but around the world."

In the spring of 2011, when Barack Obama was under pressure to release the death-scene photos of Osama bin Laden, he declined, saying he "didn't want to spike the football." A year later, conservative critics claimed that he'd done an "end zone dance" to boast about the killing when his campaign aired a political ad highlighting the action. What was perhaps even more notable than Obama's and his critics' use of those football colloquialisms was the fact that few media commentators felt the need to explain them. The use of sports metaphors in American politics is socially normative, especially for men. Listen to *National Review* editor Rich Lowry's analysis of former Virginia Senator George Allen, once a leading Republican hopeful for president and a United States senate candidate in 2012. "Football gives Allen a conversational entree with nearly any American male," Lowry writes. "And it is one he never leaves unexploited. What Shakespeare is to the sonnet, Allen is to the football analogy. Over a period of a couple of months, I heard him compare every significant event in Washington to a football play or situation."[26]

It is unfortunate but perhaps not surprising that outside of the light-hearted stories that run from time to time about what kinds of sports presidents enjoy as either participants or spectators, little attention has been paid to the relationship between sports and presidential politics, especially insofar as the dominant sports culture wields enormous influence in helping to shape ideals of manhood. It could be that the politicized use of sports metaphors is nearly invisible, even to cultural critics, precisely because they are such a part of our daily speech that they "fly under the radar" of critical consciousness. And how realistic is it to expect serious examination of this subject in media, especially when some key opinion leaders in that realm are men who themselves are frequently caught up in the masculine myth making that often passes for insightful political analysis?

But in spite of the fact that everyone from political scientists to op-ed columnists has written about our culture's obsession with seeing the political world through the lens of sports experience and language, relatively few academics or journalists have analyzed the particularly gendered aspects of sports metaphor. There is widespread agreement that men are more likely than women to appreciate statements like "So far, we've been waging this campaign between the forty-yard lines; we've got to begin to move down-field." In fact, much of the journalistic treatment of the topic of sports metaphors and politics highlights gender differences, with commentators frequently poking fun at men's sports obsessions and the way they creep into other areas of life. The Republican pollster Frank Luntz says that men's use of sports analogies "drives women insane."[27]

But it is a mistake to dismiss this subject as light fare or merely fodder for pop psychological speculation. In an era when a woman emerged as a major candidate for the presidency for the first time in US history, much more attention needs to be paid to the process through which cultural ideas about what it means to be a man—including those shaped by the dominant male sports culture— impact voters' perceptions of the people, parties, and interests that seek to attain and exercise power at the highest levels of American government.

CHAPTER 1: IT'S THE MASCULINITY, STUPID

This process includes asking some critical questions about the political function of sports metaphors. What effect does it have on our political system when mainstream commentary about politics is infused with the kind of language one hears every day on ESPN, in sports bars, and in locker rooms? To what extent can bitter partisanship in the two-party system be understood as a political manifestation of the sort of quasi-tribalism that is routinely on display in sports rivalries? What are the particularly gendered features of sports/political discourse, and how do those influence which qualities in potential leaders are regarded as important? For example, presidential debates are routinely covered by the mainstream media as if they were boxing matches. Does this subtly, or not so subtly, influence voters' perceptions of various candidates? Can a male political figure who does not embody certain traditionally masculine qualities, such as being pugnacious enough to credibly go "toe-to-toe" with our official enemies, succeed in such an environment? Can a woman? Will we get any closer to finding solutions to complex twenty-first-century problems when political commentary focuses not on what candidates say or stand for, but on the fact that the "frontrunner" failed to deliver a "knockout punch"?

Metaphors from sports such as basketball and baseball regularly surface in political speech. But arguably the two most metaphorically influential sports in presidential campaign rhetoric are boxing and football. Not coincidentally, they are both violent sports that attract a disproportionate percentage of male participants and fans. It is only possible to speculate about how much of the white male vote is determined by impressions about the relative "manliness" or "toughness" of candidates or political parties. But there is no doubt that for several decades violence—both our individual and collective vulnerability to it, and questions about when and how to use the violent power of the state to protect the "national interest"—has been an ominous and omnipresent factor in numerous foreign policy and domestic political issues (e.g., the Cold War, Vietnam, the "War on Terror," and the invasion of Iraq, as well as gun control, and executive, legislative, and judicial responses to violent crime). The frequent use of boxing and football metaphors in political discourse did not cause violence to become such an important force in our politics, but this usage is one measure of how presidential campaigns can be less about policy differences and complex political agendas than they can be about the selling of a certain kind of exec-utive masculinity, embodied (through 2004) in a particular man whom the public comes to know largely through television and other technologies of mass communication.

Boxing metaphors play a crucial role in defining presidential campaigns as the ultimate arena for masculine competition. Boxing is a prototypical working-class or poor man's (or more recently, woman's) sport that strips the notion of physical combat to its barest essence: man against man in a fight to the finish. Through the campaign of 2008, the (almost exclusively) white male candidates who have vied at the highest level for the presidency have in effect been competing to be their party's *champion*, who if victorious becomes the champion of the entire country, the man who stands in for the home team in international political competition against the champions of other countries (e.g., Saddam Hussein, Hugo Chavez, Mahmoud Ahmadinejad, etc.).

For many decades, newspapers have covered presidential debates with language taken directly from coverage of title bouts, complete with "Tale of the Tape" features that quantify a candidate's strengths and weaknesses. To this day, the political fortunes of various candidates are in part determined by whether or not political and media elites describe them as "heavyweights." Anyone who follows contemporary US politics even superficially knows that politicians and journalists constantly use boxing metaphors to describe political machinations. A few examples: before his first debate with Ronald Reagan in 1984, Walter Mondale was urged by Tip O'Neill to "come out slugging and come out fighting."[28] The *Los Angeles Times*, during the presidential primary season in 2000, ran an article about a dramatic speech by Arizona Senator John McCain under the headline "McCain Delivers Hard Left to Christian Right."[29] And in a lead-in to a jocular and substantive exchange on National Public Radio with commentator Michael Eric Dyson about the first debate between George W. Bush and John Kerry in 2004, host Tavis Smiley stated: "Once the lights and cameras are off, media pundits and voters are still left to decide which punches actually landed, which political jabs will be felt throughout the rest of the campaign."[30] Later in the discussion Dyson, commenting on a previous debate performance by Kerry, said "I ain't saying he was dancing like Ali, but at least he wasn't plodding like some ham-fisted contender for the crown."[31]

Boxing has historically been a male bastion, and it remains so in the twenty-first century. But women's boxing now occupies a small—but highly visible—cultural space. It is probably too early to tell how the increased popularity of women's boxing has affected the power of masculine symbolism associated with the sport. In any case, the 2008 political season broke new linguistic ground, at first because the presence of Hillary Clinton in the ranks of political "heavyweights" complicated the boxing metaphors. Politicians and political commentators had to choose whether or not to use language that had men metaphorically hitting a woman, and vice versa. (They largely decided in favor of using the language in gender-neutral fashion.)

Republican Sarah Palin's entry into the race as her party's vice-presidential nominee and the second woman on a major party ticket provided another watershed cultural moment. In her first nationally televised speech, at the Republican National Convention in early September, Palin sharply attacked Barack Obama's character and record. A typical headline in the media coverage read "Defiant Sarah Palin Comes Out Swinging,"[32] while the *New York Times* editorialized that Palin's rallies had become "spectacles of anger and insult," not unlike the staged media events where boxers ridicule each other in the hopes of drumming up fan interest in an upcoming title bout.[33] One of Palin's most-quoted lines on the campaign trail in the fall of 2008 was "The heels are on, the gloves are off," which she typically delivered to wild cheers of approval. In coming years, when this historic campaign and those yet to come are analyzed, it will be particularly interesting to see how female and male voters respond to language where a woman throws the "knockout punch." Does this masculinize and thus help to make them more credible as potential commanders-in-chief? Or do women who are seen as "too-aggressive"—even if only in a metaphorical sense—turn voters off? What are the differences between how the sexes view a woman "throwing punches" if she's a conservative (like Palin) or a liberal feminist (like Hillary Clinton?) More generally, how does political discourse infused with boxing metaphors influence the electoral chances of women candidates?

In the 2012 election year boxing metaphors continued to be as popular as ever. Commentators regularly scored the Republican debates like boxing matches. In a front-page *New York Times* profile of Rick Santorum, Katharine Q. Seelye wrote that Santorum's supporters "are drawn to (his) moral certitude, his fire-and-brimstone passion, his pugilistic posture of never giving up and never giving in."[34] Anticipating the start of the general election season, a headline on the cover of *Rolling Stone* magazine read "From Hope to Rope-a-Dope: Inside Obama's campaign." In early June, a *Boston Globe* headline read, "Romney Fires Up Conservatives with Spirited Jabs at Obama."[35]

Football is not only a hugely popular sport across the United States; it also provides a wealth of evocative metaphors in contemporary American politics. Journalists wonder whether a politician will do an "end run" around his/her opposition in the legislature. TV pundits preface their remarks about a candidate's debate performance by apologizing for doing a little "Monday-morning quarterbacking." Newly energized campaign volunteers claim to have been inspired to "get off the sidelines" and join the political battle. An op-ed in *USA Today* runs under the headline "Don't punt on Iran: US shouldn't throw bombs or play a soft defense."[36] And interestingly, the general election campaign season, when political ads increase exponentially and political talk fills the airwaves, corresponds to the main part of the football season. In fact, Election Day is the first Tuesday in November, right in the heart of the fall football schedule. This means that it is likely a common experience for men and women who watch football on television to be watching a game at one moment, then watching a political ad during a commercial break, followed by a panel of experts analyzing the game, and perhaps moments later watching a panel of experts analyzing the political ad, with much of the rhetoric about football and politics overlapping and interchangeable.

Since football is a violent sport, football metaphors bring violent language and imagery to political discourse. They also subtly and overtly link politics to warfare. As Howe (1988) puts it, "The element of physical conflict in football…makes football metaphors effective…because it establishes that politics is a violent exercise of power with clear winners and losers."[37] Football metaphors with military analogs that are used commonly by sportscasters and sportswriters, such as "throwing the bomb," "penetrating the zone," and "air game vs. ground game," ensure that the language of football and the language of war cross-reference each other. Establishment politicians—men and women—who use this sort of language can thus prove their mastery, or at least familiarity, with two important masculine domains: football and the military. As Reagan and many others have proven, this can be an effective way for wealthy candidates to show blue-collar males that they're one of the guys (especially if they're a man)—whether or not their economic program addresses working people's concerns or represents their interests.

It is certainly not difficult to find examples of football metaphors in the speech of contemporary politicians. During the 2004 Republican National Convention in New York City, Rudy Giuliani praised George W. Bush as a "great president" because "he turned around the ship of state from being solely on defense against terrorism to being on offense as well."[38] Speaking to reporters about the Iraq War several years later, Secretary of Defense Robert Gates made a similar point, with even more explicit football terminology. "It's important to defend this country on the extremists' 10-yard line, and not on our 10-yard line," he said.[39] Republican Senator Richard Lugar compared the Bush plan for a "surge" in Iraq to "…a draw play on third down with 20 yards to go in the first quarter. The play does have a chance of working if everything goes perfectly, but it is more likely to gain a few yards and set up a punt on the next down."[40]

The previously mentioned George Allen, a former college quarterback and the son of the late Washington Redskins coach, has taken the political use of football metaphors to a new level. As reported by Dana Milbank in the *Washington Post*, Allen filters nearly everything political through a football lens. He once said that critics of Condoleezza Rice, who went on to become secretary of state, "have used some bump-and-run defenses and tactics against her." A number of years ago, when the Republicans won a Senate seat in Louisiana, he said it "was like a double-reverse flea-flicker and a lateral." As head of Senate Republicans' campaign efforts in 2004, he called his candidates in the southern states the "NFC South."[41]

According to Milbank, "In Allen's world, primaries are "intrasquad scrimmages," his Senate staff is the 'A-team,' Senate recess is 'halftime' and opponents are flagged for 'pass interference.'" Allen accused the Democrats of "Constant delay of game, constant holding, constant pass interference and, once in a while, even piling on." Years without elections are the "offseason." Primaries are the "preseason." Senate Republicans are President Bush's "teammates." Big political donors join a "Quarterback Club" or a "Special Teams" committee.[42]

It is important to note that George Allen's near-obsessive use of football metaphors did not hurt him politically. In fact, while his football language was the object of ridicule in some quarters of mainstream journalism and also the blogosphere, until late in 2006 he was a star in conservative Republican circles and a potential 2008 presidential candidate. Interestingly, new media contributed to a major crisis in his political career, when his use of an alleged ethnic slur was caught on a handheld video camera and broadcast widely on YouTube, an incident that tarnished his reputation and contributed to the loss of his senate seat.

Allen might seem to have exhausted the genre, but in fact there seems to be no end of football metaphors that help make sense of political events. In a *USA Today* article about Obama's decision to nominate Elena Kagan to the Supreme Court, DeWayne Wickham wrote that black civil rights groups found themselves in a quandary because they weren't consulted in advance of the nomination but were expected to support it: "There's a sense among some that they're expected to support the plays being run by the White House," Wickham wrote, "even though they weren't in the huddle when they were called."[43] Before a big speech on jobs the president was preparing to deliver to the nation, Representative Emmanuel Cleaver (D-Mo), predicting the Republicans would criticize him no matter what, urged Obama to take a bolder approach: "If the player is going to get a penalty no matter what he does," Cleaver said, "why not deliver a hard hit?"[44] In the fall of 2011, the cochairman of Rick Perry's Iowa campaign said "We're doing the blocking and tackling for the Iowa caucus, we're getting people organized."[45]

The 2008 election of the first black president has already resulted in an increase in the use of basketball metaphors in politics. Since he emerged as a national figure, Barack Obama has shown a proclivity to reference basketball in his public statements. Before he delivered his famous keynote address at the 2004 Democratic National Convention in Boston, while he was running for the US senate, he boasted to a *Chicago Tribune* reporter that "I'm LeBron, baby," referring to basketball superstar LeBron James. "I can play on this level. I got some game." As president, Obama compared his vice-president Joe Biden to a basketball player "who does a bunch of things that don't show up in the stat sheet. He gets that extra rebound, takes the charge, makes that extra pass."[46]

CHAPTER 1: IT'S THE MASCULINITY, STUPID

Obama also happens to be a good basketball player, and in 2008 he often played pickup games on the campaign trail for exercise. But it is fair to ask whether this helped or hurt him politically, especially among the working-class white men whose votes the party has had such trouble attracting in presidential races for the past generation. Basketball is very popular with all races and ethnicities, but African American players dominate at the elite level in college and the pros. And although basketball is played in rural areas, in the late twentieth and early twenty-first centuries in the popular imagination it is coded as an urban sport, which for many rural voters reinforces Obama's city roots. In other words, did Obama's identification with basketball reinforce his "otherness" to the white majority, his *black* masculinity? Shared interest and experience with sports can be a catalyst for connection between a candidate and the voters—but divergent experiences can also serve as a proxy for racial/ethnic differences. As MSNBC's Chris Matthews said, "This gets very ethnic, but the fact that he's good at basketball doesn't surprise anybody, but the fact that he's that terrible at bowling does make you wonder."[47]

Maybe the politics of Obama and basketball don't all turn on race and geography. After all, playing pickup basketball has not traditionally been seen as "presidential" behavior. Unlike the more traditional presidential sport of golf, basketball is considered a young person's game. Could Obama's balling have contributed to the perception among some voters—not all of them rural and white—that he was young and inexperienced, and therefore not ready to be the patriarch of the nation?

Chapter 2
Setting the Stage: The Election of 1972

The 1972 presidential election helped set the stage for Republican dominance of presidential politics for the next generation. In a wartime election the incumbent Republican president Richard Nixon won a resounding forty-nine-state landslide victory over Democratic Senator George McGovern. The racial and gender dynamics that were catalyzed by Nixon's re-election campaign against McGovern in 1972 nonetheless continued to gather momentum throughout the 1970s, with class politics playing a central role. Historian Jefferson Cowie explains that in addition to a harsh economic climate during the seventies, with oil prices skyrocketing and record inflation and unemployment, the Democratic Party "faced a dilemma it could not solve: finding ways to maintain support within the white blue-collar base that came of age during the New Deal and World War II era, while at the same time servicing the pressing demands for racial and gender equity arising from the sixties."[1]

During the seventies white men were leaving the Democratic Party in droves—and not just in the South. In that sense, Jimmy Carter's was an anomalous term in what might otherwise have been an unbroken streak of Republican presidential victories stretching from 1968 until Clinton's win with a plurality of the vote in a three-way race in 1992. It is not possible here to examine or even outline all the reasons why working and middle-class white men abandoned the party that had been closely identified with the concerns of working men (and women) for most of the twentieth century. But white flight from the Democratic Party was at least catalyzed by the Democrats' identification with the civil rights movement, especially after President Lyndon Johnson signed the historic Civil Rights Act of 1964.

What is much less acknowledged, or understood, is the role played by gender in this cleavage. Of course, it is never entirely possible to separate race and gender. For one thing, a critical subtextual component of white male racism against blacks is white men's psychosexual anxieties and perceptions of inferiority to black men. But for the purposes of this analysis, Richard Nixon was able to identify and exploit the increasing disaffection of working-class white male voters from the Democratic Party over questions of patriotism and cultural identity that were caused in part by the Vietnam War and the movements against it. Many analyses of Nixon's strategy to woo these voters focus on class-based and racial resentments, yet fail to analyze the politics of masculinity that lurked just beneath the surface.

NIXON AND THE HARD HATS

In the late 1960s and early 1970s, a number of writers and academics began to look at the plight of the white working class. One piece that fired Nixon's imagination was journalist Pete Hamill's 1969 essay in *New York* magazine entitled "The Revolt of the White Lower Middle Class." Hamill captured the rage of blue-collar men in white ethnic communities in the urban north who felt neglected and abandoned. "A large reason for the growing alienation of the white working class is their belief that they are not respected. It is an important thing for the son of an immigrant to be respected," he wrote.[2] "It is imperative for New York politicians to begin to deal with the growing alienation and paranoia of the working-class white man," Hamill continued. He "feels trapped, and...ignored...any politician who leaves that white man out of the political equation does so at very large risk."[3] In 1970, Nixon's assistant secretary of labor Jerome Rosow delivered a report entitled "The Problem of the Blue-Collar Worker." The Rosow Report, as it came to be known, argued that white lower-class workers had a range of material needs, and were "on a treadmill, chasing the illusion of higher living standards." But echoing Hamill, it also said they felt like "forgotten people," for whom "the government and the society have limited, if any, direct concern and little visible action." Nixon dreamed of patching together a "new majority" of Republican voters to undo the reigning New Deal coalition, and he knew that in order to make this happen he needed to pull these voters away from the Democrats.

His problem was that he couldn't offer them rising wages or other material benefits, because that wouldn't be acceptable to the traditional Republican business constituency. But, as historian Rick Perlstein pointed out, Nixon figured out that if he were "to extend to blue-collar workers the hand of *cultural* recognition, that was a different ball game altogether." When a group of construction workers wielding American flags attacked an antiwar march of college students and others in New York City, called after the Kent State shootings in early May of 1970, the strategy gained further clarity. Here was a way the Republican Party could maintain its primary loyalty to the business class *and* stand with workers: by capitalizing on the cultural politics of patriotism and manhood. Perlstein explained that "the hard hat ascendancy set into motion a qualitative shift: the first concerted effort to turn the white working class, via its aesthetic disgusts, against a Democratic Party now joining itself objectively… to the agenda of the smelly longhairs who burned down buildings."[4] As Perlstein put it: "The Democratic Party: enemy of the working man. It was the political version of the *New York Times* photograph of the stockbroker and the pipe fitter joined in solidarity in the act of clobbering a hippie—their common weapon the American flag."[5] But Perlstein doesn't point to what that photo represented in terms of gender politics: The Hard Hat Riots—and Richard Nixon's divide and conquer tactics— served to accentuate the clash not only between differing class-based perceptions of patriotism but between competing visions of manhood. In the realm of cultural symbolism and identity—if not in the concrete realm of paychecks, health care, and education—the GOP positioned itself squarely on the side of the hard hats. They became the party of "real (white) men," while from that point on the Democrats were increasingly perceived as the party of pampered, feminized elites.

The Right was thus able, in the words of linguist Geoffrey Nunberg, to "convert the old populist language of class resentments into a new idiom that stripped it of any real economic content and turned America into (a society) divided only by values and fashions."[6] As *What's the Matter With Kansas* author Thomas Frank said, this was based on "a way of thinking about class that both encourages class hostility and simultaneously denies the economic basis of the grievance."[7] It was also a way to shift attention off the Republican Party's loyalty to Wall Street plutocrats and the ownership class and make it seem as if it was perfectly natural for blue-collar white guys to side with blue-blooded aristocrats. For forty years this strategy of defining liberalism as a lifestyle brand has been electoral gold for the GOP, which has, to the consternation of many on the Left, successfully sold itself as the party that cares about (white) working people. Decades later, John McCain could mention "Joe the Plumber" twenty-five times in a 2008 debate with Barack Obama, with few in the political commentariat noticing or commenting on what a stretch it was to think that the party of the 1 percent was actually concerned about the plight of most Americans.

ABORTION, AMNESTY, AND ACID

During the 1972 campaign the conservative journalist Robert Novak reported in one of his columns that an unnamed Democratic senator had lamented that George McGovern's candidacy was characterized by "abortion, amnesty, and acid." In conventional journalistic analysis, this alliterative phrase was taken as a metaphor for the capture of the McGovern campaign by the political and countercultural Left. By rejecting McGovern, a large majority of the voting public—Nixon's "silent majority"—was registering its disgust with sixties-era cultural and political radicalism and its supposed new home in the Democratic Party. But "abortion, amnesty and acid" was more than a metaphor for the Left. It was also a metaphor for the feminization of the Democratic Party by its association with sixties-era social movements that catalyzed direct challenges to traditional (white) male power and offered new cultural meanings of masculinity. Each of the terms—"abortion," "amnesty," and "acid"—suggests distinctly gendered qualities. By describing the McGovern campaign with these terms, the implicit message from his adversaries was that McGovern, and the Democratic Party under his leadership, had been emasculated.

Considering the gendered subtext of the three issues, each can be read as a critique of the masculine shortcomings of the McGovernites.

Abortion

The national movement for legalized abortion, which culminated in the 1973 United States Supreme Court ruling in *Roe vs. Wade*, was a feminist movement to secure women's right to reproductive decision making. Since *Roe vs. Wade*, antiabortion activists in and outside of government have been successful in their efforts to shift the focus of abortion discourse away from women's rights and onto the rights of the fetus. The logical progression of this shift in recent years has been the introduction of fetal "personhood" amendments that right-wing activists have successfully placed on the ballot in several states. The Right has been abetted in its efforts to roll back women's reproductive rights by a weakened women's movement and an often timid Democratic Party, which prefers to couch the terms of the debate in (seemingly) non-controversial words like "choice" and "privacy" when discussing fundamental questions of women's reproductive freedom. The term "reproductive freedom" itself, while technically accurate as a description of the stakes in the abortion debate, is itself slightly euphemistic. The feminists who catalyzed the abortion rights movement understood that safe, legal abortion represented a major step toward women's sexual freedom—their freedom from *men's* control of their sexuality. In that sense, early 1970s agitation for abortion rights was part of a much larger movement for women's rights, a movement that was gaining momentum and securing legal and political victories before the 1972 election. The backlash against the women's movement gathered political momentum throughout the 1970s, culminating in Ronald Reagan's election to the presidency in 1980. But as early as 1972 and even earlier, a substantial portion of the electorate, whom historian Ruth Rosen calls "neo-traditionalists," resisted any change that altered familiar gender relations.

> For them, feminism symbolized the decadence of the 1960s, and the loss of women's moral guardianship of the family. Fearful of an uncertain future, they yearned for a mythic past in which men earned a family wage and ruled a patriarchal family, when women bore many children and stayed at home to care for them, when homosexuals prayed for conversion or absolution and stayed out of sight, when African-Americans didn't ask for special reparations, and when schools and universities taught the superiority of Western European culture.[8]

The Republican Party had a long tradition of support for women's rights, and in the early 1970s many Republicans at both the state and national level were active supporters of the Equal Rights Amendment and progressive reform of the abortion laws. But as the parties continued to realign, the Democratic Party was clearly becoming the party of women's rights, just as it had emerged in the decade prior as the party of civil rights. While countless political analysts and commentators have examined the phenomenon of the Democrats losing white votes as a result of championing civil rights legislation, there has been much less attention to the cost they paid with men due to their embrace of the major tenets of liberal feminism. As Frank Rich pointed out in 2012, "It's not news that the GOP is the anti-abortion party, that it panders to the religious right, and that it's particularly dependent on white men with less education and less income, a displaced demographic that has been as threatened by the rise of the empowered modern woman as it has been by the cosmopolitan multiracial male elites symbolized by Barack Obama."[9] In the early seventies the Democrats sought to address the growing movement of women into the workforce and political life, and as a result the Democratic "brand" became increasingly identified as a "woman's" brand. This happened just as Nixon was shifting the focus of the GOP's appeal to working people from bread and butter economic issues to questions of cultural identity. The GOP was becoming the party devoted to holding the cultural line against changes in the racial, gender, and sexual order; the Democrats were fast becoming known as the party that sought to enshrine these changes in law. In a culture in which citizens' decisions about which parties and candidates to support had increasingly become analogous to consumers' decisions about which brands to remain loyal to or which products to purchase, it is no wonder that Democratic presidential candidates would find it harder to attract white men's votes.

Amnesty

South Dakota Senator George McGovern had a distinguished military record as a World War II fighter pilot. He flew thirty-five B-24 bomber missions and earned the Distinguished Flying Cross. But he turned against the Vietnam War early in his Senate career and in 1972 ran as an opponent of continued US military aggression in Vietnam. He also proposed deep cuts in military spending, and announced that he supported amnesty for draft evaders. In the Vietnam-era, "amnesty" meant legal amnesty for men who dodged the Vietnam-era draft by illegal means, such as living underground, or fleeing to

Canada. As a result of his stances on issues related to the war, McGovern attracted support from the antiwar Left, and opposition from pro-war Republicans and Democrats, and other defenders of a US hard line against "communist expansionism." There was a pronounced class dimension to Vietnam-era tensions around the role of the US military and the mandatory draft, tensions that were on full display in the Hard Hat Riots in New York City May, 1970. These demonstrations featured hundreds of blue-collar male construction workers protesting throughout the month and culminated on May 20 in a rally of 100,000 that was sponsored by a major New York labor organization. In the riots and rallies, the construction workers, carrying aloft a sea of American flags, violently expressed a resentment widely felt by many working-class whites toward what they considered entitled, unpatriotic college students who were ungrateful for the sacrifice of so many working-class young men who had already died or been wounded in Vietnam in service of their country. This class-based resentment was exploited skillfully by Nixon and then by subsequent Republican Party strategists and their allies in media for the next four decades, who rhetorically allied the GOP with white working-class voters against the "latte-sipping, *New York Times* reading" Democratic elites who supposedly looked down upon the heartland values and simple patriotism of working people. (In contemporary conservative media the most skilled practitioner of this brand of right-wing cultural politics is the talk radio and cable TV host Sean Hannity, who is also a best-selling author. Hannity, a former contractor from Long Island, New York, routinely has guests like Marine Lieutenant Colonel Oliver North and other blue collar icons on his radio and TV show, decrying liberal snobs and reasserting the moral righteousness of traditional American values.) Ironically, many conservative movement leaders in the 1980s, 1990s, and 2000s, including many senior officials in the Reagan administration and both Bush administrations, were middle-class college students in the 1960s and early 1970s who avoided military service using any means at their disposal. But in 1972, with troops on the ground and nightly news reports and video footage of US casualties, emotions ran high, and the suspicion that McGovern would side with the "wimpy" opponents of the war instead of the brave men who were fighting it cost him dearly with voters, especially white men. In the general election, only one in five white male adults voted for McGovern.

CHAPTER 2: SETTING THE STAGE: THE ELECTION OF 1972

Acid

"Acid" can be read as a metaphor for the sixties counterculture, and the explicit critique of white middle-class values and lifestyle that it represented. To the extent that the McGovern campaign could be framed by Republicans and mainstream media commentators as guilty by association with the likes of drug guru Timothy Leary, whose famous advice to young people was "tune in, turn on, drop out," the more Democrats appeared out of step with average, hard-working Americans, including millions of parents who worried about their kids getting involved with drugs. Of course the Democratic Party was the party of the counterculture only in the fevered imaginations of the counter-countercultural Right. In fact, the very notion of a countercultural politics elides the significant tensions within sixties-era left-wing social movements between political and so-called cultural radicals, where the former critiqued the amorphous rebellion of the latter, and the white, middle-class privilege and self-absorption of hippies, flower children, and sundry antiauthoritarians. To the extent that one could speak of a "countercultural politics," at a minimum it rejected the inherent conservatism, stifling conformity, and corporate influence in the two-party system. Notably, as McGovern progressed toward the nomination, much of the "Triple-A" criticism his campaign received came from fellow Democrats. The journalist Hunter S. Thompson captured the dilemma this posed for McGovern.

> In three of the last four primaries (Ohio, Nebraska and California) he has spent an alarmingly big chunk of his campaign time *denying* (emphasis in original) that behind his calm and decent façade he is really a Trojan Horse candidate—coming on in public as a bucolic Jeffersonian Democrat while secretly plotting to seize the reins of power and turn them over at midnight on Inauguration Day to a Red-bent hellbroth of radicals, Dopers, Traitors, Sex Fiends, Anarchists, Winos and 'extremists' of every description.....Toward the end of the Nebraska campaign he was spending most of his public time explaining that he was Not for abortion on demand. Not for legalized Marijuana, Not for unconditional amnesty…and his staff was becoming more and more concerned that their man had been put completely on the defensive.[10]

As Timothy Noah (2007) observes in a review of Bruce Miroff's book *The Liberals' Moment: the McGovern Insurgency and the Identity Crisis of the Democratic Party*, to this day "it is an article of faith among centrist Democrats (and nearly all Republicans) that the Democratic Party blundered badly when it nominated McGovern," who was thought by many to be a dangerous radical. Since 1972, powerful forces within the Democratic Party have sought to fashion the image of the party in opposition to the image conjured up by the McGovern campaign. Because his opponents were successful in linking McGovern with the counterculture, they were able to associate him with what was perhaps the most threatening message of sixties-era counterculture: the revolutionary idea captured in the popular bumper sticker slogan Question Authority. The phrase suggested the necessity of questioning all forms of established power, but the various influential social movements of the time were determined most of all to challenge the centuries-old power and privilege of the white male patriarchs. Thus an embrace of countercultural values was tantamount to a rejection of white men's rule, most recently manifest in television culture as the Father Knows Best ethos of the 1950s. McGovern, Noah writes, is often (unfairly) blamed "for taking a Democratic Party that represented the working man and refashioning it into a party of blacks, women, gays, environmentalists, college professors, criminals, movie stars, software engineers and personal-injury lawyers." The historical processes that occasioned this shift were clearly much larger than one man's campaign. As Bill Clinton said in 2004, the polarization in American politics began with the civil rights, women's rights, gay rights, and abortion rights struggles of the 1960s. "If you look back on the 60's and on balance, you think there was more good than harm, then you're probably a Democrat," he said. "If you think there was more harm than good, you're probably a Republican."[11] But if it is true that since 1972—and perhaps since the mid-1960s—white working-class men felt increasingly disaffected from a Democratic Party they were led to believe expressed the values of the counterculture, one of those values was a new form of feminized masculinity that rejected not only patriarchal authority but any displays of traditional masculine aggression. While a generation of feminist activists and historians has documented the sexism of men in the New Left, the hippie movement, and other sixties-era social and political movements led by men, conservatives were repulsed by the feminine

CHAPTER 2: SETTING THE STAGE: THE ELECTION OF 1972

characteristics of countercultural masculinity, such as long hair and opposition to war. It is revealing, for example, that one of the most common epithets directed toward men with long hair in the 1960s and early 1970s was "hippie fag," which conflated the transgression of masculine gender norms with deviation from normative heterosexuality, but which nonetheless demonstrated how much the counterculture was seen as a threat to traditional masculinity.

Chapter 3
1980: Reagan vs. Carter

The 1980 election was a watershed election in American politics for many reasons, not least of which is that Ronald Reagan's superlative performance of presidential masculinity continues to loom large in contemporary presidential politics. But 1980 was not the first electoral contest between competing versions of masculinity, nor was it the first election in which media figured prominently. Among political historians there is widespread agreement that the 1960 race between Richard M. Nixon and John F. Kennedy was the first presidential campaign in which television played a decisive role, mostly because in a televised debate the camera loved Kennedy and showed Nixon's sweaty brow and less-than-endearing five o'clock shadow. Constructed and mediated images of presidential masculinity had long been important in presidential races, even before the mass media technologies of the twentieth century. But since the invention of television, and particularly since 1960, the way a candidate for president performs his manhood in the media spectacle of presidential campaigns has not merely been an important part of his "electability"; it has arguably been the most important part. Especially since the 1980 Electoral College landslide victory of Reagan—a former Hollywood actor—effective televisual performance, including the ability to project "manly" strength, has become the sine qua non of success at the presidential level.

The Republican Party has understood since at least 1972 that the key to winning working-class and middle-class white male votes (to complement the party's huge historic advantage with wealthy white men) is twofold: (1) appeal to the racial resentments of white voters by coded references to the Democrats as the party of blacks and other racial minorities, and to the GOP as the party that is on "your" side; and (2) frame politics, especially presidential politics, in terms of a contest about manhood, where the Republican side represents the true home of red-blooded, flag-waving, red-meat eating, heterosexual "real men." Until the 2008 election, the Republican Party had been fabulously successful with this strategy, as Jimmy Carter in the post-Watergate election of 1976 and Bill Clinton, in a three-way race in 1992 with the weak incumbent George H. W. Bush and the independent and eccentric candidacy of H. Ross Perot, were the only two Democrats—both from the South—to be elected president in the past thirty-six years.

THE COLD WAR

The central and overarching foreign policy issue for American presidents since the end of the Second World War was the Cold War with the Soviet Union, which lasted from the mid-1940s through the demise of the Soviet state in 1989. For four decades Cold War politics dominated foreign policy discourse in government, media, and academia. Each election cycle, presidential candidates of both major parties were judged by how effectively they would be able to "stand up" to the Soviet leader, with the individual men serving as embodied proxies for the fight between two "superpowers" with competing and incompatible economic/political systems. In the US, Cold War battles were fought in the ideological realm ("capitalism vs. communism," "freedom vs. tyranny") and in the news and entertainment media. But it is also important to note that fear of nuclear war—on both sides—was pervasive and well-founded. Each country possessed enough nuclear weapons to obliterate entire cities and kill tens of millions of people in the enemy nation, wreaking historically unprecedented death and destruction. The Cuban Missile Crisis in 1962 is widely regarded as the closest the US and the Soviets came to actual nuclear war, but nonetheless for several decades realistic fear of superpower conflict pervaded public consciousness.

In 1964, one of the most famous political ads in history took advantage of this fear—specifically by capitalizing on public fear of hypermasculine overreaction to the perceived threat. The presidential campaign of Lyndon Johnson ran a television ad entitled the "Daisy" ad, which featured a four-year-old girl in a field pulling petals off a flower. As the girl innocently counts to ten, an adult male announcer cuts in and begins his own countdown, leading to a bomb exploding and a mushroom cloud rising. As the sky fills with smoke, Johnson's voiceover warns: "These are the stakes! To make a world in which all of God's children can live, or to go into the dark. We must either love each other, or we must die." The ad was shown only one time but was widely regarded as an important aspect of the Democrats' successful strategy to frighten people about the prospect of electing as president the right-wing Republican Arizona Senator Barry Goldwater. Goldwater lost the 1964 election to Johnson in a landslide of historic proportions. The Goldwater campaign in 1964 was one of the few instances in postwar American politics where hypermasculine posturing arguably cost a politician political support, in this case because Goldwater's bombastic anticommunist rhetoric and aggressive militarism raised fears among many voters that his immoderation could result in nuclear annihilation.

It is important to consider how presidential masculinity played out against the backdrop of the US-Soviet struggle. Since at least 1972, conservative hardliners in politics and media routinely accused liberals and Democrats of being "soft on communism," a tactic used not only to win elections by feminizing the opposition but to justify escalating military spending. Cold War politics, rhetoric, and propaganda played a powerful role in many elections in the fifties, sixties, and seventies, both because of the nuclear arms race and because the US government mobilized popular support for the Vietnam War by describing it as a war against communist expansionism. When the Soviet Union existed, it also served the purpose of giving the US president a powerful adversary against whom to demonstrate his masculine bona fides in staged media events. The Soviets played this adversarial role masterfully, in part because of their own leaders' need for public demonstrations of militarized virility, exemplified by their semiannual parades through Red Square on May Day and the anniversary of the revolution in November, where thousands of soldiers marched in rigid military formation behind dozens of tanks and large missiles in an unmistakably phallic display of Soviet military might. Since the end of the Cold War, no US president has had the opportunity to shine—like Ronald Reagan—as the champion of our side in a clearly defined competition with our declared enemy. This is not possible in today's world of asymmetrical warfare and terrorist attacks from faceless enemies, where the "other side" is a loosely organized and diffuse collection

CHAPTER 3: 1980: REAGAN VS. CARTER

of non-state actors whose leaders never appear in public, much less pose for pictures in staged media spectacles. As Stephen Colbert put it on his fake news show, "I miss the Cold War. That was an enemy I could wrap my head around."[1]

During the Cold War, candidates for president were judged, in popular parlance, in part by whether they could go "toe-to-toe" with the Soviet leader—a boxing metaphor that conceptually linked superpower conflict to heavyweight title fights. In fact, US-Soviet "summits" that were conducted between the US president and the Soviet premier during the 1970s and 1980s were media spectacles that had much in common with prizefights, including the verbal fisticuffs and rhetorical positioning prefight, the sensationalized media coverage, the boxing metaphors that characterized commentary about both events, and most importantly, two larger-than-life men who represented opposing sides in a competition where the stakes were high.

At US-Soviet arms control summits, which were covered extensively in the media, the American president was not only the official leader of our side, he literally embodied our national virtues. His performance on that public stage said something about *us*—how strong we were, how self-assured. Reagan's stage managers understood this well. As much as any modern presidency, the Reagan administration successfully sold itself—in the person of the cowboy hero Ronald Reagan—as synonymous with the United States. President Reagan himself was aware that for many people, he *was* America. His biographer Edmund Morris, who enjoyed unprecedented access to Reagan during his second term, confirmed this. "Reagan," he said, "strangely combined modesty... with... a sense of himself as the embodiment of the state."[2] The Cold War was also the backdrop to the legendary 1980 US Olympic hockey team victory over the heavily favored Soviet team in Lake Placid, New York, a media spectacle that featured a potent mix of sports, white masculinity, and nationalism, and helped to usher in the Reagan era. According to a representative article in the *St. Petersburg Times* (2005), the US victory touched such a nerve and "People reacted so emotionally because they needed something to feel good about. American hostages were being held in Iran. The Soviets had invaded Afghanistan, and President Carter was threatening a boycott of the Summer Olympics in Moscow."[3] The victory of the young Americans against the older and more experienced Russians was later judged to be the most outstanding sports moment of the twentieth century by *Sports Illustrated* magazine.

Ronald Reagan won the White House later that year and came into office in 1981 as a militant anticommunist and staunch Cold Warrior who opposed Richard Nixon's policy of détente with the Soviet Union. Much of Reagan's political appeal can be attributed to his (at the time) uncompromising stance toward the Soviet government, such as when in 1983 he called the Soviet Union the "focus of evil in the modern world," in what came to be known, with a nod to Reagan's cartoonishly cinematic worldview, as his "evil empire" speech. Reagan campaigned for president in 1980 and 1984 on the clever slogan of "peace through strength," which identified conservative Republicanism directly with muscular masculinity, and provided rhetorical cover for his administration's massive transfer of federal spending from health, education, and human services programs to the military. Throughout the Reagan presidency, the haunting specter of an expansionist communist Russia was used to rationalize massive increases in military spending, which, together with a reorganization of the tax code that redistributed wealth upward, created huge deficits and thus added hundreds of billions of dollars to the national debt. The Right effectively used media at opportune moments to stoke the American public's fear of the Soviets. For example, in 1984 the Reagan presidential campaign ran an ad entitled "Bear in the woods," which became one of the famous political ads of the 1980s. The ad's unconventional narrative depicted a large brown bear—a stand-in for the Soviets—running in the woods, as a somber-toned but authoritative male announcer warned: "There is a bear in the woods. For some people the bear is easy to see. Others don't see it at all. Some people say the bear is tame. Others say it's vicious. And dangerous. Since no one can really be sure who is right, isn't it smart to be as strong as the bear? If there is a bear." There was no need for the ad to further spell out its message beyond the visual metaphor, because its essence by that time was so well known: vote for Ronald Reagan if you're a man (or woman) who understands the elemental dangers in the world, and you want a government led by a man who will not hesitate to use the overwhelming power of the United States military in order to protect you, your family, and your country.

It is important to note that Republican propaganda about the Democratic Party being "weak on defense" is a tactic the GOP has used since 1972 with repeated electoral success, despite the demonstrable absurdity of the charge. There was a long-standing bipartisan consensus in American politics in the postwar era that the major foreign policy objective and budgetary priority in foreign policy was the arms race and military competition with the Soviet Union. Even after 1972, the differences between Republican presidents' budgetary requests for the military and those approved by Democratic-controlled congresses have been relatively miniscule, especially as a percentage of the federal budget. The often heard Republican charge that America's defenses would be imperiled by the level of military spending proposed by the Democratic Party has been even more hyperbolic in the post-Soviet era, when US military spending is annually larger than the next twenty-five countries' military budgets *combined*. Ironically, much of Ronald Reagan's political legacy is built on the notion that he "won the Cold War," but he reached historic agreements with the Soviets toward the end of their crumbling empire in the late 1980s only when he went against the hard right wing of his own party and negotiated far-reaching reductions in nuclear weapons.

JIMMY CARTER

Conventional commentary about the historic nature of the 1980 election focuses on the political ascension of Ronald Reagan, and the triumph of the conservative movement that his election represented. But the rise of Reagan arguably would not have been possible were it not for the presidency of Jimmy Carter. Thus I would like to begin this discussion not by inquiring about why Reagan won, but about why Carter lost. For it is against the negative example of Jimmy Carter that post-Vietnam era conservatives created their masculine ideal of the American president, in a process that began with Reagan and culminated in the two-term presidency of George W. Bush. Jimmy Carter was elected as a kind of national "healer" in the first post-Watergate election in 1976; notably he won 47 percent of the white male vote, which to this day remains the high-water mark for Democrats since Lyndon Johnson's landslide victory in 1964. Just four years later he lost the presidency to Ronald Reagan in an Electoral College landslide, winning a mere 32 percent of white males.

Historians have enumerated the litany of economic woes that contributed to Carter's political demise: high interest rates, double-digit stagflation, long gas lines. They point to his political failures, such as his inability to push energy legislation through a Democratic-controlled Congress, or his ultimately disastrous so-called "malaise" speech. These troubles alone might have caused the voters to reject his bid for re-election, but to his numerous critics—especially on the Right—it was the hostage crisis that exposed Carter's fundamental shortcoming: he was too conciliatory, too nice. He wore cardigan sweaters, had big teeth, and smiled too much. He was not tough enough to lead America in a world where our enemies could pounce at any moment. He was deficient in the one quality that mattered most—he wasn't man enough for the job.

When radical Iranian students took US embassy personnel hostage in Tehran on November 4, 1979, it was a rude awakening to many Americans that we were vulnerable—at home and abroad—to terrorism arising out of Middle East conflicts in which our government and military had long played a central role. It is also important to note that the hostage taking took place only four years after the final pullout of US troops from Vietnam, an event documented in media by video footage of US personnel being airlifted by helicopter off a rooftop in Saigon, bringing an ignominious and televised end to the first war our country had ever lost. The long, bloody debacle in Vietnam, and the deep social cleavages at home it had laid bare, cast a giant shadow over President Carter's missteps with Iran, because the hostage taking confirmed what many people—especially white men—already suspected: the US had lost its way in the world, had passed its peak. It seemed no longer to be, in the words of former Secretary of State Madeleine Albright, the "indispensable nation."

Jimmy Carter was never known for having a tough-guy persona, but he did come into office in 1976 with a resume that attested to his traditional masculine credentials. As William Pollack, the author of *Real Boys*, explains, "Carter was misunderstood. He was caring, thoughtful, in ways that were perceived as not masculine, tough, and strong enough...I think some white men voted for (Carter) because they thought they would get a nuclear sub commander but instead they got the preacher who their wife drags them to Sunday lessons with."[4] In a 1984 *Wall Street Journal* article, John Mihalic elaborated on that theme and took the premise a step further.

Jimmy Carter first presented himself to the nation as a masculine person-

CHAPTER 3: 1980: REAGAN VS. CARTER

ality. Naval academy. Submariner. Nuclear engineer. Farmer. Loner. Tough governor. But once in office, he lost no time revealing his true feminine spirit. He wouldn't twist arms. He didn't like to threaten or rebuke...And we watched how far this approach got him in the jungles of Washington and the world. So in a sense, we've already had a woman president: Jimmy Carter.[5]

The Iranian Hostage Crisis was the chief development in Carter's presidency that set the stage for the subsequent characterization of him—and by association the entire Democratic Party—as "soft" and emasculated. Carter's popularity, already hovering at near-record lows due to the nation's myriad economic problems, initially soared in the months after the embassy seizure, as the American people followed the standard script and rallied around their leader in response to threats from without. But time wore on with no imminent release in sight. What was in sight, night after night on television, were scenes of American flags being burned by angry young Iranian men in the streets of Tehran, and blindfolded Americans being dragged around in ritual displays of public humiliation. This continued for 444 days. As demand for more news and commentary about the ongoing crisis grew, ABC News began to broadcast a news program after the late local news, which they called *America Held Hostage: Day 72*, and so on. (In order to capitalize on the audience they had developed for that show, at the end of the hostage crisis *America Held Hostage* became *Nightline, with Ted Koppel*.) *America Held Hostage* featured updates on hostage negotiations and related political developments, as well as commentary and debate from guests, typically representatives of US diplomatic and military elites. It also featured the latest video footage from Tehran. The late 1970s media universe in which the hostage crisis took place was dramatically different from the one today. It was just before the widespread advent of cable TV, so most homes only had access to television news on the three major networks, as well as radio and newspapers. Although communications technology was primitive by digital era standards, the limited range of media options meant that tens of millions of Americans witnessed the same events, filtered through the same media lens, and hence experienced the hostage crisis together. Aside from the human interest stories it generated about individual hostages, and their terrified families anxiously awaiting news each day about their loved ones, perhaps the most powerful political story mainstream media coverage told about the hostage crisis concerned Americans' newly acknowledged vulnerability to terrorism. There had been other terrorist incidents that affected Americans in the 1970s, but none remotely as high-profile and consequential as this full-blown media spectacle.

Because the Carter administration made it a priority to secure the release of the hostages unharmed, its options were limited. For the duration of the ordeal, the awesome military power of the United States was rendered inconsequential, which contributed to the narrative, advanced by conservatives, that America itself had suffered a great humiliation. We had been metaphorically emasculated. This point was accentuated with the failure of a hostage rescue attempt authorized by President Carter on April 24, 1980, when eight US service members were killed when their helicopter crashed in the desert. Because of the symbolic position of the president as the masculine embodiment of national power, Jimmy Carter's folksy religiosity, cerebralism, and excessively polite personal style became increasingly the object of public criticism and scorn. It was much easier to maintain that Carter's supposed weakness *as a man* had somehow allowed this debacle to occur than it was to blame US policy in Iran stretching back decades, under both Democratic and Republican rule. This personalization of policy matters was facilitated by the fact that coverage of US foreign policy in the corporate media routinely obfuscates the economic interests and imperial motives of US elites in favor of wholesome-sounding narratives about the "promotion of democracy," as well as the ever-shifting dynamics of interpersonal relationships among national leaders. In the latter case, the ubiquitous photos that appeared in media coverage of the stern, authoritarian Iranian Islamist revolutionary leader Ayatollah Khomeini reinforced the idea that in a battle for masculine supremacy, our weak president was no match for their ruthless leader.

This narrative was validated with classic cinematic timing as the Iranian students contributed immeasurably to the eventual mythification of Ronald Reagan when they released fifty-two Americans hostages just five minutes after Reagan—playing the no-nonsense national sheriff in what his biographer Lou Cannon called "the role of a lifetime"—rode into town and was inaugurated on January 20, 1981. By most accounts, the timing of the

CHAPTER 3: 1980: REAGAN VS. CARTER

hostage release was intended to humiliate Carter further. To Reagan supporters who deeply identified with the idea of their hero's masculine prowess and
the muscular foreign policy his administration promised to pursue, the radical
students were once again afraid to push the US around now that we once
again had a real man in charge. In either case, the conventions of media
coverage of these historic events as they unfolded contributed to the growing
perception that a resurgent American manhood as personified in the president
was a central factor in the furtherance of foreign policy goals and the national
interest of the United States.

Jimmy Carter has had a particularly active and productive post-
presidency, writing books, lecturing, overseeing the Carter Center, and monitoring elections around the world. Still, to this day, conservatives openly
ridicule his manhood, and use him as a foil to bolster their own presumptive
masculine prowess. As Glenn Greenwald writes:

> ...right-wing tough guys who never spent a day in the military protested
> and mocked endlessly when it was announced, in 2005, that a submarine
> would be named after Navy veteran Jimmy Carter. Carter is a graduate of
> the Naval Academy, having attended during World War II. In the Navy he
> became a submariner, serving in both the Atlantic and Pacific fleets, and he
> rose to the rank of lieutenant. He was personally selected by Admiral
> Hyman Rickover, known as the "Father of the Nuclear Navy," for the top-
> secret nuclear submarine program...
>
> Despite a history of military service that few right-wing warriors can
> come close to matching, conservatives heaped endless scorn and ridicule on
> the decision that a nuclear submarine would bear Carter's name. At
> *National Review* alone—filled to the rim with absurd, swaggering, pretend
> tough guys—Steve Hayward referred to the "oxymoronic Jimmy Carter
> attack submarine"; Jonah Goldberg published an e-mail spouting that
> "naming this boat for Carter resounds with irony" and another stating
> that... "If a Russian sub attacks undefended ships, will the *USS Jimmy
> Carter* immediately boycott the US-Russian softball game in Guam?" His
> colleague Kathryn Jean Lopez sneered: "I can't get over how ridiculous the
> sound of a Jimmy Carter attack sub is. The enemy trembles."[6]

It should be noted that while scholarly and mainstream media accounts of US foreign policy during Jimmy Carter's presidency routinely emphasize the successful Camp David negotiations he brokered between Israel and Egypt, as well as his promotion of human rights, critics on the Left point to numerous instances of the Carter administration's financial and military support for murderous regimes in El Salvador, Haiti, Indonesia, and elsewhere. In addition, the Nobel Peace Prize winner with a decidedly dovish image since he left public office is the same person who, as president, reinstated draft registration, funded the neutron bomb, and increased military spending beyond the inflation rate each year of his presidency. Contrary to the popular misconception that Carter "weakened" US defenses, Reagan's massive military buildup in the 1980s did not reverse Carter-era policy; it merely accelerated it.

RONALD REAGAN

Ronald Reagan grew up in the Midwest but was marketed to the public as a leader who embodied one of the enduring masculine myths of the United States: the strong, unwavering, moral cowboy riding in from the west to save the day. After the economic crises of Jimmy Carter's presidency, and especially after the Iranian Hostage Crisis prompted criticism from some quarters that the US had become an "impotent giant," a significant portion of the electorate was ready to turn the government over to the former governor of California, an aging right-wing ideologue who positively radiated a belief in old-fashioned American military supremacy.

On his third attempt at the presidency, Ronald Reagan appeared on the presidential scene in 1980 as if he had been sent to the Republican Party straight from central casting. It was not simply that he was a former actor who was skilled at memorizing his lines and making his marks when the cameras rolled. His entire persona was tailor-made for the task of remasculin-izing both the GOP and, for those who supported him, the country itself. If Jimmy Carter's "soft" masculinity had failed to inspire the nation at home and allegedly deepened our vulnerability to threats from abroad, Ronald Reagan's "hard" masculinity would seek to take care of business on both fronts—literally and metaphorically—and in the process create a new conservative template for white male leadership after two decades of epochal cultural transformation catalyzed by the civil rights, women's liberation, and gay and lesbian movements.

This soft-hard dichotomy offers a useful way to think about tensions, contradictions, and shifts in the meaning of American manhood that arose in reaction to the rise of those progressive movements, followed by the debacle and defeat in Vietnam. Of course, these dynamics were manifested not only in politics but in art, perhaps most notably in the popular cinema of the 1970s, 1980s, and early 1990s. In *Hard Bodies: Hollywood Masculinity in the Reagan Era* (1993), Susan Jeffords analyzes popular movies like *Rambo*, *The Terminator*, and the revisionist Clint Eastwood western *Unforgiven*, and argues that these and many other Hollywood films both reflect and produce ideologies and narratives of manhood that in a media culture exert influence over which feature films become popular and iconic, and even which candidates and qualities of candidates are constructed as masculine, and in some cases as mandatory for political leadership. Conflating the roles of actors and politicians, she says of Reagan:

> He was able to portray himself as both a 'real man' and a 'real president,' as both a father and a king…he was able to foster a (conservative) revolution that would define the nation's identity for the next eight years…It was a revolution defined by what it was not. It was not Jimmy Carter or the Carter policies, which it rewrote as weak, defeatist, inactive and feminine…Ronald Reagan and his administration (were able to) portray themselves successfully as distinctly masculine, not merely as men but as decisive, tough, aggressive, strong and domineering men.[7]

In this section, I will examine key aspects of the construction of Ronald Reagan's masculinity in media culture during his 1980 run for the presidency, his reelection campaign in 1984, and select moments during his two-term presidency. Reagan's political influence was enormous and far-reaching. Recent revisionist histories, such as Will Bunch's *Tear Down This Myth*, make a compelling case that Reaganomics was largely a failed economic experiment that required more than a decade of economic policy to undo, and that Reagan's signature foreign policy triumph, helping to usher in the end of the Cold War with the Soviet Union, was only possible due to Reagan's willingness to discard his earlier right-wing bellicosity and negotiate with the leader of a country he had formerly called the "evil empire." Nonetheless, Reagan's presidency shifted federal spending priorities away from social welfare to the military, and pushed regulatory policy, taxation, civil rights enforcement, criminal justice policy, the federal judiciary, and much more significantly rightward. More than twenty years after Reagan left office, and eight years after his death, Reaganism remains a powerful ideological force in the conservative movement and Republican Party through its officeholders at the local, state, and federal level.

But Ronald Reagan's cultural influence was also considerable. As I have argued, the president plays an important pedagogical function in that (he) helps to establish and maintain masculine norms; as the highest-status man in the country, the qualities a president possesses help to influence the very idea of what is considered masculine. I am especially interested in how Ronald Reagan was able to perform as president a kind of retro white masculinity in an era when white men's continued cultural dominance faced ideological and political challenges on numerous fronts—especially from modern multi-cultural women's movements that have done so much in recent decades to transform the social landscape. In other words, Reagan's popularity—especially with white men—offers insight into the backlash not only against the civil rights movement but also against feminism and how it expressed itself politically. And because of the skill and sophistication with which his administration managed Reagan's image, it is imperative that analyses of his political success feature a deconstruction of its media components. Most people, after all, "know" presidents not as a result of personal contact with them, but through the consumption of their televisual performances and other media constructions. Thus to "know" and identify with them is to know and identify, in a sense, with a character they have created on television.

For purposes of brevity and practicality, I have narrowed the focus of this brief analysis of Reagan's masculinity in media to three areas, some of which overlap: the relationship between the idea of "John Wayne" in the movies and the idea of "Ronald Reagan" as president; the construction of Ronald Reagan as a plain-spoken cowboy; and the role of anti-intellectualism in presidential politics. In each case, I pay special attention to media constructions as they relate to issues of violence at home and abroad.

CHAPTER 3: 1980: REAGAN VS. CARTER

Reagan/Wayne

When discussing Ronald Reagan's masculinity, it is difficult if not impossible to avoid talking about questions of appearance versus reality, because the "President Reagan" who appeared in public and on television screens throughout the 1980s bears only faint resemblance to the man with whom people close to him were familiar. In fact, many members from both of his administrations have written memoirs in which they candidly admit how little they knew or understood about the actual man himself, as distinct from the powerful leader who came across in the scripted performances that defined his presidency. Former president Gerald Ford said Reagan was "one of the few political leaders I've met whose public speeches revealed more than his private conversations."[8] In this way, Reagan was not unlike many actors who create larger-than-life personae on the big screen, but whose private lives often fail to live up to anything close to the nobility or heroism of the characters they manage to project. The classic example of this was John Wayne, whose career had much in common with Reagan's, from their size and masculine good looks, to the cowboy paraphernalia they were both frequently photographed wearing, to their right-wing political views. Like Reagan was later to become, Wayne was a much-larger-than-life cultural presence, whose image stood for something that transcended the mundane details of his acting career or his personal life. In *John Wayne's America*, Garry Wills traces the history of "John Wayne" as an idea, not of John Wayne (or Marion Morrison) the man. Central to the idea of "John Wayne"—or "Ronald Reagan"—was a "compound idea of what American manhood is in the minds of the vast majority of Americans."[9] Wills differentiates Wayne from both Nixon and Reagan because while the latter had their handlers, the "projectors and protectors of their image," ultimately they were elected officials and leaders of their party. Wayne on the screen was nothing *but* image—an image that nonetheless carried enormous political weight. And whereas politicians had speechwriters, Wayne had scripts. These scripts were "the tools for making the myths that go into our self-understanding as a people." Although he was writing about the cultural politics of John Wayne's artistic contributions, Wills could have been writing about Reagan when he said:

Naturally, so political an art caused political resistance from those who disagreed with or feared its meaning—women, for instance, opposing the ethos of masculine supremacy. But the Wayne idea drew so deeply upon the largest myths of our past—of the frontier, of a purifying landscape, of American exceptionalism, of discipline as the condition of rule—that some had trouble resisting the idea even when they renounced its consequences.[10]

Reagan's appeal also drew upon the largest myths of our past, especially the myth of the strong, stern, white male patriarch who could restore order to a world gone mad—a theme in many of Wayne's most popular films. A culture that still embraced John Wayne as its favorite movie star in a Harris poll as late as 1995—and who was still at number three in 2009—was in a sense primed to support Ronald Reagan for president in 1980, just slightly more than a year after Wayne's death from cancer. The idea of "John Wayne," in the way that Garry Wills meant it, clearly outlived the actor in the person of his fellow actor, Ronald Reagan.

Ronald Reagan's political persona and the characters that John Wayne played on the silver screen are so symbiotically connected, in an era when visual media are central to the construction of presidential narratives, that any serious historical analysis of the Reagan era must of necessity include at least some discussion of the overlapping myths of these two towering cultural figures. In fact, it is striking that Sean Wilentz's *The Age of Reagan* (2008) does not even *mention* John Wayne, an omission that speaks, perhaps, to a deficit of basic cultural studies insights in mainstream historiography. Wayne's success on the big screen foreshadowed—and might even have contributed to—Reagan's success on the small screen. Reagan's political handlers understood this; at the 1984 Republican National Convention, clips from John Wayne films provided the opening for a film celebrating Reagan's life and the achievements of his first term.[11] It is impossible to know how much Reagan himself was influenced by Wayne, but some important clues to Reagan's political success can be found in John Wayne's box office success—and the way millions of white men responded to his swagger and projection of old-fashioned masculine confidence, backed up by the implicit threat of violent force. To this day, much of the mainstream cultural commentary about Wayne explains the actor's popularity in terms of his supposed devotion to

CHAPTER 3: 1980: REAGAN VS. CARTER

old-school values in a time of cultural upheaval—which is, of course, also an explanation of Reagan's reactionary appeal. Both Wayne and Reagan represented a version of white masculinity that literally stood in defiance of sixties-era social transformation. Consider this hagiographical tribute to Wayne by Ronald L. Davis in *American Cowboy* magazine:

> Duke felt progressively more uncomfortable with prevailing values in the late 1960s. As he grew older, his determination to play characters who were courageous and honorable intensified. He felt that it was essential for him to set an example for a society racing toward permissiveness. He became convinced that a radical minority was leading the nation's youth astray. He was appalled at the widespread use of drugs and the counterculture's defiance of established conventions. "There doesn't seem to be respect for authority anymore," Wayne said. Through a turbulent time of nasty demonstrations Duke remained vitally concerned about America's reputation. He believed in the importance of the individual but maintained that his countrymen must express gratitude for the freedom they enjoyed with responsibility. Showing little sympathy for the changing world around him, Wayne refused to accept that his thinking was obsolete. In his mind he was simply a concerned patriot…he mirrors his culture's expectations of heroism; he is a cultural receptor that successive generations can remake to meet the requirements of their changing society. For millions the Duke continues to be emblematic of strong, silent manhood, of courage and honor in a world of timidity and moral indifference.[12]

Now compare the previous passage to what Haynes Johnson says about Ronald Reagan and the 1960s, in his book *Sleepwalking Through History: America in the Reagan Years*:

> With the emergence of Reagan, many disaffected political groups found a force of counterreaction around which to rally…In Vietnam the trickle of bloodshed had turned into a torrent as the dispatch of American troops increased…In the United States civil disobedience was in the air. Students took to the streets and rioted on campuses, holding rallies to burn draft cards and American flags….Political consensus was replaced by embittered

dissent. A resurgence of old American strains began to appear: ideological certitude; patriotism; nationalism; America's God-given mission in the world. These were Reagan's themes...Nor was the war the only divisive new factor threatening national stability. The nonviolent civil rights movement that brought together blacks and whites in marches across the segregated South had turned violent. In northern cities U.S. military force was required to quell riots, and new racial polarization developed. Fear of disintegration of American society was widely expressed. All this, too, produced reaction on campuses and led to savage denunciations of all authority, especially the authority of the president of the United States...Such outrageousness, taking place amid the shattering of consensus, led to the greatest national reaction of all: a strong counterreaction against these events...it was a reaction created in equal measure by disgust, fear, and desire for bringing order out of disorder. Through Reagan the public had a vehicle to express resentment at both national disorder and political leadership.[13]

The characters played by John Wayne and Ronald Reagan—on screen and off —embodied a full-throated response to social upheaval in the 1960s and 1970s, in a society where media was increasingly central not only to the construction of social reality but to politics, as well. Each of them achieved iconic stature because they tapped into something much larger than themselves, which was the nagging suspicion among millions of American men *and* women that the erosion of white male authority was at the heart of our cultural decline. There is more to the popularity of John Wayne and the political appeal of Ronald Reagan than their ability to perform like "real men" from days gone by when the camera starts rolling. But that is surely an important factor in their success.

Ronald Davis, whose work from *American Cowboy* is quoted above, seems to disregard accounts that call into question whether John Wayne the real person lived up the ideals that his characters displayed on the big screen. Davis, like so many of Wayne's fans, seems to accept at face value the conflation of the actor and the roles he played, as if the heroic men that John Wayne portrayed in many of his films were really thinly veiled self-portraits. The author and blogger Glenn Greenwald takes a different view. In his book *Great American Hypocrites* (2007), Greenwald devotes the entire first chapter

CHAPTER 3: 1980: REAGAN VS. CARTER

to a dissection of the difference between the actual man, John Wayne, and the cultural symbol that has wielded so much influence. Greenwald argues that Wayne was a "trailblazer of deceit," whose example has influenced a generation of right-wing men, including Reagan. Greenwald writes:

> Beyond his acting career, John Wayne has long been famous as a symbol of the ideal, supermasculine American right-wing male. From his all-American name to his cowboy swagger, from his numerous film roles as a war hero to his hard-core right-wing politics and steadfast support for American wars, the image of the Duke has remained the model of masculine American strength and wholesomeness.
>
> Yet the gap between Wayne's image and the reality of his life is enormous. While Wayne adopted uber-patriotic political positions and held himself out as a right-wing tough guy, he did everything he could to avoid fighting for his country during World War II.
>
> Although he spent the 1950s enthusiastically promoting Joseph McCarthy and the 1960s excoriating war opponents as traitors and cowards, when his country needed him most, Wayne preferred that others fight and die—including the country's wealthiest and most famous actors—so that he could remain in Hollywood and, as one of the only leading men not to fight—become very rich making one war film after another.
>
> …John Wayne flamboyantly paraded around as the embodiment of courage, masculinity, patriotism, wholesomeness, and the warrior virtues. He adopted right-wing political positions that he claimed demonstrated his thorough, tough, and resolute patriotism. This man who ran away from war then spent the rest of his life loudly cheering for every American war he could find. And as he left a series of broken marriages characterized by ugly divorces involving allegations of abuse, and as he further entered multiple adulterous relationships, he insisted—with increasing shrillness—that he was devoted to wholesome, American, Christian values …like the right-wing warriors who would idolize him and follow in his path, Wayne excelled at playacting the masculine virtues but failed miserably at adhering to them in his life.[14]

Like John Wayne, Ronald Reagan benefited from the perception that in real life he was the same man as the "character" he played in politics. This perception was fed by Reagan's tendency to confuse events in movies he had acted in or seen with events in which he had actually been involved, such as when in 1983 he allegedly told Israeli Prime Minister Yitzhak Shamir how moved he had been when he was filming the liberation of concentration camps in Europe at the end of World War II, when in reality his wartime service (which included *watching* film of the death camp liberations) only brought him as close to Europe as Culver City, California. As the playwright Arthur Miller put it, Reagan's ability to move back and forth between his current situation and the movie reel running in his head was

> Unknowingly, of course, a Stanislavskian triumph, the very consummation of the actor's ability to incorporate reality into the fantasy of his role. In Reagan the dividing line between acting and actuality was simply melted, gone. And what we want from leading men is quite the same thing as we demand of our leaders, the reassurance that we are in the hands of one who has mastered events and his own uncertainties. Human beings, as the poet said, cannot bear very much reality, and the art of politics is our best proof.[15]

The character—President of the United States—that Reagan played to perfection was a physically imposing and self-assured leader who restored American confidence through his bold decision making and moral clarity— especially his willingness to take on the Soviet Union. An important part of Reagan's public image was that he was in control and would assert his authority, and America's, when necessary. No equivocation or self-doubt; he was a man who took action. This was especially attractive in the period following the protracted debacle in Vietnam and the crisis of confidence in the nation's civilian and military leaders that the disastrous war engendered. Reagan further earned the admiration and respect of millions of Americans across the political spectrum when he survived a serious assassination attempt—and managed to laugh about it—just two months into his presidency in 1981.

However, since he left office in 1989 one of the most powerful, and misleading, media narratives about Reagan has described him as a genial, avuncular man who promised "morning in America" and was beloved by millions—even those who didn't share his political beliefs. But this portrait of Reagan elides the leadership role he played in the radical right wing of American politics since the 1960s, a movement seething with animosities and assorted bigotries which drew much of its energy from white middle-class resentment and rage. As Will Bunch puts it:

> ...the Ronald Reagan that we saw in the fall of 1964 wasn't the 1980s model—the hair was more slicked back, face less jowly and more angular, and there was more of a scowl than a smile. Indeed, 'the sunny optimist' Reagan was mostly angry in the middle 1960s. Today it is mainly political junkies who remember that without that simmering rage, cloaked in the often harsh rhetoric of backlash of that tumultuous decade, Ronald Reagan might today be only an answer to a movie trivia question.[16]

One moment on the primary campaign trail in 1980 seemed to exemplify what it was about Reagan's persona that his supporters found so appealing—and it wasn't his sunny optimism. It was in New Hampshire, before a Republican debate, and there was some confusion about whether the sponsors wanted all of the candidates to appear or just the frontrunners, George H. W. Bush and Reagan. Bush wanted a two-man debate; Reagan favored an extended roster. At one point in the deliberations, as the moderator threatened to turn off his microphone, Reagan grabbed the microphone and shouted, angrily, "I am paying for this microphone, Mr. Green (sic)." With a flash of righteous anger, Reagan reminded the GOP faithful that he could bare his teeth and get tough when he needed to. He went on to win 51 percent of the vote in a seven-man race.

But the assertive leader in public was a very different man in private. It was not just that, like Wayne, Reagan was an especially hawkish supporter of the Vietnam War, even though he managed to avoid deployment despite being of age during World War II, claiming difficulties with his eyesight. (Unlike Wayne, Reagan did serve in the military, making propaganda films for the Air Force at Hal Roach Studios in Culver City, dubbed "Fort Roach" by its personnel.)[17] Away from the cameras, the man whom Rush Limbaugh anointed with the majestic name of "Ronaldus Magnus" was nothing like the forceful leader that appeared in public. He wasn't even a strong leader in his own family. In fact, Michael Deaver, his long time media consultant, claimed he "had never known anyone so unable to deal with close personal conflict. When problems arose related to the family, or with personnel in his office, Nancy had to carry the load."[18] The old right-wing lion William Casey, CIA director under Reagan, told Bob Woodward that he continued to be struck by the overall *passivity* of the president—*passivity* about his job and about his approach to life."[19] Casey also considered Reagan to be "lazy...comparatively friendless and 'strange'." David Stockman, the chief of Reagan's Office of Management and Budget in the first term, described Reagan as "*serene*" and "*passive*." The conservative historian Richard Pipes wrote in his diary about the first National Security Council meeting he attended in 1981, that Reagan "seemed *lost, out of his depth, uncomfortable*...both the substance (of the discussion about national security) and human conflict...is above and beyond him. He has not enough of either knowledge or *decisiveness* to cut through the contradictory advice that is being offered to him...[20] The writer Gail Sheehy paraphrased one White House staffer who said he "came to understand that the president's *natural passivity* had been reinforced by his movie career: twenty years of taking direction."[21]

This man who so many of his staff and political allies considered passive and disengaged nonetheless often appeared to act decisively in foreign affairs. For example, on October 25, 1983, Reagan authorized the invasion of the tiny Caribbean island of Grenada. This was just two days after 241 US service members, mostly Marines, were killed by a suicide bomb while stationed in Lebanon as part of a multinational peacekeeping force. As numerous critics on the Left observed, the invasion of Grenada forced the dramatic loss of American lives and the failed policy that was responsible for it off the front pages. Reagan also ordered the bombing of Libya in retaliation for an incident in a German discotheque where two American service members were killed by suspected Libyan-backed terrorists. At the time, Reagan said with characteristic public bravado, "Quadaffi counted on America to be passive. He counted wrong." Reagan was also a masterful speech maker who many times sounded quite convincing in the role of the fearless, powerful leader, such as the historic moment when, during a speech at the Berlin Wall in West Germany, he thundered, "Mr. Gorbachev, tear down this wall!" Visitors to the Reagan library in Simi Valley, California, can see clips of these speeches and others endlessly replayed on video loops, on the countless Reagan DVDs in circulation, or on thousands of clips on YouTube posted on right-wing websites. In spite of the clear contrast with the personal reflections of the people who knew the actual man, these media spectacles constitute the public record of Reagan and the kind of manhood he symbolized.

What this disjuncture between the public and private Reagans demonstrates is that the pedagogical function of the presidency in the shaping of a masculine ideal is dependent upon the success of the president's public performance, rather than on what kind of person he might be in private. When Reagan misstepped politically, his most fervent supporters tended to blame it on his handlers, who, it was said, needed to "let Reagan be Reagan." But the conceit of this premise is that the true Reagan was the one who made forceful public declarations—not the one who could never bring himself to fire anyone in his administration, or the one who doodled in national security meetings, where he rarely asked any questions, and when he did speak, was more likely to tell Hollywood anecdotes than to weigh in thoughtfully on questions of policy or politics. Millions of Americans believed in the powerful, assertive Ronald Reagan for the same reasons they believed that John Wayne in real life was the same person as the characters he played on the silver screen: they wanted to believe that strong, white masculine leadership which seemed anchored in an earlier, simpler era could guide us through a period of significant and anxiety-producing social instability.

In a discussion of John Wayne's jingoistic and transparently pro-Vietnam War film *The Green Berets* (1968), Garry Wills offers an explanation for how such a poorly made film, where Wayne himself is totally miscast, could be a commercial success despite attracting a great deal of critical ridicule.

> For Wayne fans, its very unrealism may have been its selling point. People who did not want to know about the actual Vietnam War could feel that the national unity and resolve of World War II might turn around this strange new conflict in the far-off jungles of the East. Wayne was fighting World War II again, the only way he ever did, in make-believe; and that make-believe was a memory of American greatness that many still wanted to live by.[22]

That memory of American greatness, of glory restored, was validated for millions of Wayne fans and Reagan voters when the TV cameras captured pictures of US hostages being released in Iran just a few minutes after Ronald Reagan took the oath of office. The myth that Reagan intimidated the Iranian students into releasing the hostages persists among Reagan supporters, even after the disgrace of the mid-1980s Iran-Contra affair, when Reagan not only capitulated to Iranian terrorists but actually traded arms with them. In fact, during the Iran-Contra period, Reagan had his own hostage crisis, which he dealt with in a manner that directly contradicted the right-wing idea that our enemies understand only force. In 1986 Reagan's national security advisor, Robert McFarlane, traveled on a secret mission to Tehran to meet with Iranian officials carrying a Bible that contained a handwritten verse from President Reagan along with a cake in the shape of a key to signify an opening to Iran. This highly unusual tactic was aimed at convincing the Iranians to secure the release of American hostages held by Hezbollah in Lebanon. It did not succeed. To this day, this and other sordid details of the entire Iran-Contra scandal, for which Reagan could have been impeached, are conveniently overlooked by Republicans seeking to enhance their masculine credibility in the reflected glare of their cowboy hero. Facts that don't support the legend are discarded or forgotten. As Rudolph Giuliani said during the 2008 campaign, Iranian president Mahmoud Ahmadinejad "has to look at an American president and he has to see Ronald Reagan. Remember, they looked in Ronald Reagan's eyes, and in two minutes, they released the hostages."[23]

COWBOY MASCULINITY IN THE WHITE HOUSE

With expert assistance from movie directors and campaign consultants, both John Wayne and then Ronald Reagan each came to be identified as the embodiment of the all-American cowboy, and of the hardworking, straight-talking virtues that signified. Reagan was hardly the first American president to employ cowboy imagery to help construct his image and sell his program, but he was certainly among the most skillful. To this day, one of the most famous images of Reagan is a smiling headshot of him in a cowboy hat. There are countless photos in circulation of him on horseback or in jeans and cowboys boots chopping wood or clearing brush on his ranch in Santa Barbara.

A famous slogan from his campaigns, on mass-produced and do-it-yourself signs that were highly visible on campaign stops in 1984, read "This is Reagan Country," in a not-so-subtle allusion to the ubiquitous cigarette ad campaign from Phillip-Morris for "Marlboro Country" that featured the Marlboro Man, a powerful symbol of white working-class masculinity and once the leading advertising icon in the world. Because he acted in six westerns during his Hollywood career, photos of Reagan in cowboy chaps or a deputy US Marshal's uniform burnishing a Smith and Wesson circulated on postcards, T-shirts, and posters throughout his presidency and beyond. Perhaps the most common editorial cartoon caricature of Reagan during his years in office portrayed him as a reckless, gun-toting cowboy. Even his Secret Service nickname was born from the myth: Rawhide.

Although Reagan's major domestic policy objectives were cutting taxes for the rich, rolling back the rights of workers, and shifting federal spending from human services and education to the military, he was repeatedly photographed in rugged outdoor settings—especially on his ranch—that furthered the impression of him not only as a man's man, but a (white) man of the people. This was true even though when horseback riding, Reagan preferred to ride in English saddle, the style of the British aristocracy, and not western style, more common to cowboys and other working people in the American West. His longtime aide Lyn Nofziger recounted a revealing anecdote about this particular disjuncture between the man and his image. Reagan was running for governor of California, and was scheduled to go riding with a woman reporter from a local TV station. He went into the ranch house to change into riding clothes, and when he came out he was wearing jodhpurs. Nofziger recoiled. "What the hell are you wearing?" he said.

"This is what I always wear when I ride," Reagan responded.

"Ron," Nofziger said. "We're trying to win an election. You wear jodhpurs and people will think you're one of those eastern sissies. I want you to be a westerner, a cowboy. California voters want you to be a cowboy." Reagan reluctantly changed into Levis, put on cowboy boots, and threw western saddles on his horse and the one for the reporter.

Saddles notwithstanding, Reagan's common touch was one of his best public relations assets, especially as GOP partisans increasingly railed against the "elitist" Democrats, who, conservative commentators never tired of saying, were "out of touch" with ordinary Americans. This trope was repeated with the marketing of George W. Bush in 2000 and 2004 as a kind of folksy Texas cowboy, with similar though less impressive electoral success. It is worth noting that despite Bush's attempts to mimic Reagan's faux-cowboy performance, after the debacles in Iraq and with Hurricane Katrina, and then the massive bank failures at the end of his second term, Bush never came close to the iconic stature achieved by Reagan.

Reagan's performance of presidential masculinity and its resonance with the public owed a great deal to the special role of the cowboy in the national psyche. According to ethnic studies scholar Steven M. Lee,

> Since the 1880s, one of the most powerful symbolic figures to occupy what Lisa Lowe calls the "terrain of culture" essential to the construction of an American identity has been the cowboy hero. Through over a century of mass marketing and media production, the cowboy hero (and his forerunner, the frontiersman) has materialized as a conspicuous embodiment of the national ideal. Indeed, the cowboy is so ubiquitous in the culture, so ingrained in the collective consciousness, that Americans might not even realize the extent to which this image is both cause and effect of a nationalism both racialized (white) and gendered (masculine).[24]

The cowboy aura was also suffused with violence. As the historian Richard Slotkin writes, "violence is central to both the historical development of the frontier and its mythic representation."[25] Slotkin further maintains that regenerative violence is a powerful and even constitutive feature of twentieth-century American life, a theme that recurs in American literature and cinema. The role of the frontier and its mythic representation in Reagan's rise to power—and the violence that lurked both beneath and above the surface of his right-wing politics—is thus prototypically part of the twentieth-century American story.

It is important to remember that Reagan's ascension to the presidency came at a particularly gloomy juncture in post-World War II US history. In the text accompanying a special exhibit in 2008 at the Autry National Center in Los Angeles entitled "Cowboys and Presidents," Byron Price writes that "Conditions were perfect for the return of a cowboy president when Ronald

CHAPTER 3: 1980: REAGAN VS. CARTER

Reagan arrived in Washington. Emerging from the traumas of the Vietnam War, the Watergate scandal, and the Iran hostage crisis, the US was again in search of itself and obsessed with the cowboy. Fueled by 'outlaw' country-and-western music, the popular television series *Dallas* (1978-1991), and the John Travolta/Debra Winger film *Urban Cowboy* (1980), Western gear had again entered mainstream fashion."[26]

Of the many narrative themes generated by the Reagan presidency, perhaps none is as ubiquitous—and as largely unchallenged in mainstream discourse—as the one in which Reagan led a revival of the American spirit, and made Americans "feel good about themselves once more." But even this idea of national revival had a gendered character. As Michael Kimmel writes in his cultural history *Manhood in America*:

> We've often thought of the 1980s as a decade of the reassertion of pride, the retrieval of political and metaphoric potency for America and, hence, for the American man. In a replay of the frontier cowboy myth, America was once again sitting tall in the saddle, willing to take on all comers, asserting its dominance in world affairs. 'Americans are now standing tall and firm,' Reagan commented after the invasion of Grenada; columnists praised him for 'stiffening our foreign policy'—as if this masculine country had been suffering from a nationwide bout of impotence.[27]

James William Gibson's *Warrior Dreams: Violence and Manhood in Post-Vietnam America* (1994) analyzes the class, race, and especially gender-based insecurity and compensatory hyper-masculinity that characterized the male supremacist and highly militaristic radical right wing in US politics that emerged after the US defeat in Vietnam. He writes: "American men—lacking confidence in the government and the economy, troubled by the changing relations between the sexes, uncertain of their identity or their future—began to *dream*, to fantasize about the powers and features of another kind of man who could retake and reorder the world. And the hero of all these dreams was the paramilitary warrior."[28] Gibson argues that Ronald Reagan was politically successful because he tapped into these anxieties and offered a salve: "He was a shaman of sorts who wanted to restore and build upon America's fundamental creation myths through presidential performances."[29] Members of Reagan's administration were candid about the degree to which the president actively performed his role. Reagan chief of staff Kenneth Duberstein said in 1987 that for the Reagan White House to function effectively, there had to be "a very strong stage manager-producer-director" and "very good technical men and sound men." As Gibson said, "the White House was a movie set, a sound stage."[30]

Voting for Reagan in 1980 and 1984 gave individual white men the opportunity to vote for a "real man" they could proudly support, and identify with, as president. It also gave millions of (mostly) white men collectively the chance to disidentify with and revoke the 1970s "Sensitive New Age Guy," that breed of caring soul—endlessly mocked to this day—who responded to the women's liberation movement not with defensiveness and sexist disdain but with introspection and a determination to be less encumbered by trying to live up to the (false) standards of performance required of "real men." Even before Reagan was elected, the pump had been primed for the triumphant cultural revitalization, in legend and in fact, of the rugged individualist cowboy who could lead the political backlash against seventies feminization. Westerns were the most popular genre of film in the twentieth century, with over four thousand titles. In 1959 there were forty-eight television shows with western themes, and in the 1950s, Reagan himself had been the TV host of *Death Valley Days* on General Electric Theater. In addition to John Wayne and Gary Cooper movies, many of the men (and women) who later voted for Ronald Reagan grew up watching *Bonanza, Gunsmoke, The Lone Ranger,* and other shows. So not only did the cowboy tap into a deep wellspring and a link to our national mythic past as an archetype of (white) American masculinity. The resurgent popularity of the cowboy at the dawn of the Reagan era also suggested a reactionary refutation of feminism, just as the cowboy president and the conservative movement he led sought to block and roll back women's progress in the legislative and judicial realms.

The racial politics of white backlash that contributed significantly to Reagan's rise to power have been well-documented; what has received far less attention in mainstream political commentary is the antifeminism that energized Reaganism. The 1970s, after all, was a decade of dramatic gains for women's rights. Political scientist and feminist Jo Freeman wrote that women's rights and the sexual revolution became the "driving engine of partisan polarization," with the 1973 *Roe vs. Wade* abortion decision a particularly important realigning issue.[31] As Thomas Edsall points out, on every issue of importance to liberal women's rights groups, the Democratic Party is overwhelmingly more supportive than the GOP: "Abortion rights, affirmative action, access to the morning-after pill, sexual harassment, gay rights, hate crime legislation, Title IX mandates for gender parity in college sports, criminalizing violence against women, government-funded day care— all of these receive stronger backing from Democrats than Republicans at every level, from regular voters to political elites," a process that accelerated in the 1970s.[32] At the same time the Democrats were incorporating feminist ideas into their party's political program, the Republicans were doing the opposite. One of the more stunning political developments in the 1970s was how far the GOP moved away from its historic support for women's rights. In 1971-1972, 90.6 percent of House and Senate Republicans voted for the Equal Rights Amendment. In 1978, 68.5 percent voted *against* it. Even before the election of Reagan, the Republican Party had become the home of white men—and women—who were unsettled by epochal changes in the gender culture, and wanted a restoration of the perceived stability of the old patriarchal order.

If foreign policy hawks were concerned about the seeming diminution of America's military power in the post-Vietnam period, and traditionalists of various sorts were uncomfortable with the rise of feminism and the breakdown of male authority in the family, neoconservatives made the link between the two. Neoconservative "founding father" Norman Podhoretz identified a "culture of appeasement" that threatened to weaken America's role in the world. Garry Wills wrote that another founding neocon, Irving Kristol, believed "it was time to assert a 'new nationalism,' and that muscle-flexing and being unafraid to say 'We're Number One' required sacrifices to make that boast come true against increasing Soviet advantage." Wills continued "Thus Midge Decter joined forces with George Gilder or with Phyllis Schlafly against the women's movement, and with her husband (Podhoretz) against the gay rights movement. Both movements, they felt, were literally emasculating the nation."[33] For millions of white voters who had already been falling away from the Democratic Party, the "new man" of the 1970s—whom

Jimmy Carter seemed to symbolize in part because of his soft-spoken personal manner, and in part because of his political image as a champion of human rights—was no match at all for our violent adversaries, especially communists and Arab terrorists, who, right-wing commentators maintained, only understood the language of brute force and violence. It is all well and good to talk about getting in touch with your feelings, but not when the other guy is about to blow your head off. For these voters, the old cowboy gunfighter in the person of Ronald Reagan provided a more reassuring, and time-tested, model of manhood.

ANTI-INTELLECTUALISM

Anti-elitism and its cousin, anti-intellectualism, have a long history in the US, and as Richard Hofstadter showed, are intertwined with the ever-shifting politics of masculinity. While many people in the educated classes and in media were horrified by Reagan's simpleminded pronouncements and clear lack of intellectual depth, these were actually an important part of his political strength—especially with white men. To many of them, disproportionately but by no means exclusively in the South and parts of the West, a deficit of formal education and bookish knowledge in a presidential candidate was hardly a liability and could even be a political advantage, as if it proved that a man was more grounded in the "real world," and hence more of a "regular guy," unlike the "pointy-headed intellectuals" the populist racist Governor of Alabama, George Wallace, railed against in the 1960s and 1970s. When critics mocked Reagan's mangled syntax, or the superficiality of his understanding of issues, it actually bolstered the notion that he was a man of the people. Criticism of Reagan backfired even more when he was accused not only of being intellectually shallow and lazy, but also of being a "cowboy," and as a result unsophisticated and not qualified to be a leader. Millions of white men took it personally when cowboys were ridiculed, because for a variety of reasons the "cowboy" in the era of civil rights and feminism had in mainstream political discourse come to represent certain idealized qualities of traditional (white) masculinity—especially rugged individualism, eye-for-an-eye justice, belief in moral absolutes, straight talk, and no-nonsense problem solving. For Democrats, who have been losing among white male voters by wide margins for decades, criticizing Reagan and later George W. Bush as reckless cowboys was shortsighted and self-defeating. As Danny Goldberg advised progressive readers of *The Nation* after George W. Bush beat John Kerry in 2004, in future elections the (Democrats) need candidates "who understand that part of the job description for political leadership is fluency in mass American cultural language, a language in which, for example, the word 'cowboy' is a compliment, not an insult."[34]

As Richard Hofstadter wrote in his 1964 classic *Anti-Intellectualism in American Life*:

> ...the Jacksonian conviction that the duties of government were so simple that almost anyone could execute them downgraded the functions of the expert and the trained man to a degree which turned insidious when the functions of government became complex....the estrangement of training and intellect from the power to manage and decide had been completed.[35]

Although in the passage above he was writing about a much earlier period, Hofstadter might just as well have been describing late-twentieth and early twenty-first century presidential politics, especially the Republican presidencies of Ronald Reagan and George W. Bush. Both men won overwhelming majorities among white male voters in part because they were not intellectuals, and hence were seen more as "one of the guys," in contrast to Democrats like Jimmy Carter, Al Gore, and John Kerry, whose cerebralism and erudition were coded—in the case of Gore and Kerry—not only as effeminate but as condescending. Hofstadter's detailed analysis is particularly relevant to this one in the way it links the role of anti-intellectualism in presidential politics to historical shifts in the economy and gender order. For example, anticipating Rush Limbaugh's attacks on the masculinity of liberals in the 1990s and 2000s, Hofstadter describes how established politicians and political bosses at the end of the nineteenth century resisted political reform and the attempt to upgrade standards and instill a meritocracy for the civil service and political office by mocking the manhood of the reformers themselves.

> As the politicians put it, they, the bosses and party workers, had to function in the bitter world of reality in which the common people had to live and earn their living. This was not the sphere of morals and ideals, of education

and culture: it was the hard, masculine sphere of business and politics. The reformers, they said, claimed to be unselfish...but ...in the hard-driving, competitive, ruthless, materialistic world of the Gilded Age, to be unselfish suggested not purity but a lack of self, a lack of capacity for grappling with reality, a lack of assertion, of masculinity."[36]

Ironically, it was the Republican Teddy Roosevelt who helped to remasculinize the idea of good government by bringing to the political "arena" his self-created identification with the rugged West and his love of ranching, hunting, and other vigorous outdoor pursuits. According to Hofstadter, Roosevelt paved the way for the Progressive era

> ...by helping to restore prestige to educated patricians who were interested in reform, by reinvesting their type with male virtues. American men, impelled to feel tough and hard, could respond to this kind of idealism and reform without fearing that they had unmanned themselves...(For) T.R. and his generation...the role of the scholar in politics was founded upon his possession of certain serviceable skills that were becoming increasingly important to the positive functions of government...the era of the scholar as expert was about to begin.[37]

Reagan was no intellectual, but neither was he as dumb as some of his critics believed. In 2001, a book of his writings, entitled *Reagan in His Own Hand*, prompted much discussion in the media about whether or not this proved there was intellectual substance behind the sound bites and staged performances that had done so much to burnish his image as a right-wing hero and a national treasure. (Most of his writings were the scripts for his weekly radio addresses in the 1970s.) It is for the reader to decide whether Reagan's writings revealed his depth or merely confirmed his superficial grasp of the complex issues of modern society. But it is undeniable that from his days as governor of California, Reagan's aides provided him with three-by-five index cards, on which they would summarize the key points of whatever issue he was supposed to be addressing. When in public settings he strayed far from these summaries, he often stumbled badly, frequently misstating facts and his administration's position, forcing his communications directors and handlers

CHAPTER 3: 1980: REAGAN VS. CARTER

to issue hastily composed "clarifications" to the media. But whether or not he understood the fiscal principles embedded in his own budget, or the far-reaching effects of his administration's foreign policy positions, Ronald Reagan certainly possessed an intuitive grasp of what Americans expected of their president's performance that was almost savantlike. As Drew Westen wrote:

> Reagan did not create the agenda of the radical right on his own, but he created, packaged, marketed and embodied in his own persona a 'brand' so simple and emotionally compelling that it was able to sustain itself through eight years of moderate Democratic leadership (Bill Clinton) far closer to the values of the average American. What distinguished the conservative ideology of Reagan was its crystal-clear narrative coherence and its emotional resonance.[38]

In that sense, Reagan possessed a kind of emotional intelligence that provided him with uncommon insight into what millions of Americans expected out of the public performance of their leader in a media era. It is important to remember in this regard that Reagan's ideology and political program were much less popular than he was personally. In particular, Reagan knew how to act the part of the reassuring patriarch to the nation, even if he was to a great extent physically and emotionally absent from the lives of his own children and grandchildren.

In light of the way George W. Bush in the 2000s was the target of relentless ridicule, it is interesting to speculate about whether Ronald Reagan's stage managers would have been as successful in heroicizing him in the 1980s if programs like *The Daily Show* were around to run video replays of his numerous gaffes, factual misstatements, and inarticulate ramblings. There is reason to believe that Reagan's timing was fortuitous, as he left office just before the explosion of 24/7 media, the Internet, and the blogosphere revolutionized media discourse about politics. Neil Postman recounts a 1983 article in the *New York Times* headlined "Reagan Misstatements Getting Less Attention." The article begins:

> President Reagan's aides used to become visibly alarmed at suggestions that he had given mangled and perhaps misleading accounts of his policies or of current events in general. That doesn't seem to happen much anymore.

Indeed, the President continues to make debatable assertions of fact, but news accounts do not deal with them as extensively as they once did. In the view of White House officials, the declining news coverage mirrors a decline in interest by the general public.[39]

Postman speculates that the public was not outraged by Reagan's errors and falsehoods because they were an audience that was not paying attention, in large measure because they were bored. He wrote,

Perhaps if the President's lies could be demonstrated by pictures and accompanied by music the public would raise a curious eyebrow...We do well to remember that President Nixon did not begin to come undone until his lies were given a theatrical setting at the Watergate hearings. But we do not have anything like that here. Apparently, all President Reagan does is *say* things that are not entirely true. And there is nothing entertaining in that.[40]

Postman's focus on politics-as-entertainment fails to recognize that many people overlooked Reagan's deficits because they were emotionally invested in his myth: the aging white male patriarch who emerged after two decades of racial, gender, and sexual upheaval to restore American pride through masculine assertions of discipline at home and military muscle abroad. Contrary to the rational-emotional binary that enshrines the assumption of male rationality, it is important to recognize that Reagan's appeal to millions of white men was *emotional.* For some it surely was their longing for a reassuring father-figure. Many others wanted him to succeed in part because he stirred something in them. They identified with him. Their manhood was tied up in his perform-ance. In a culture where media increasingly structured social and political reality, he was the heroic leading man whom decades of Hollywood cinema had con-ditioned them to idolize. Why let a few facts get in the way of the satisfactions of idolatry? Reagan himself seemed viscerally aware of this dynamic between him and his followers/fans. In his 1989 book *The Acting President*, the veteran television journalist Bob Schieffer offers this insight into Reagan's appeal:

Once, when asked why the president had 'cited' a non-existent British law in order to discredit arguments for gun control, (White House spokesman)

Larry Speakes breezily responded: "It made the point, didn't it?" By then, Speakes had learned what Reagan had known intuitively for years: that it was the punchy line and performance that 'made the point,' not substance or accuracy.[41]

Or as *Fox News* chief Roger Ailes, a veteran of Reagan's media team in 1980 and one of the architects of the "Morning in America" campaign in 1984, told Reagan, "You didn't get elected on details. You got elected on themes."[42]

Richard Slotkin argues that in contrast to Teddy Roosevelt, whose personal heroic aura was proved by reference to his actual deeds as a stockman, sheriff, and Rough Rider,

> Reagan's claim to heroic character was based entirely on references to imaginary deeds performed in a purely mythic space. The difference between them indicates the change that has occurred in our political culture over this century: the myths produced by mass culture have become credible substitutes for actual historical or political action in authenticating the character and ideology of political leaders....At the height of his powers, (Reagan) was able to cover his actions with the gloss of patriotic symbolism and to convince his audience that—in life as in movies—merely symbolic action is a legitimate equivalent of the 'real thing.'[43]

In fact, the political and popular success that Reagan enjoyed in life and death demonstrates quite clearly one of the central conclusions of this study: there is no way to understand presidential politics in the present era without understanding—or the very least interrogating—the confluence between myth, entertainment, semiotics, and politics, and the complex relations among them. As Garry Wills wrote:

> Reagan runs continuously in everyone's home movies of the mind. He wrests from us something warmer than mere popularity, a kind of complicity. He is, in the strictest sense, what Hollywood promoters used to call 'fabulous.' We fable him to ourselves, and he to us. We are jointly responsible for him.[44]

Chapter 4
1988: George H. W. Bush vs. Michael Dukakis

CLASS AND EFFEMINACY IN THE GOP

By the time Ronald Reagan was elected in an Electoral College landslide in 1980, the ascendant right wing of the Republican Party—based largely in the South and West—had for many years been disparaging the fiscally conservative but socially moderate East Coast "Rockefeller Republicans" with family trust funds and Ivy League pedigrees who had defined the GOP for most of the twentieth century. Right-wing Republicans had many ideological differences and policy disputes with the established leaders of their party, but on a visceral level they were also uncomfortable with the masculinity of the men in the old Republican establishment. Many were small business owners and blue-collar workers who by class and temperament were more comfortable with *Bare Knuckles and Back Rooms*, the title of a memoir by Reagan's 1984 campaign manager Ed Rollins, than they were with the genteel bipartisanship of the old money, country club Republicans they were rapidly supplanting. This posed a problem for George H. W. Bush, who had served loyally as Reagan's vice president for two terms and was his heir apparent as leader of the party and 1988 presidential candidate. Bush was seen by many conservative Republicans as both ideologically unreliable and too aristocratic in his speech and personal mannerisms to appeal to the white working- and middle-class men who were increasingly an important segment of the party's base. To make matters worse, although he had an impressive resume on paper, Bush, a decorated fighter pilot in World War II, damaged his personal reputation when he went overboard in his attempts to ingratiate himself to right-wing Republicans. Perhaps the most egregious example of this was when Bush sought the support of the late William Loeb, the hard right-wing publisher of the *Manchester Union Leader*, the most influential newspaper in New Hampshire. Bush was so obsequious in his courting of Loeb, whose endorsement in the first-in-the-nation primary had long been considered crucial for candidates in pursuit of the GOP presidential nomination, that conservative commentator George F. Will mocked him as a "lapdog of the right." Compounding Bush's problems was that he was seen by many in the GOP as a high-profile representative of the old Northeast Republican establishment, just as the party under Goldwater/Reagan had consolidated its geographic shift to the South and West. It didn't help when the story (perhaps apocryphal) circulated during the campaign that he had asked for a "splash" of coffee at a New Hampshire truck stop, which revealed his patrician roots and thus opened him up for ridicule. According to Stephen Ducat, author of a 2004 book entitled *The Wimp Factor*, in the United States, from the very beginning, "if a politician wanted to attack the masculinity of a candidate, he would often accuse him of being aristocratic. The affectations of aristocracy were seen as markers of effeminacy."[1] Bush was afflicted with the same problem that led Teddy Roosevelt early in the century to remake himself with a trip out west to celebrate the "manly virtues" and proclaim himself the "Cowboy of the Dakotas."

Despite his attempts to remake himself by claiming to love country music and pork rinds, Bush's upper-class mannerisms presented a challenge for a party that was seeking to solidify and build on its already large lead among white working- and middle-class men. The conundrum was summed up by a famous *Newsweek* magazine cover story in 1987 entitled "Bush's Wimp Factor."

Bush's political dilemma foreshadowed the struggles of Mitt Romney more than two decades later, when the former Massachusetts governor and wealthy private equity manager was trying to sell himself to working-class white male voters in the 2012 Republican primaries. A comment by a Party official in central Illinois prior to the 2012 Illinois primary foregrounded class divisions in the GOP but also reinforced the idea that perceptions about a candidate's manhood are central to the electoral calculus of the modern Republican Party: "I'm tired of rich guys running for office because it's a mountain to be climbed for them," said Tony Libri, chair of a Republican County committee. "He [Romney] probably spends more on a shirt or a haircut than most Americans make in a week. I want a guy who can roll up his sleeves and talk about being on the front lines in Afghanistan or being a welder on a factory floor."² *Newsweek* reprised its 1987 cover and reminded voters of the similarities between the upper class Bush 41 and Romney when it published a cover story in August 2012 with the taunting headline "Romney: The Wimp Factor: Is he just too insecure to be president?"

Fortunately for George H. W. Bush, his Democratic opponent in the 1988 general election was the governor of Massachusetts, Michael Dukakis. Dukakis was an intelligent and principled politician, but also a technocratic leader who failed utterly to understand the symbolic side of the presidency and what that demanded of him. Former New York governor Mario Cuomo quipped that Dukakis had mastered the prose of government, but not the poetry. Not the least of Dukakis's flaws as a presidential candidate was that he could not—and did not—ever present himself convincingly as a tough enough man to be president, especially when he was running to succeed Ronald Reagan, who with the help of expert media consultants and stage managers had successfully created a new archetype of a late-twentieth century warrior statesman. It did not help that Dukakis was small of stature, eschewed excessive ceremonial displays of patriotism, and had a reputation as an opponent of the death penalty and an advocate of gun control, all symbolically significant issues in the construction of presidential masculinity.

In spite of these political shortcomings, Dukakis held a commanding seventeen-point lead over Bush in public opinion polls early in the 1988 campaign. But then, under the leadership of the young political consultant Lee Atwater, whose aggressive campaign tactics are influential to this day in the Republican Party, the Bush campaign went on the offensive against Dukakis, seeking to bolster Bush's suspect projection of streetsmart masculinity by destroying what little Dukakis had to begin with. As Atwater said, "I'm going to scrape the bark off that little bastard."³ Atwater had achieved notoriety earlier in the decade by running negative attack campaigns for clients in congressional races that included personal attacks and phony polls. A native South Carolinian, he seemed to understand intuitively that presidential elections turn in part on cultural attitudes about (white) masculinity, and that if you can successfully attack a candidate's manhood, he'll have a difficult time winning the votes of (white) men, whose own identities are wrapped up in the party and man they support. Like many Republican Party activists, Atwater talked the language of populism as he set out to brand the Democrats as the party of elites who look down on hardworking (white) Americans. But for him as for many conservatives, populist appeals always had a gendered edge. In the 1988 campaign, for example, Atwater identified three issues he could use against Michael Dukakis, all of which centered on themes of masculinity and violence: patriotism, prison furloughs, and national security.

In two of these issues the Bush campaign, abetted by coverage and commentary in the pre-Internet media and the Dukakis campaign's ineptitude, successfully feminized Michael Dukakis: patriotism and the Willie Horton ad/crime issue. In the third, Dukakis's wound was self-inflicted: the infamous "Tank" commercial. Each of these three key issues in the 1988 presidential race was driven by media and turned in its own way on the masculinity of the respective candidates, and how they had, and would, handle threats of violence at home and abroad. Atwater's strategy was vindicated by the result: George H. W. Bush won forty states and beat Dukakis in the Electoral College 426-111.

PATRIOTISM

Michael Dukakis was a proud liberal who had long been immersed in Massachusetts politics, where Democrats enjoy a vast numerical advantage to this day and where the Republican Party until recent decades was dominated by blueblood Yankees with old money and moderate social views who lived in the wealthy white suburbs of Boston. His house in Brookline, Massachusetts, was less than a mile from John F. Kennedy's boyhood home. In those environs, a statement by Dukakis that he was a "card-carrying member of the ACLU" would hardly cause a raised eyebrow. However, in the national political landscape that had been shaped most recently by nearly a decade of jingoistic Reaganite theatrics, this self-identification, and the similarities it had with "card-carrying member of the Communist Party," was enough to cast doubt not only on Dukakis's ethnicity (he was the son of Greek immigrants) but on his commitment to American values. Seizing on this perceived weakness of Governor Dukakis, George H. W. Bush repeatedly referred to Dukakis as "way out in left field" and out of step with ordinary Americans. Right-wing opinion makers had a field day with an item developed by opposition research: in 1977, Dukakis had vetoed a bill that would have required teachers to lead their students in the Pledge of Allegiance, and would have fined them if they refused. When he vetoed the bill, Dukakis cited a Massachusetts Supreme Judicial Court advisory opinion that held that the measure violated teachers' First Amendment rights to freedom of speech and religion. Bush ignored Dukakis's principled stance when he said to an enthusiastic, cheering campaign crowd, "What is it about the Pledge of Allegiance that upsets him so much? It is very hard for me to imagine that the Founding Fathers—Samuel Adams and John Hancock and John Adams—would have objected to teachers leading students in the Pledge of Allegiance to the flag of the United States." Later in the campaign, Bush actually spoke at a flag factory in New Jersey, as an unsubtle reminder to voters that he was the "patriotic" candidate in the race. "The flags you make still inspire Americans," he said, "and those who love our values the world over."

What many political scientists and mainstream commentators alike miss in their discussion of the role of "patriotism" in presidential campaigns is the gendered nature of that discourse. For example, the 1988 debate about patriotism can be understood as a proxy debate for a contest between the candidates about masculinity. The question wasn't really about patriotism per se; it was about which brand of patriotism would attract the most votes— especially white men's votes. Dukakis was intensely patriotic, but like most liberals, his patriotism was based in reverence for the constitution and the processes of democracy, and not on flag-waving jingoism and martial displays of patriotic fervor. But on the campaign trail, process liberalism is no match for flag-waving conservatism, especially when the other side had, among other celebrities, the likes of Charlton Heston (aka Moses) leading crowds of red-meat Republicans in reciting the pledge. If members of the audience didn't already get the connection between liberals' notions of patriotism and their supposed "weakness" on issues of national security, Bush was careful to remind them. In speech after speech, he made the absurd claim that Dukakis "would leave America totally defenseless."

Two decades later, Dukakis told the reporter David Paul Kuhn that he ran a lousy campaign, largely because he didn't respond "while the other guy is trying to define you. Here I am the son of Greek immigrants, and they are painting me a cultural elitist running against a Yankee Brahmin who went to

Milton Academy. I let that happen!"[4] While the older and wiser Dukakis displayed an admirable level of self-reflexivity and political self-awareness, he still seemed not to get that what Bush did in 1988 when he openly questioned Dukakis's patriotism was not so much to define him as an elitist as it was to define him as effeminate by attacking his masculinity. What Dukakis failed to do, which cost him dearly with white male voters, was to fight back more forcefully. If the president embodies the national (white) masculinity, it follows that patriotic white men would want to identify with the man who holds the office. Countless polls over the past generation confirm that voters, especially men, want political candidates who are fighters, as Hillary Clinton most recently proved when her approval ratings with white men increased as she persisted in her 2008 primary race against Barack Obama long after the odds suggested her cause was hopeless. This was an era, after all, when a fictional losing boxer who fought to the finish, Rocky Balboa, became a household name and cultural icon. It didn't help Dukakis that his nickname was "The Duke," which triggered cinematic fantasies and invited unflattering comparisons between the diminutive liberal politician and the larger-than-life John Wayne. What Dukakis seemed not to comprehend until it was too late was that in the hands of the Bush strategists and a compliant media, the 1988 campaign was not about competence or ideology; it was about manhood as it had been traditionally understood. In that contest, the better man wins far less often than the more aggressive one.

THE RISE OF VIOLENT CRIME AS A POLITICAL ISSUE IN THE 1960S AND 1970S

The rise of crime as a political issue in the 1960s and 1970s had powerful racialized and gendered dynamics. During that time, the graphic depiction of violence rapidly increased as a part of media culture, insinuating its way into the psyches of millions of Americans. From the mid-to-late 1960s through the end of the Vietnam War, nightly news reports featured disturbing footage of American soldiers and marines in the war zone carrying dead and wounded buddies as explosions went off and villages burned. Unlike today, when Pentagon censors have largely succeeded at keeping the gore and suffering in the Iraq and Afghanistan wars out of middle-class Americans' living rooms, viewers actually saw blood and fresh corpses on screen. At home, urban riots and nightly news reports of armed robberies, murders, and rapes grew more common, leading to a sense among what Nixon termed a "silent majority" that American society was unraveling.

Ronald Reagan, whom recent hagiography portrays as a relentlessly upbeat, gentlemanly soul, drew much early political support by tapping into and articulating white middle-class rage at the social disruptions of the 1960s. The experienced actor knew well how to portray *in public* the role of stern, authoritarian father, literally laying down the law to ensure domestic tranquility. In 1970, during his first term as governor of California, he angrily denounced student protesters at the University of California. His anger captured the growing rage of the white middle-class in the face of social unrest and what many saw as a generation of ungrateful, unpatriotic young people. Just a month before the Kent State shootings, when asked a question about how he would respond to the increasingly unruly student antiwar demonstrations at the University of California, Reagan coldly stated, "If it takes a bloodbath, let's get it over with. No more appeasement." Reagan also gave voice to white middle-class rage at the increased assertiveness of blacks. Outside the 1968 Republican convention, Reagan got into a shouting match with a black woman; during his campaign in 1980 he shouted down a black woman heckler in the South Bronx. As Jeremy Mayer argued, "the powerful image of an infuriated Reagan shouting at blacks was highly unusual for a white politician."[5]

Starting in the 1960s, numerous Hollywood films with law enforcement themes did big box office; detective shows on TV were a staple of prime time on the major networks. In the 1970s, communications scholar George Gerbner produced pioneering research that quantified acts of violence on television; the number of acts per hour in prime time increased nearly every year. Gerbner coined the term "mean world syndrome" to describe the media-induced fears that result from excessive television-watching, and he warned that the resultant insecurity and anxiety provided fertile ground for intolerance, extremism, and a paranoid style of politics. This insecurity and anxiety had a powerful racialized dimension, in part because prior to the Internet (and even today) millions of suburban voters got the majority of their news from television. As communication scholars have written, "a steady drumbeat of frightening information and images dominates television news,

CHAPTER 4: 1988: GEORGE H. W. BUSH VS. MICHAEL DUKAKIS

and of course crime drama is a staple of television entertainment…Not only does local news depict life in America as pervaded by violence and danger; this genre also heightens whites' tendency to link these threats to Blacks."[6] In this anxious cultural climate, politicians increasingly sought to prove they were "tough on crime" to assuage the fears of white middle-class voters and the resentments of white working-class voters. Of course the crime they had to be tough on was not white-collar crime, or industrial polluting, or various forms of corporate malfeasance. "Tough on crime" meant tough on violent crime—and it still does. Even so, certain types of violent crime didn't qualify for political concern. For example, domestic violence, sexual assault, and child abuse are all crimes of violence that plague white communities as well as communities of color, but politicians and judges were not criticized for being "soft on crime" if they failed to crack down on abusive husbands. For many reasons, some of which I will discuss below, "violent crime" was often used interchangeably with "street crime," with street crime being unmistakable code language for threatening black men. Thus the political discourse on violent crime had a racialized subtext, a subject that has been examined extensively in communications literature. It also had a gendered subtext. Since the late 1960s, conservative white male politicians have played to white anxieties and fears of black crime by adopting stances that ensure they are regarded as "tough on crime," which explicitly reinforces not only their whiteness but also their masculine credentials.

The resentment felt by many white Americans about urban riots and rising rates of violent crime in the 1960s and 1970s surfaced as a major presidential campaign issue in 1968, and was succinctly and euphemistically captured in phrases like the "silent majority's" concern about "law and order." Of course, cultural norms and expectations around presidential masculinity have always had unspoken racial implications: until the election of Obama, everyone just assumed the president was a white man. Race was clearly the major factor in the South's transition from being solidly Democratic to solidly Republican, a transition that has made an enormous difference in presidential politics for more than a generation. But the South is not the only place where race mattered. US presidents have embodied white masculine authority in a way that transcends region both during and after the civil rights movement; "Reagan Democrats" were characteristically from the Northeast and upper Midwest.

One of the clearest fault lines in the "culture wars" is the way people respond to fears of violent crime, including those fears that are racially coded. At the risk of oversimplification (and the exclusion of more radical analyses of crime), the basic difference between liberals and conservatives in response to violent crime is that liberals see entrenched poverty and the social and psychic alienation it engenders as major contributing factors to much criminal behavior, including that which is linked to illegal drugs. Thus (elusive) improvements in urban education, universal health care, government action to foster economic growth in depressed areas, and radical reform of the drug laws are all necessary steps toward reducing crime. By contrast, conservatives typically downplay factors such as economic inequality and instead attribute crime to a "breakdown in morals" that fosters a climate where criminal behavior is tolerated. They emphasize "personal responsibility" for bad behavior and seek to redouble efforts at authoritarian methods of social control. It is no coincidence that the rate of incarceration has quadrupled during the past three decades of conservative ascendancy.

One of the key racialized aspects of the ongoing debates about crime and punishment is that many liberals attribute the disproportionate perpetration of violent crime by African American men to deeply-rooted institutional racism and poverty, which many conservatives dismiss as excuse making, motivated by political correctness or misplaced liberal guilt. They insist that the choice to engage in criminal acts boils down to questions of personal morality and individual choice. This entire debate is based on an artificial and false dichotomy; there is no necessary contradiction between understanding and seeking to change the economic and social factors that lead to crime and holding individuals responsible for their actions. It is also unfair for conservatives to suggest that because people to the left of center often advocate for the rights of defendants and decry police brutality and the inequities of the judicial system and the prison industrial complex, that they necessarily take the criminals' side against the rights of victims, as if "getting tough" through enforcement and prosecution is the only reasonable policy response to the perpetration of violent crime or other forms of criminality.

Outrage at high rates of violent crime is hardly the sole province of conservatives, and by no means is it inherently racist. It has nonetheless been well-established in public opinion research and reported in popular journalism

CHAPTER 4: 1988: GEORGE H. W. BUSH VS. MICHAEL DUKAKIS

for nearly half a century that concerns about (read: fear of) violent black male crime, and anger at politicians who fail to support harsh punishment for offenders, has been a key factor in driving many whites to the right—especially white men. One of the founding figures of the neoconservative movement, Irving Kristol, a former Trotskyist, affirmed the political importance of violent crime to this shift when he famously stated that "a conservative is a liberal who's been mugged by reality." What Kristol didn't have to say was that for the white majority—and for many people of color as well—the imagined mugger is most likely dark-skinned. In *The New Jim Crow: Mass Incarceration in an Age of Color-blindness*, Michelle Alexander documents how conservatives used the war on drugs and other "tough on crime" measures as part of their strategy to attract white working-class voters to the Republican Party, in the process arresting and imprisoning hundreds of thousands of black men, often for minor drug offenses that many whites committed with impunity, with predictably disastrous results in communities of color that persist to this day and will continue to for years to come.

"White flight" from the Democratic Party over the past forty years was the result of many factors, foremost among them the passage in 1964 of the Civil Rights Act, which was signed into law by a Democratic president, Lyndon Johnson. But beginning in the mid-1960s, popular discourse about how to address the crime problem grew increasingly gendered, a development that can be seen quite clearly in the case of public support for the death penalty, which rose dramatically in those years. As Stephen Ducat argues, "Support for the death penalty is now an article of faith that must be endorsed by any politician who hopes to draw male voters. The rare male candidate who fails to enthuse over state-sanctioned killing has his phallic credentials questioned, is seen as "soft" on crime, and bears the taint of effeminacy."[7] The United States Supreme Court during the Warren Era in the 1950s and 1960s issued a series of landmark decisions, such as the *Miranda* decision (1966) that established the rights of criminal suspects and sought to curb police abuses of state power. Predictably, conservative advocates of "law and order" recoiled at the shift in jurisprudence toward the rights of defendants. For the purpose of this study, I am interested in how "liberal" responses to crime were gendered feminine, and how the feminization of liberal jurisprudence and criminal justice practice was manifest in political discourse. For example, by the late 1970s, the Right had developed a gendered line of attack against liberal Democrats who were running for office by accusing them of favoring liberal judges who wanted to "coddle" criminals. The use of the term "coddle" in this context is instructive. The word is typically used to describe a mother who is coddling her infant. Thus a difference in judicial and criminal justice philosophy became yet another platform from which to ridicule and feminize liberal men and correspondingly associate the Republican brand with law and order (white) masculinity.

The Case of Willie Horton

Willie Horton was a black man who had been convicted of a 1974 murder in Massachusetts and was out on a weekend furlough in 1986 when he escaped and fled south to Maryland, where he ended up raping and brutalizing a white woman and stabbing her fiancé. The furlough program had been initiated by Republican Massachusetts Governor Frank Sargent in the 1970s and had an impressive track record for over a decade, but when the Bush campaign learned about the *Horton* case they quickly realized that it provided a huge opportunity to paint Dukakis as soft on crime. Because he was black and had raped a white woman, Horton was literally picture-perfect for the story the Bush campaign wanted to tell: that Michael Dukakis was weak, naïve, and in the words of Stephen Ducat a "failed protector" who could not be trusted to shelter law-abiding citizens (read: white women) from predatory criminals (read: black men).

In an early example of a new trend in the financing, production and distribution of campaign ads, an independent producer with ties to the Bush campaign produced an ad under the auspices of the National Security Political Action Committee that showed Horton's face and blamed Dukakis's policy for the violent assault. Bush had "plausible deniability"; his campaign could claim that it had nothing to do with what they knew was going to be a controversial ad. While calling attention to Dukakis's positions on crime was the stated rationale for the piece, racial fear was inarguably the subtext. Using racially coded language, the ad's creator, Larry McCarthy, said he wanted to use a mug shot of Horton that made him look like "every suburban mother's greatest fear." Roger Ailes, a longtime TV producer who worked as a campaign media consultant for George H. W. Bush in 1988 and went on to start the Fox News Channel in 1996, said "The only question is whether we depict Willie Horton with a knife in his hand or without it."

Just after the NSPAC ad aired, the Bush campaign released its own commercial, entitled the "revolving door," which showed a procession of convicts circling through a revolving gate, and a flashing sign that read "268 escaped." As the political communication theorist Kathleen Hall Jamieson points out, the juxtaposition of the Willie Horton ad and the revolving door ad created the impression that Dukakis had let 268 rapists and murderers go free, when in fact the furlough escape rate under Dukakis (268 escapes out of 67,378 furloughs) was almost identical to the one under his Republican predecessor, and that only one convict, William Horton, had been charged with rape after escaping on furlough. But together with public appearances by Horton's victims and relatives of the boy he had murdered fourteen years before, the ads created the powerful impression that Dukakis was weak and as president would let (black) criminals run free in the streets and terrorize innocent people. Dukakis did not help his cause, or counteract the perception that liberals care more about the rights of criminals than they do about the innocent, when he did not meet with the families of Horton's victims.

The power of the Willie Horton ads to dominate media coverage of the 1988 presidential race was a product of the historical trend toward entertainment values in news media and politics. As Hall Jamieson explains,

> ...we have conventionalized journalistic norms that reward messages that are dramatic, personal, concise, visual, and take the form of narrative. In 1988, the psychological dispositions of the public coupled with the news norms to produce an environment in which an atypical but dramatic personification of deep-seated fears would displace other issues and dominate the discourse of the campaign. That dramatic, visual, personalized narrative told the 'story' of William Horton.[8]

Hall Jamieson also explains that ads, news, campaign rhetoric, and audience psychology interact in powerful ways that evoke varying responses, but that, crucially, people tend not to remember where they initially heard the campaign messages. "Voters gather bits and pieces of political information and store them in a single place," she writes. "Lost in the storage is a clear recall of where this or that 'fact' came from. Information from news mixes with that from ads…"[9]

NATIONAL SECURITY/DUKAKIS IN THE TANK

A few hours before he was assassinated in Dallas, John F. Kennedy was presented with a cowboy hat as a memento of his trip to Texas. To the disappointment of the crowd that had just heard him deliver a breakfast speech, Kennedy declined to try it on, but offered to model it at a later date at the White House. We might never know why Kennedy chose not to don the cowboy hat, but his reticence finds strong support among contemporary political consultants, who advise candidates to be cautious about putting something on their head when there are cameras present; there is simply too big a risk that it will look inauthentic, and perhaps much worse.

Clearly, someone was asleep at the switch in the Dukakis camp when the decision was made to visit a General Dynamics tank factory as part of an effort to prove that—contrary to the derision he was facing from the Bush campaign and conservatives in media—the Massachusetts governor was a credible commander in chief. In a scene that was so close to self-caricature it resembles a *Saturday Night Live* skit more than it does an actual campaign moment, Dukakis put on a combat helmet and went for that ill-fated ride in an M1 tank with the cameras rolling, while the theme music from the movie *Patton* blared in the background. As Stephen Ducat quipped, "instead of the formidable battle-hardened leatherneck he wished to present himself as, Dukakis looked more like a frightened four-year-old boy on his first bumper car ride."[10] This monumental gaffe in campaign stagecraft badly damaged Dukakis's reputation for personal integrity. It also confirmed visually what Republicans had been doing rhetorically to Democrats since at least 1972— accusing them of being "weak" on defense and thereby threatening the safety and security of Americans. Because their standard-bearer Michael Dukakis appeared so out of place in a US army tank, it left the powerful misimpression that not only was the Democratic Party politically unsupportive of a strong military; its leaders were personally uncomfortable in the role of leading the armed forces. Even if he hadn't faced—and lost—other challenges to his manhood on the campaign trail, such as the death penalty question at the presidential debate with Bush or the Willie Horton ads, there was only a slim chance that a Democrat could win a national election—during the Cold War—if tens of millions of voters judged him to be unsure of himself on military matters.

It is important to note that the perception by many voters that Dukakis was "weak on defense" does not correspond to any actual "weakness" that is provable empirically. Contrary to the misleading notion that Democratic policies would weaken America's defenses, a refrain repeated endlessly by Republicans and many media commentators since 1972, the difference between the two major parties on matters related to military spending is relatively minor. Military spending levels do fluctuate between various administrations, but for reasons less ideological than practical. As international relations expert and American University professor Gordon Adams points out, since 1945 military budgets have tended to rise during wartime and fall as conflicts end—under presidents of both major parties. For example, Republican presidents Richard Nixon and Gerald Ford cut 37 percent from the defense budget after the Vietnam-era high in 1968, and President George H. W. Bush had cut 14 percent compared with the 1989 Cold War budget by the time he left office. Meanwhile, Adams notes that after adjusting for inflation, the most expensive defense budget in more than sixty years belongs to Democratic President Barack Obama.[11]

The simplistic mainstream debate about which presidential candidate or party is "strong" or "weak" on defense is especially absurd when you take into account the size and scope of the US military budget and how much it dwarfs the military expenditures of the rest of the world *combined*. But there is very little substantive debate in the corporate media about the level of military spending actually necessary for America's "defense," and even less debate about the structural effects of our militarized economy on the ability of government to adequately fund health care, education, mental health treatment, infrastructure improvement, environmental protection, and many other services to the majority of the population. In the absence of thoughtful public dialogue on this subject, superficial arguments about "weakening America's defenses" and schoolyard taunts on talk radio and elsewhere about "wimpy Democrats" acquire disproportionate influence.

Chapter 5
1992: Bill Clinton vs. George H. W. Bush and Ross Perot

By all accounts, the election of 1992 was not a foreign policy contest. However, a number of cultural and political developments were catalyzed by the election of Bill Clinton that have direct bearing on the central concerns of this book. These include Clinton's project to remasculinize the Democratic Party by pulling it to the right on issues related to crime and punishment; the emergence of Hillary Clinton as a First Lady whose independence and outspokenness sparked a cultural conversation about the shifting roles of women—and men—at the highest reaches of power; and the emergence of conservative talk radio as a potent force in American politics. Also, the Clinton presidency was marked by the rapid rise of the right-wing of the Republican Party and a corresponding acceleration of polarization in US politics, a process with gendered dimensions.

BILL CLINTON

William Jefferson Clinton was elected president in 1992 with 43 percent of the vote in a three-way race with the incumbent Republican president George H. W. Bush and the eccentric billionaire H. Ross Perot, running on the Reform Party ticket. Because Clinton won only a plurality of votes in a badly divided electorate, it is necessary to temper any claims about the broader cultural significance of his victory. Nonetheless, the ideological shift in the Democratic Party that Clintonism represented, as well as events during his two terms in office, constitute an important part of the story about presidential masculinity over the past generation. To be sure, increasing corporate influence in the party was a major factor in the Democratic Party's move to the right. But there were electoral considerations as well. Simply stated, Clinton's attempts to lead the Democratic Party in a more conservative direction can be understood, at least in part, as attempts to reassure voters—especially but not exclusively white men—that the party was not as soft as the popular stereotype suggested. It is important to keep in mind the historical context. Clinton was the first Democrat to be elected president after twelve years of Republican rule. Before Clinton, the last Democrat to win the White House was Jimmy Carter in 1976. Carter, as we have seen, had been rhetorically emasculated from the moment he was voted out in 1980 after serving only one term in office and suffering a humiliating defeat at the hands of Ronald Reagan. The last Democratic presidential nominee had been Michael Dukakis, whose patriotism, commander in chief credentials and manhood had been viciously—and successfully—attacked in 1988 by the campaign of George H. W. Bush and its surrogates.

Clinton was not the perfect candidate for Democrats who were eager to win back some of the white male voters whom the party had lost to Republicans in the past several elections. Politically he might have been a cautious centrist whose propensity to compromise with conservatives infuriated liberals. But as a young man he participated in protests against the Vietnam War, situating him somewhere vaguely to the left of center in the ongoing "culture wars" that heated up in the 1980s and 1990s as the conservative backlash against the counterculture of the 1960s reached political maturity. The young Clinton was not an antiwar leader, but his sympathies clearly aligned with the antiwar Left, and he did attend antiwar rallies when he was a student at Oxford. This personal history created an opening for conservative talk radio hosts and right-wing pundits to question whether he had forfeited the standing to lead the armed forces. Furthermore, he was married to a strong, assertive, professionally successful woman, which gave rise to speculation and snickering about the balance of power in his marriage. But when it came to the cultural politics of white manhood—an area long mastered by the Right—Clinton brought a number of strengths. Perhaps most prominent among them was that despite his educational accomplishments, he came from a dysfunctional, blue-collar family in the South and was neither ashamed nor reluctant to talk about it. He talked openly about having to defend his mother from his abusive stepfather. His interpersonal communication skills and ability to connect with average people came across in his public speeches and in media interviews. But it wasn't just his often caricatured ability to "feel people's pain"; Clinton also made populist pronouncements like "I am tired of seeing the people who work hard and play by the rules get the shaft." As the linguist Geoffrey Nunberg pointed out, with statements like that he also conveyed his ability to feel their anger.[1]

Bill Clinton's physical stature was also a plus; at six feet two inches and with a stocky build, he cut an imposing figure. When Clinton chose for his vice-presidential running mate Senator Albert Gore of Tennessee, another Southerner who at the time had a reputation as one of the more conservative Democrats in the senate, it sent a message that the Democrats were ready to fight back against the assumption that they had irretrievably lost the white male vote. It didn't hurt that Gore, although a son of privilege (a senator's son) was a Vietnam veteran. Furthermore, when the two strapping Southern white men appeared together in photos that ran on the front page of newspapers and on magazine covers, such as the November 1992 cover of *GQ* magazine that ran with the headline "Huck and Tom," it seemed certain that the Right would have a harder time turning these Democrats into the "liberal wimps" they had so successfully caricatured since the late 1970s. Even Clinton's nickname confounded the right-wing stereotype of Democrats— especially liberals—as effete snobs and elitists. It's tough to make that case against someone with the nickname "Bubba."

From the 1992 campaign onward, Clinton's presidency was immersed in the politics of race on both a policy and a symbolic level. The Nobel Prize-winning novelist Toni Morrison famously called Clinton "the first black president," and he enjoyed high approval ratings from African Americans throughout his two terms in office. Many volumes have been written about the complexities of race in American electoral politics. For this discussion, I am interested in how Clinton's handling of two racially-charged incidents during the 1992 campaign—one that involved his signing a death warrant for the murderer Ricky Ray Rector, and the other concerning his response to provocative statements by the rapper Sister Souljah—helped to define him as a "New Democrat." Conventional wisdom about those events holds that

CHAPTER 5: 1992: B. CLINTON VS. G. H. W. BUSH & R. PEROT

Clinton's actions sent a powerful signal to white voters—especially but not exclusively in the South—that he would not be hemmed in politically by the party's lockstep allegiance to the old civil rights coalition.

But as we have seen, racial issues often have a gender subtext. In these two cases, the decisions Clinton made—whether or not this was his or his campaign's conscious intent—served not only to reassure white voters that the era of liberal permissiveness on crime was over. They also bolstered Clinton's—and thus the Democratic Party's—manhood credentials with white male voters.

The first event took place in late January 1992, just weeks before the New Hampshire primary, when Bill Clinton, still the sitting governor of Arkansas, interrupted his presidential campaign to return home to sign a death warrant for Ricky Ray Rector, a mentally impaired thirty-year-old African American man who had been convicted in the 1981 murder of a white police officer. The move was widely seen as sending a signal that Clinton was indeed a "New Democrat" who would not be burdened by the liberal legacy of his party. Part of this legacy was the perception among many in Richard Nixon's "silent majority," the seventies' "forgotten middle-class," and the legions of Reagan Democrats that liberals' response to violent crime was a misplaced compassion for violent criminals and a lack of concern for the victims of crime.

It is notable that Clinton's apostasy from liberal orthodoxy was successfully highlighted on the issue of the death penalty, part of whose symbolic potency derives from its status as the most dramatic form of premeditated, state-sanctioned violence. If the state holds the monopoly on the legal—and therefore "legitimate"—use of violence, then in a democracy voters are charged with selecting the person whom they trust to exercise that ultimate power. In the 1970s and 1980s, as the conservative backlash against sixties-era permissiveness deepened *and* campaign advertising and other forms of unpaid media coverage increasingly drove political narratives, electoral debates about crime and punishment became both more personalized and more gendered. Is a candidate tough or soft on crime? Does a governor, or a prospective president, have the nerve to pull the switch, or are they just another mushy liberal? As the political scientist Merle Black pointed out in 1992, in Southern states—where the vast majority of executions have occurred in recent decades—the death penalty was often used as a litmus test for executive leadership.[2] As Bill Clinton understood, this litmus test translated neatly to presidential politics. And despite his Georgetown, Oxford, and Yale Law School pedigree, Clinton was determined to project an image of himself as something of a good ol' boy from the South, albeit one with generally progressive views on gender.

In addition to the issues it raised about the morality of the state killing a mentally impaired inmate, the *Rector* death penalty case—like many questions of crime and punishment—was also unavoidably about the electoral politics of race. As the political scientist Jeremy Mayer said, "In killing Ricky Ray Rector, Clinton was exorcising the ghost of Willie Horton from the Democratic Party." But as we have seen, the *Horton* case was not just about white fears of black men; it was also subtextually about the manhood of white male politicians who are responsible for protecting their women and children. So when Clinton authorized the execution of Rector, he metaphorically provided the answer that Michael Dukakis failed to give Bernie Shaw in that fateful CNN debate: unlike some of his fellow national Democrats, he was tough enough to kill a killer.

A few months after the *Rector* case, Clinton's manhood was once again put to the test on what seemed to be a straightforward racial issue. This time the contretemps surrounded a controversial statement by rapper Sister Souljah, followed by Clinton's indignant response. The African American artist and social activist had casually suggested that "if black people kill black people every day, why not have a week and kill white people?" Clinton defied the advice of the Reverend Jesse Jackson and publicly chastised Souljah in a speech at the NAACP convention, in which he suggested that if you reverse the words, it sounded like something KKK leader David Duke might have said. Clinton's statement impressed conservative Southern white Democrats like then-Georgia governor Zell Miller, who praised Clinton for "taking on" the angry rapper. The moment touched such a chord that it entered the political lexicon; a "Sister Souljah moment" describes situations in which politicians calculatedly denounce a member of a group that has historically supported them or their party in order to win votes in the political center.

Mainstream media commentary about the Sister Souljah affair emphasized Clinton's effort to push the Democratic Party to the right in part by showing white voters—including Reagan Democrats in the North—that

CHAPTER 5: 1992: B. CLINTON VS. G. H. W. BUSH & R. PEROT

he was willing to take the risk of criticizing a prominent black figure even if it meant offending the core Democratic constituency of African Americans. But there was also a gendered subtext at play that surfaced in the language used to describe Clinton's action. Clinton was praised—or criticized—for having "stood up" to Sister Souljah, or for "taking her on." The implication was that for the past few decades, Democrats had remained seated in similar circumstances. They had been passive—and therefore feminized—in their unwillingness to challenge African American leaders on matters related to race and violence. Through this largely symbolic act, Clinton was able to masculinize his image, along with that of the Democratic Party, because a politician who stands up to someone, whether an adversary or an ally, develops a reputation as a fighter: a boxer or a street brawler. As we have seen, being identified as a fighter is political gold for a politician—especially one who is seeking the votes of working-class white men. Clinton sent yet another traditional message of strength to these voters when he promised to put one hundred thousand new police officers on the streets, a promise he fulfilled in his first term.

As the first Baby Boomer president, it is perhaps befitting that Bill Clinton would embody many of the tensions and contradictions that accompanied shifting notions of manhood in his generation. He came of age, after all, during an era in which heterosexual white men faced unprecedented challenges to their social position and privilege from the civil rights, women's, and gay liberation movements. If Ronald Reagan (and to a lesser extent, George H. W. Bush) fulfilled a kind of romantic yearning among a segment of the electorate for the reinstatement of old-school patriarchal masculinity in a time of rapid social transformation, Clinton was more a man of his times. Communication scholar Brenton Malin placed descriptions of Clinton's manhood in historical context:

> President Clinton offered the '90s a conflicted masculinity characterized by ambiguous, mobile and conflicted notions of sensitivity, sexuality, class and race. Sensitive and tough, impotent and highly sexualized, Oxford educated and dirt poor, white trash and the first black president, President Clinton was a bundle of contradictions and conflicts. These conflicts allowed him to maintain high popularity ratings despite accusations of waffling and repeated attacks against his character.[3]

To be sure, Clinton's own behavior left him vulnerable to a great deal of criticism, especially his conduct surrounding his relationship with the White House intern Monica Lewinsky. But the vitriol he received from the Right—from the earliest days of his presidency—seemed to stem from something deeper than mere disapproval of his personal actions. It is perhaps impossible to say with certainty why the Right was so unrelenting in its attacks on him, culminating in his impeachment in 1998 for lying to a grand jury in connection with the Paula Jones sexual harassment case. Although right-wing provocateurs like Rush Limbaugh regularly called him a liberal, Clinton governed more like a centrist than a liberal Democrat. But it is notable that during Clinton's presidency, right-wing media exploded in popularity; in 1994, dubbed the "Year of the Angry White Male," the Republican Party took over control of the US House of Representatives, elevating Newt Gingrich to Speaker; the fiercely antigovernment militia movement grew across the country; and in 1995 the right-wing extremist Timothy McVeigh carried out the bombing of the Alfred P. Murrah Federal Building in Oklahoma City, killing 168 people in the bloodiest act of homegrown terrorism in US history.

Did the rise of organized and sometimes explicitly violent right-wing white masculinity during Clinton's presidency have anything to do with the cultural shift represented by a man in the White House who—despite his appropriation of Republican positions on welfare and crime—represented, at least symbolically, a new and more progressive masculinity? One clue might lie in the recent rise of the Far Right, antigovernment "sovereign" movement, which has proliferated since Barack Obama's election in 2008. The Southern Poverty Law Center estimates that a national antigovernment network of "patriot" and "militia" groups has increased from 149 in 2008 to 1274 in 2011.[4] The evidence is mounting that when Democrats become president—even centrists or moderate liberals like Clinton and Obama respectively—some of the most hypermasculine elements in the political universe—far-right-wing men—become increasingly agitated and anxious about their perceived loss of power. They are also vulnerable to the influence of political movements—and media personalities—that offer them a way to reclaim their fragile manhood by joining the fight for liberty and against tyranny, which not coincidentally resembles the title of right-wing talk radio

CHAPTER 5: 1992: B. CLINTON VS. G. H. W. BUSH & R. PEROT

host Mark Levin's 2009 *New York Times* bestseller. *Vanity Fair* writer James Wolcott had this to say about the anti-Obama anger from the Tea Party that surfaced in town hall meetings in the summer of 2009:

> Part of the crazy cognitive dissonance of this summer is the rabid conviction the tea baggers and conservative bloggers possess that Obama is a suave-talking, solid-core radical socialist who practices Chicago-thug hardball, when in fact if Team Obama was the steamroller they claim, they never would have acquired the momentum they've mustered this summer—a true Lenin would have squashed them out of the gate and hardly would have allowed this much slippage this fast. They want Obama to be ruthless and authoritarian because they want to think of themselves as a heroic resistance.[5]

Many right-wing white men respond to the election of Democrats by purchasing more firearms; gun sales increased dramatically after Obama was elected in 2008, just as they did after Clinton was elected in 1992. It is not enough to say that these gun sales reflected a growing (and largely paranoid) concern that Democrats would enact gun control legislation and "take away" people's guns. That might be the proximate cause for some gun purchases, but it does not adequately convey the fear and anger among a notable segment of white men who see progressive gains as threats to their very identity as men.

RUSH KNOWS BEST: WHITE MANHOOD AND THE POLITICS OF CONSERVATIVE TALK RADIO

If the rise of militantly antigovernment conservatism in the 1990s was catalyzed in part by white men's continuing loss of economic power and an accompanying loss of familial and cultural authority, especially in the working and middle classes, similar dynamics contributed to the rise of right-wing talk radio, as well as cable talk TV. A number of charismatic white male talk show hosts have risen to prominence in recent years by selling a brand of authoritarian, bellicose, and at times verbally abusive white masculinity, which for reasons of identity politics and history has touched a nerve with millions of listeners—especially white men. These hosts do much more than simply recite talking points and dispense highly partisan conservative Republican commentary. They speak with an old-school masculine authority that recalls an idealized past, when (white) men were in control in the public and private spheres, and no one was in a position to actively challenge their power. They also provide their listeners with an alternate media universe where the old order of male dominance and white supremacy is still intact, even if they've (sometimes) cleaned up the cruder rhetorical expressions of sexism and racism. In the real world of the twenty-first century, white men's unquestioned dominance in the family and workplace might be in the process of a long term decline—but not when you turn on right-wing AM talk radio or Fox News Channel. People don't generally travel to those precincts to seek out diversity of thought or perspective. It is both fitting and revealing that one of the signature on-air promotions for Rush Limbaugh's radio program features an announcer boldly proclaiming that Rush is "America's anchorman," one who has it all figured out and whom you can trust to expound upon, in the title of one of his bestselling books, *The Way Things Ought To Be*.

Conservative talk radio's influence has grown in recent years, to the point that a radio personality like Limbaugh could be described by the conservative writer David Frum as "the unofficial spokesman for the Republican Party."[6] This extraordinary development has its roots in the election of 1992. If 1960 was the year that television made its debut as a decisive factor in presidential politics, 1992 was the year that ushered in the political power of talk radio. During that campaign Rush Limbaugh in particular emerged as a major force in presidential politics. Limbaugh was so influential that President George H. W. Bush, who was running for reelection, invited Limbaugh to accompany him to the Kennedy Center and to spend a night at the White House. Limbaugh's biographer Zev Chafets reported that Bush personally carried Limbaugh's bag from the elevator of the White House residence to his room, "a gesture Rush never forgot."[7] In 1993, *National Review* ran a cover story about Limbaugh entitled "Leader of the Opposition."

Since the early 1990s Limbaugh's astounding political influence on the right—and in the Republican Party—has been an open secret. He has been the top-rated radio talk show host in America since *Talkers* magazine started the rankings twenty-one years ago.[8] His audience is made up not only of casual listeners and die-hard "dittoheads" but of a significant percentage of the political class both inside and outside of the Washington Beltway, especially conservatives. In 1994, dubbed "The Year of the Angry White Male,"

CHAPTER 5: 1992: B. CLINTON VS. G. H. W. BUSH & R. PEROT

when Republicans gained control of Congress for the first time in forty years, Limbaugh was asked to address the new GOP legislators and was named an honorary member of the freshman class. For two decades he has regularly been the subject of mainstream media interest, and concern. One *Time* magazine cover story that appeared as far back as 1995 was headlined "Is Rush Limbaugh Good for America? Talk radio is only the beginning. Electronic populism threatens to short-circuit representative democracy."[9] A 2008 cover story in the *New York Times* magazine profiled Limbaugh's political influence, as well as offered readers a glimpse at the lavish lifestyle afforded him due to his financial success.[10]

But until recently few people on the left or center of the political spectrum took Limbaugh seriously. Some refused to accept that he had real political power that had to be reckoned with; others foolishly dismissed him as a master vaudevillian showman. When the controversy over Limbaugh's misogynous tirade against Georgetown law student Sandra Fluke erupted in 2012, Al Neuharth, founder of *USA Today*, wrote, "The real problem with Rush Limbaugh is that people take him seriously. He's a clown. If you listen to his radio program regularly, it should be to get your daily laugh."[11] However, many have not clearly understood that distinctions between entertainment culture and political culture collapsed long ago in our media-saturated society. In fact, talk radio occupies a privileged cultural space in the sense that it provides a wealth of information, misinformation, and political analysis, but ultimately is judged by the values of entertainment. Good ratings are what matter, not good scholarship or journalism. As a result, hosts like Limbaugh can put forth all manner of intellectually shallow arguments and repeatedly say silly things—not to mention grossly misstate facts—and still maintain their standing and popularity.

Right-wing talk radio, which accounts for nine out of the top ten talk radio programs, plays an important role in pushing political discourse to the right. This is in part because the hosts with the loudest voices and biggest audiences, such as Limbaugh, Sean Hannity, and Mark Levin, routinely denounce moderation and compromise as surrender, and instead champion the most reactionary policies and candidates. Furthermore, the hosts control the microphone—and hence the conversation—for an enormous amount of time: three hours per day, Monday through Friday, fifty-two weeks of the year. (Hannity also has a nightly television presence on Fox News Channel.) Many stations with conservative talk radio formats offer a lineup of national and local hosts from early in the morning through the night. Thus, unlike Sunday morning political news shows, prime-time cable TV talk shows, or even the more substantive (though largely centrist) analysis that appears on nightly television news programs such as *The News Hour* on PBS, conservative talk radio is on close to all the time. If one accepts the premise that thirty-second political ads can shape political discourse, what about thousands of hours of broadcast radio, where charismatic hosts tightly control whose voices are heard, which ideas get respectful treatment, and which are mocked and dismissed? In terms of its ability to deliver political propaganda, there has never been anything like conservative talk radio in the history of communication.

But conservative talk radio does more than provide an unprecedented platform for the promotion of right-wing ideology. It also plays a powerfully regressive role in gender politics. This is not only because hosts like Limbaugh repeatedly make sexist and patronizing comments about women, belittling those who disagree with them by comparing them to their nagging ex-wives, or reducing young women to crude stereotypes as sexual objects, as Limbaugh did with Fluke in the controversy that flared around insurance coverage for contraceptives. It is also because right-wing talk radio provides an ongoing forum where the virtues of traditional masculinity are celebrated, and where male presidents—and presidential candidates—who do not subscribe to conservative precepts are often mercilessly ridiculed and feminized. In this way Limbaugh and some of his lesser-known rivals play a crucial role in the shaping of presidential masculinity. They function as arbiters for their listeners of what is considered "manly," both in terms of lifestyle and consumer choices and more specifically in terms of political allegiances and voting habits. In addition, while each culture at a given moment in history has conceptions of what is considered "masculine," in order for dominant definitions of masculinity to be sustained they must be reinforced. Talk radio personalities like Limbaugh have outsized influence in this regard, largely because they have millions of listeners and a daily platform to provide running narrative commentary on social life and politics, including which party and politicians "true conservatives" should support, which they should oppose, and perhaps most importantly, what "real men" should think and believe. Karl Rove said

CHAPTER 5: 1992: B. CLINTON VS. G. H. W. BUSH & R. PEROT

as much when he told the *New York Times* that he thought Limbaugh's greatest influence in the 2008 election cycle would be as a backbone stiffening agent. "He's a leader," Rove said. "If Rush engages on an issue, it gives others courage to engage." Thus, when Limbaugh attacks the manhood of liberal men in the course of defining the "conservative" position on an issue, it helps set a tone for political discourse that reverberates in barrooms and back halls, but also in the corridors of Republican power at the local, state, and national level.

It is notable, although hardly surprising, that Rush Limbaugh's audience is 72 percent male, over 90 percent white, and skews age fifty and older. Presumably, a key part of the appeal of conservative talk radio to its predominantly older white male audience resides in its reinforcement of traditional masculinity in the face of a culture where epochal economic transformations and progressive social movements have shaken old certainties about what constitutes a "real man." Limbaugh not only articulates a set of conservative moral precepts and reactionary politics, he also performs a kind of cartoonish masculinity from an era gone by. For example, Limbaugh loves to talk about football; he is frequently photographed smoking expensive cigars. He champions the military and was a prominent defender of the conduct of US service members in the disgraceful episode of the Abu Ghraib prison in Iraq, which he dismissed as a "fraternity prank." According to his biographer, he has "a fair amount" of Hugh Hefner in him.[12] In the media persona he has constructed for himself, his unrestrained narcissism drives him to broadcast to his audience an inflated sense of himself as a "man's man," while his political agenda seeks to reinforce the link between manly strength and political conservatism. He accomplishes this rhetorically, in part, by relentlessly attacking the femininity of feminists, and the masculinity of men who support gender equality.

In Limbaugh-land, Democratic women who demand to be treated as men's equals are castrating "feminazis," and Democratic men are either neutered wimps, or gay. In fact, homophobia is never far from the surface when right-wing politicians and media personalities ridicule the supposed effeminacy of liberals. In 1992, the editor of the *American Spectator* magazine R. Emmett Tyrrell noted the closure of New York bordellos before the Democratic convention. Tyrrell opined that "the convention is going to be pretty dreary for the handful of heterosexual men who still attend the Democratic assemblage."[13] On his show in early September 2008, Limbaugh, echoing Tyrrell, reported a news item about how business at Denver strip clubs was supposedly slow during the Democratic National Convention, held the previous week. "There is other news out there, ladies and gentlemen," he said. "…The political convention is kind of a bust for downtown strip clubs." But instead of playing to the socially conservative segment of his audience by praising male Democratic delegates for not participating in the sexual exploitation of women, Limbaugh took the opportunity to ridicule their manhood and, presumably, their heterosexuality. "This is easily understood by me," he boasted. "How many real men were in Denver this past week? That's the question you need to ask."

Socially conservative women who consider him a hero might want to ask Rush Limbaugh if he thinks "real men"—who in Limbaugh's moral universe are all conservative Republicans—were out in the strip clubs in Minneapolis-St. Paul during the 2008 Republican National Convention, getting lap dances from naked women even as their party nominated a woman for vice president who the thrice-divorced and four times married talker repeatedly referred to as a "babe."

In discussions about presidential politics, contempt toward men who do not identify as conservatives surfaces in the kind of schoolyard name calling that Limbaugh and others have made a stock-in-trade. Limbaugh is the most influential of an entire fraternity of right-wing talk radio hosts who use child-ish taunts about bodily characteristics and other tactics to question the man-hood of Democrats. Limbaugh likes to hone in on personal characteristics of liberal men whom he then dismisses as feminine, such as when he labeled former Senator John Edwards the "Breck Girl" because of his famously stylish hair, or when he traded in a popular stereotype about the supposed effeminacy of the French by derisively referring to Senator John Kerry as "Looks French" Kerry. Limbaugh calls the thoughtful and even-keeled TV commentator David Gergen "David Rodham Gergen," a reference that serves both to indict him for going easy on "liberals" like Hillary Clinton and to question his manhood. He calls the former chairman of the Democratic National Committee Terry McCauliffe a "punk." He dubbed PBS commentator Mark Shields "Maxi-Shields." He uses the term "PMS-NBC" to refer to MSNBC,

CHAPTER 5: 1992: B. CLINTON VS. G. H. W. BUSH & R. PEROT

the cable network which is owned by the conservative General Electric corporation but features male on-air personalities who do not march in lock-step to right-wing talking points, such as Lawrence O'Donnell and Ed Schultz, and only in 2008 added a liberal woman, Rachel Maddow, to its prime-time lineup. It is ironic, to say the least, that Limbaugh mercilessly ridicules liberal men as "linguini spined," emasculated wimps, when he himself avoided military service in Vietnam by claiming an anal boil rendered him unfit for service.[14]

Limbaugh's avoidance of the draft didn't stop him from bashing Bill Clinton as a draft dodger throughout the 1992 presidential campaign, but for reasons of his own history, as Zev Chafets generously puts it in *Rush Limbaugh: An Army of One*, "his heart wasn't in it." Presumably his heart was more invested in a later attack on Barack Obama's manhood that Limbaugh launched after the killing of Osama bin Laden.

When the news broke on the evening of May 1, 2011 that a team of Navy Seals had killed Osama bin Laden, it was a gigantic news story—and the Right's biggest nightmare. One of their main narratives about President Obama had been dealt a devastating blow. Even before he was elected president, Barack Obama had been the target of relentless mockery and ridicule on conservative talk radio. The line of attack varied from issue to issue, but its essence was usually the same: Obama was Jimmy Carter II: a weak and vacillating leader who (in Obama's case) gave good speeches but was in way over his head.

The bin Laden killing posed a problem for Limbaugh. How would he respond? The man whom Limbaugh and others on the Right had relentlessly mocked and ridiculed as a lightweight and a wimp had quietly and systemati-cally led and authorized the killing of bin Laden in such a militarily impressive way that crowds in sports stadiums cheered "USA! USA!" and spontaneous rallies erupted at the White House. Limbaugh would have to go on the air just a half-day later when the entire infotainment universe was abuzz in this signa-ture moment of American triumphalism—with the former community organizer and law professor Barack Obama looking tough and standing tall at the epicenter of a patriotic revival. In another era, conservatives would have been measured, and even generous, in crediting Obama with a job well done. But not in the era of conservative talk radio, and not on *The Rush Limbaugh Show*.

From the first moment he went on-air, Limbaugh attempted to strip Obama of any military/manhood credentials he might have earned from his leadership in the killing of public enemy number one. He, and other talk radio hosts with a similar agenda, could not tolerate the thought that a moderately liberal Democrat could be a "real man" and a "strong leader" of the US Armed Forces. It is worth noting that countless second-and third-tier talkers look to Limbaugh for cues about what to say and not to say.

In the hours and days after the killing, Limbaugh and other conservative talk radio hosts attempted to downplay Obama's role in the operation and denigrate his potentially rehabilitated manhood. They did this with a series of arguments:

"I, me, my." One of Limbaugh's first lines of attack on May 2 was to accuse the president of focusing on himself, as if the killing of bin Laden was primarily about Obama. Numerous commentators across the political spectrum praised Obama's televised statement the evening of the raid as a model of dignified understatement. They acknowledged that he hit all the right notes and spread the credit around, especially to the military and intelligence services. Many people said they felt proud and patriotic listening to him. Not Limbaugh. He counted the times Obama used words like "I," "me," and "my," and emphasized one of his running themes about this president: that he is a full-fledged, pathological narcissist.

"Congratulations?" Limbaugh did sarcastically "congratulate" Obama, but not for anything the Democrat did. He congratulated Obama for having the good sense to follow Bush's policies "in the Middle East." Limbaugh made a point of not congratulating Obama for his own bold act of leadership. From the beginning, Limbaugh helped to shape what emerged as one of the Right's strongest talking points—that Obama was claiming credit when it was really Bush who got bin Laden. Bush was the decisive, risk-taking conservative who made the tough choices; it was just a coincidence that final justice came on the vacillating liberal's watch.

Limbaugh also repeatedly praised the Navy Seals and the special counter-terrorism operations run by the Department of Defense—as if Obama had nothing to do with the armed forces who carried this out; as if he wasn't the commander in chief who oversaw and ordered the operation; as if he wasn't in charge.

CHAPTER 5: 1992: B. CLINTON VS. G. H. W. BUSH & R. PEROT

"Obama opposed the hard-line, hyperaggressive policies that made success possible." In the first hours after the country awoke to news of bin Laden's death, Limbaugh and other right-wing opinion leaders quickly pivoted to the position that the al Qaeda founder's killing had been made possible by actionable intelligence the military procured from torturing prisoners back in the early 2000s. This allowed them to argue that Obama had tried actively to undermine the tactics that made this entire raid possible, which made it even more unseemly for Obama to be pounding his chest in pride at the killing. Supporters of the president, on the other hand, refuted this line and argued that the intelligence used was gathered using nontorture methods. The implication was that Obama's way was less brutal—but more effective.

All of this is part of a contentious, high-stakes political debate about presidential manhood. Obama has been criticized by the Left for largely continuing Bush's counterterrorism and national security strategy. Even so, he and Bush represent starkly contrasting masculine styles: the Decider vs. the Consensus-seeker, the leader who goes with his gut versus the one who goes with his head, the Texas good ol' boy versus the urbane intellectual. These binaries also fit neatly into conservative versus liberal and Republican versus Democrat. Rush Limbaugh and a large percentage of his audience have an enormous stake in one side of that binary being the one that makes people safe in the real world—and it isn't the side of the urbane intellectual. If Obama's style of manhood appears to make us safer, it's a blow to the cultural appeal of white male conservatism.

"Obama had no choice but to authorize the raid." As days passed by and Limbaugh gathered steam in his continued attack on Obama, he went from arguing that Obama was claiming credit for something Bush was responsible for to an even pettier argument: that Obama never even had a choice. All the pieces were in place; there would have been hell to pay, as Rush reminded his listeners, if Obama hadn't green-lighted the operation. In other words, the president deserves no credit for this huge victory because he was pressured into approving it.

"Obama's failure to release the photos of a dead bin Laden proves that he's a wimp." Conservative talkers loved the fact that Obama deliberated on and then decided not to release the photos of bin Laden. That gave them the opportunity to argue that Obama cared more about some potentially hurt

feelings in the Muslim world than about the right of Americans to gloat. In other words, it fit neatly into the right-wing narrative, fed daily on talk radio, that Obama is an effete elitist who looks down at average Americans (who want a photo that satisfies their lust for revenge). Mostly, the debate about the death-scene photos of bin Laden helped shift the conversation away from a discussion about Obama's steely and bold leadership and back toward the president's supposed failures. As the conservative Boston talk show host Michael Graham wrote, "…the mishandling of the details of the raid, the waffling on the photo release, the pandering to the Arab street—is enough. Americans demand better, and we will get it."

In the universe of conservative talk radio, the killing of bin Laden happened coincidentally on Barack Obama's watch. Obama had to be pressured into authorizing it, and even then he made lots of mistakes. Democrats still can't be trusted on issues of national security. In order to get the bad guys and keep America safe, we need to elect red-blooded, red state conservative men (or a gun-toting Sarah Palin). What conservative talk radio listeners were unlikely to hear were legitimate questions raised by some—mostly those on the left, but also Republican Congressman Ron Paul—about the legality and morality of targeted assassinations. The idea barely registered that some people were less impressed by Obama's manly action and more troubled by what appeared to be the precedent he set by playing a central and highly visible role in an extrajudicial killing.

Unlike most talk radio hosts, Rush Limbaugh rarely has guests on his program and almost no one who dares to criticize or even mildly disagree with him. On the infrequent occasions when he does have a guest, they are usually right-wing politicians seeking a large and generally sympathetic audience—and a compliant host—to defend a policy choice of some kind, such as when then-vice president Dick Cheney came on the program to refute media reports critical of the Bush administration's conduct of the war in Iraq. Most of Limbaugh's daily three-hour show is devoted to the host's clever and entertaining monologues, punctuated by callers who shower him with gratitude and praise before making a point or soliciting his opinion. While he can be charming and witty in on-air conversation, the host's volcanic anger is never far from the surface. Sometimes he raises his voice in anger at a caller or when he's reporting the comments of a "liberal" whose news-making comments get under his skin. Limbaugh often cuts to a commercial at the peak of his angry outbursts, cautioning his listeners that if he doesn't rescue himself with this commercial intervention, he might totally lose his cool and utter obscenities which would bring down the wrath of the Federal Communications Commission. Perhaps the most frequent victims of Limbaugh's rants are liberals, whom he derides as "libs," mercilessly demeans, and blames for just about every imaginable social problem. Like many of the demagogic right-wing populists of the past century, Limbaugh relentlessly ridicules liberals as out-of-touch elitists, devoid of the kind of common sense that he, and his listeners, presumably possess in abundance. Apparently most of his working and middle-class listeners are unfazed by the absurdity of the fact that the enormously wealthy Limbaugh, who flies around the world in private jets, forcefully defends corporate power and big business interests, and has a salon in his secluded Palm Beach mansion meant to suggest Versailles, unselfconsciously positions himself as an antielitist.

Critics of Rush Limbaugh and other right-wing talk radio hosts often point to the coarsening of political discourse to which the talkers have contributed. Former vice president Al Gore describes what he terms the "Limbaugh-Hannity-Drudge axis" as a kind of "fifth column in the fourth estate" that is made up of "propagandists pretending to be journalists."[15] Gore claims that what most troubles him about these right-wing polemicists is their promotion of hatred as entertainment—particularly their mean-spirited hostility toward liberals and progressives. But what most of right-wing radio's progressive critics overlook or downplay is the gendered nature of Limbaugh and company's contempt for liberals.

Embedded firmly within the talk radio host's scathing critique of liberalism is a barely suppressed well of anger at the progressive changes in the gender and sexual order over the past forty years and the concomitant displacement of traditional patriarchal power. Limbaugh is perhaps the most overt in his open hostility toward feminist women, and the men who support them. He calls these men the "new castrati," and ridicules them for having "lost all manhood, gonads, guts and courage throughout our culture and our political system."[16] This antiwoman and antifeminist anger finds expression in the commercial world of talk radio in a way that is inconceivable in other forms of mainstream political discourse.

LEADING MEN

In fact, the source of Limbaugh's immense popularity on AM radio has some interesting parallels to Howard Stern's popularity on FM, and later on satellite radio. Under the guise of self-consciously constructed personae—Limbaugh as the fun-loving conservative truth-teller, Stern as naughty rock and roll bad boy—both men function as the id of their respective audiences. They say things that men in more responsible or respectable contexts simply would never say *out loud*. For example, survey data for the past quarter century shows that many men resent the changes in workplace environments brought about by federal and state sexual harassment legislation, largely championed by the Democratic Party. But few men in public life, particularly Republican candidates and officeholders, would dare criticize sexual harassment laws when women comprise 53 percent of the electorate. Rush Limbaugh, on the other hand, repeatedly refers to accomplished women, including women in politics, as "babes," female journalists as "infobabes" and "anchorettes," and boasts that a sign on his door reads "Sexual harassment at this work station will not be reported. However, …it will be graded."[17] As an entertainer, he is clearly allowed a certain license to offend. However, it is disingenuous for conservative organizations, including the Republican Party, to deny that he is their most important—if unofficial—spokesman, especially when you consider that in addition to his daily distribution of conservative talking points via his radio program and website, Limbaugh is regularly invited to address conservative gatherings like the Conservative Political Action Conference.

Rush Limbaugh has the biggest national stage, but many right-wing hosts in local markets have mastered the technique of feminizing liberal and progressive male opponents. A noteworthy example is Boston radio host Howie Carr, also a longtime columnist with the right-wing tabloid *Boston Herald*. Carr, whose syndicated show reaches into heavily populated southern New Hampshire and thus every four years plays a role in the first-in-the-nation presidential primary, repeatedly ridiculed former governor and 1988 Democratic presidential nominee Michael Dukakis as "Pee-Wee," mocked John Kerry as the "War Hero" in an attempt to undermine the authority of the senator's impressive military record, referred to the former Secretary of Labor Robert Reich as "the 59-inch Robert Reich," and used to call the diminutive former president of the Massachusetts state senate William Bulger the "Corrupt Midget."

CHAPTER 5: 1992: B. CLINTON VS. G. H. W. BUSH & R. PEROT

Of course many other right-wing media personalities have engaged in these sorts of tactics, and not all of them have been men. Most notably, in her frequent talk radio and cable TV appearances, and in her speeches on college campuses and elsewhere, the provocative conservative commentator Ann Coulter routinely accuses male liberals of being gay or effeminate.[18] In 2007, in a speech at the Conservative Political Action Conference that was widely replayed on cable TV shows and on YouTube, Coulter implied that then-Democratic presidential candidate John Edwards was a "faggot," a comment which drew robust applause.

No discussion about the power of conservative media to narrow the range of a president's political operating space through bullying tactics and raising questions about his masculinity would be complete without some discussion of the top-rated *Fox* cable TV host Bill O'Reilly. According to author and media critic Jeff Cohen, O'Reilly is an "imposing TV presence whose face exudes emotion— annoyance, frustration, fury—better than most TV actors," allowing him to tap into and articulate the anger and resentment of conservative white men toward a culture many of them no longer recognize as their own.[19] A key part of the fight he wages is against liberal elites in Washington and Hollywood, but perhaps his strongest venom is reserved for progressive intellectuals, whom he delights in skewering, even if he routinely has to resort to verbal bullying tactics to "win" an argument. Jeff Cohen, who appeared as a guest on *The O'Reilly Factor* several times in the late 1990s, surmises that Bill O'Reilly is someone who knows, at least subconsciously, that research and inquiry might erode his beliefs. "With O'Reilly," Cohen wrote, "his beliefs are bedrock, immovable. Everything else—facts, logic, perhaps someone's jaw—can be rearranged."[20]

Like Limbaugh, O'Reilly has been at this a long time and has mastered the art of framing policy debates—especially on issues of homeland security and foreign policy—as tests of manly resolve. Consider: in December of 2008 President-elect Barack Obama was in the process of selecting a person to nominate as head of the Central Intelligence Agency. O'Reilly asserted on his TV and radio programs that unless Obama backed off his campaign pledge to end "enhanced interrogations," he would have trouble finding someone to accept the job of CIA chief, because, he said, everyone knows that we have no chance of beating the Islamist radicals without resorting to such "unpleasant" tactics. O'Reilly then upped the ante by arguing that if Obama stuck with the "loony left" (O'Reilly absurdly included the *New York Times* in this designation) and failed to accept the need for enhanced interrogations, and Americans die as a result ("which they will"), the new president would lose O'Reilly's support for good, and presumably the support of millions of Americans who look to the *Fox* host as a source of cultural insight and political guidance.

As always, O'Reilly's pronouncements were infused with the pretense that what he believed was just common sense; he wanted to test whether the newly elected president was going to measure up. In fact, the issue of torture exemplifies the manner in which conservative talk show hosts with large audiences of older white men help to set the parameters of debate about what constitutes manly presidential leadership in the twenty-first century. O'Reilly's position boiled down to a simple narrative that made for great dialogue on TV and radio: bad men with dark skin and exotic religious beliefs will harm American citizens unless the skinny president-elect has the guts to get tough with them. O'Reilly didn't use the word "torture," but he strongly implied that the standard he favors is whatever it takes to get necessary information. The top-rated *Fox* host threatened repercussions if Obama honored his campaign pledge and brought US policy in line with the Geneva Conventions and other international human rights treaties that the George W. Bush administration treated with contempt.

It seems fair to assume that media-driven right-wing pressure of this sort posed a political dilemma for the newly elected president. By sticking to a principled opposition to torture, he won applause and respect around the world and at home among liberals, progressives, and other civil libertarians. At the same time, he faced relentless criticism in the conservative media and blogosphere for capitulating to terrorism, criticism that was only slightly muted after his successful authorization and leadership of the raid that killed Osama bin Laden. The vitriol aimed at Obama from the Right often gets personal, because a time-honored tactic on the Right is to demean the masculinity of men whose political positions do not conform to conservative orthodoxy, especially on matters of national security. Politicians who have been branded as weak on national security, *who have been feminized*, have a very difficult time winning the votes of white men, especially during times

CHAPTER 5: 1992: B. CLINTON VS. G. H. W. BUSH & R. PEROT

of war. It doesn't matter whether the charge of weakness/feminization has any validity; it has been a successful political tactic. It might not be possible to prove that a specific president pursued a more aggressive policy than he wanted to in order to fend off criticism from the Right, but can there be any doubt that Democrats have felt pressure for many years to take aggressive positions on national security questions, lest they be dismissed as dreamers and idealists who can't be trusted to protect America's interests?

The challenge for Democrats running for president—in a culture in which talk radio and cable reach daily into tens of millions of people's cars, homes, and psyches—is to present a compelling counternarrative to the reactionary story about masculinity and social change that Limbaugh and his fellow right-wing talkers tell every day. One of the most powerful themes in right-wing social commentary today—reprising a popular theme in right-wing social thought from early in the twentieth century—is the supposed "feminization" of American culture, where American men have grown weak and passive in the face of women's increased social and political assertiveness. The right-wing radio personality Michael Savage, author of four *New York Times* bestsellers and host of the third most popular talk radio program, *The Savage Nation*, claims that "Today in America we have a 'she-ocracy,' where a minority of feminist zealots rules the culture." He defends the nastiness of his on-air persona and his far-right views by maintaining that "Only a more savage nation can survive…not a more compassionate nation."[21] Limbaugh blames the emasculating forces of feminism and liberalism for everything from declining male enrollments on college campuses to reaction to the "stupid torture" at Abu Ghraib prison. Limbaugh himself summed it up well in a typical monologue.

…Who do liberals consider real men? Michael Kinsley, Alan Alda, the guy that played … the character Frank Burns on M*A*S*H … how long ago that was, and this guy was practically a pet on a leash for 'Hot Lips' Houlihan. And I think they've become Democrats. Some Republicans, too. Tom Daschle, Harry Reid, soft-spoken, concerned about everything. They're little wusses and they're constantly voicing their concern over every little thing that fits their template into a Democrat America. Snerdley, as you would say, it's time to man up, grow a pair …Any man with onions, as you say, is voted off the island these days since he doesn't fit the feminist chickified template and agenda. And so what we're left with is a collection of sniveling, whining Frank Burns-type guys who 'Hot Lips' Houlihan was running around on a leash. These are the people apologizing to the world for America. These are the people seeking the approval, the Richard Holbrookes of the world. These are the people that run around Europe and the Middle East, "Please like us … what have we done to make you hate us, please like us." What?…Why do you think I'm so hated by the feminists? Cause I am not feminized.[22]

The masculinist fear of feminization that is a recurring theme on Limbaugh's program and other right-wing talk shows has a rich lineage in American history. According to the historical sociologist Michael Kimmel, a powerful strain in nineteenth-century American thought held that something happened to American society that had led to "a loss of cultural vitality, of national virility" which necessitated men's "retreat from feminization." Kimmel explains that the term "feminization" refers "both to real women, whose feminizing clutches as teachers, mothers, and Sunday school teachers were seen as threatening to turn robust boyhood into emasculated little pipsqueaks, and also to an increasingly urban and industrial culture, a culture which increasingly denied men the opportunities for manly adventure and a sense of connectedness with their work."[23] One of the many institutions that were created to counter this perceived feminization was the Boy Scouts, founded in the US in 1910 as a way to socialize boys into a more robust and quasimilitary masculinity. Kimmel recounts a passage from the 1886 Henry James novel *The Bostonians*, which but for the elegance of the language could have been uttered by Limbaugh in 2008. The speaker is the dashing Basil Ransome, a displaced Southern gentleman, railing against modern society.

The whole generation is womanized; the masculine tone is passing out of the world; it's a feminine, nervous, hysterical, chattering, canting age, an age of hollow phrases and false delicacy and exaggerated solicitudes and coddled sensibilities, which, if we don't soon look out, will usher in the reign of mediocrity, of the feeblest and flattest and most pretentious that has ever been. The masculine character, the ability to dare and endure, to know and yet not fear reality, to look the world in the face and take it for what it is…that is

CHAPTER 5: 1992: B. CLINTON VS. G. H. W. BUSH & R. PEROT

what I want to preserve, or rather…recover; and I must tell you that I don't in the least care what becomes of you ladies while I make the attempt.[24]

Is it mere coincidence that white male conservative talk radio has flourished in an era when progressive women's movements have transformed the social landscape? In the late twentieth and early twenty-first centuries, Limbaugh and his conservative talk radio cohorts have used technologies of mass communication to reach millions of American men with the deeply misleading message that many of their worst economic and social problems are somehow linked to the twin evils of liberalism and feminism, and the concomitant loss of (white) men's power. They have also managed to plug the medium itself as a vehicle for fighting back. Los Angeles-based conservative talk radio host Dennis Prager writes that because of innovations such as talk radio and *Fox News*, the "Left" no longer enjoys the same "monopoly" over mass information it once had, "and the Republican Party is no longer emasculated."[25] Because the ultimate source of talk radio's power is an advertising-driven corporate media industry that benefits from the stability of the two-party system, the implicit and explicit curative the conservative talkers prescribe for their listeners is to support conservative political candidates—overwhelmingly Republicans, and predominantly white men—who understand the genesis and scope of the problem, and have the will to fix it. It hardly matters whether the specifics of their analyses are reasoned soundly or even if they are factually accurate. What matters is that as long as they can maintain their ratings, Limbaugh and company will have the power not only to interpret social and political reality on a daily basis for millions of listeners, but in so doing to reinforce a narrow and constricted definition of masculinity, with powerful implications for what is considered "strong" presidential leadership.

THE ROLE OF FIRST LADIES

During the 2012 Republican primaries, James Dobson, influential founder of the right-wing organization Focus on the Family, suggested that Calista Gingrich was a "mistress" who would not be a suitable First Lady. Dobson's comment seemed intended to remind socially conservative voters that they were electing not only the politician who would be a preeminent symbol of

American manhood but also the woman who would become a symbolic leader of American femininity. What kind of message would it send to young women if America's First Lady had carried on a six-year affair with a married man?

But cultural conversations about first lady femininity are significant beyond the messages they might send to women. They are also, by definition, conversations about the president's manhood, because the woman (he) is partnered with reveals a great deal about *him*. Voters make judgments about his manhood in part by the type of woman to whom he is drawn—and who is drawn to him. A 2004 *USA Today* poll found that 54 percent of respondents said that a candidate's spouse is an important factor to consider when choosing who to support for president.[26] When pollsters have asked voters in recent elections about whether a specific candidate's wife is an asset or liability to her husband's candidacy, they are not only asking people about their impressions of prospective first ladies, they are also in a sense asking them to pass judgment on *his* judgment and decision-making in one of the most intimate areas of his life.

Over the past several decades a great deal of scholarly and journalistic attention has been paid to the role of first ladies. Here, I am interested in what cultural conversations and debates about first lady femininity teach us about presidential masculinity. Hillary Clinton is a good starting point, because her tenure in the White House produced the most cultural chatter, and controversy, since Eleanor Roosevelt. With the notable exception of Rosalynn Carter, who consulted with her husband Jimmy Carter on speeches and appointments, and sometimes sat in on cabinet meetings, First Ladies since Roosevelt had generally presented themselves—in public, at least—as helpmates to their husbands and exemplars of traditional feminine virtues. Some first ladies, such as Betty Ford, publicly took positions in support of abortion rights, legislation such as the Equal Rights Amendment, and women's rights more generally. But when they attached themselves to a cause, it was usually something noncontroversial, such as Lady Bird Johnson's campaign for highway beautification, Nancy Reagan's "Say No to Drugs" initiative, or Laura Bush's efforts to promote literacy.

Hillary Clinton became First Lady when her husband Bill took office after twelve years of conservative Republican rule. Her two immediate predecessors—Nancy Reagan and Barbara Bush—were both women from a prefeminist generation whose husbands projected a *Father Knows Best*, 1950s-style white masculinity. In that traditional script, the president was the powerful white patriarch and his wife the super helpmate whose loving supervision of the domestic sphere of hearth and home attested to the intact family values of the First Family. Mrs. Reagan and Mrs. Bush were both skilled at playing the role of supportive wife in public, although accounts that surfaced both during and after their time in the White House confirmed that each wielded considerable influence in their husbands' administrations. Like her husband, Nancy Reagan was a trained actor. The adoring gaze that she affected toward Ronald Reagan whenever they were photographed together in public—especially when he stood before a microphone and she was positioned off to the side or behind him—obscured the awkward truth that she played a critical role in the nonceremonial side of the Reagan White House, especially on matters of personnel, on which her publicly assertive husband found it difficult to act decisively.[27] The reality of Nancy Reagan's power in both her marriage and her husband's administration conflicted with the legend of Ronald Reagan as a man's man at home and at work—and Nancy wasn't about to disrupt that mythology.

Barbara Bush also played dual roles in public and private. She was a popular First Lady, a composed and reassuring matriarch who presided over the sprawling Bush family. She was also well aware of the limitations of her position. "Your hands are tied in some ways," she told *USA Today*. She "curbed her tongue" and stuck to noncontroversial causes during her four years in the White House in an effort to "not cause George huge embarrassment."[28] Just the same, in a review of the 1990 book *Running Mates: The Making of a First Lady*, by Ann Grimes, Lynda Gorov writes that "the 'Silver Fox' emerges as a shrewd tactician who pursued the presidency for her husband as aggressively as other women do professional careers."[29] While Mrs. Reagan and Mrs. Bush were strong women who clearly had power in their marriages *behind the scenes*, both were careful in public not to be seen as undermining their husband's authority. Sheila Tate, former press secretary to Nancy Reagan, provided the rationale in her description of what Americans expect of a first lady. "They expect her to comport herself with style and dignity. They expect her to dress well. They expect her to represent them in international settings. They do not expect her to step over the line into her husband's domain."[30]

LEADING MEN

Hillary Clinton, on the other hand, became a lightning rod for controversy from the earliest moments of Bill Clinton's 1992 presidential campaign precisely because she refused to *act* like a traditional woman and promote the illusion that she was subservient to her husband. It all started in January during a joint interview with Bill on CBS's *60 Minutes*. During a discussion of her husband's alleged infidelities, she said that she was "not some little woman standing by my man like Tammy Wynette." A couple of months later she responded to a charge by Jerry Brown that her legal work represented a potential conflict of interest with her role as First Lady of Arkansas by saying sarcastically that she "could have stayed home and baked cookies and had teas."

Clinton's widely circulated "cookies" comment was regarded by many conservatives as an insult to traditional homemakers and became a rallying cry for many years for women on the right. The backlash forced Clinton to retreat and present a more traditionally feminine and thus less threatening image, but the genie was out of the bottle. Bill Clinton's wife had become an inspiring and polarizing cultural icon, and a major campaign issue. In his infamous "culture war" speech at the Republican National Convention, Pat Buchanan mocked Bill Clinton's suggestion that by electing him, Americans would get "two for the price of one," and then he scornfully announced, "Hillary believes that 12-year-olds should have a right to sue their parents, and she has compared marriage as an institution to slavery and life on an Indian reservation...Friends, this is radical feminism."[31] By the time the general election got fully underway in September, *Time* magazine would be running a cover story with the headline "The Hillary Factor: is she helping or hurting her husband?" In the story, the reporter Margaret Carlson described Hillary as a remarkable woman and an accomplished lawyer. "There is no doubt that she is her husband's professional and intellectual equal. But is this reason to turn her into 'Willary Horton' for the '92 campaign, making her an emblem of all that is wrong with family values, working mothers and modern women in general? The Republicans clearly think so."[32]

The "Hillary factor" continued to be a major theme during the 1992 campaign, and remained a big story throughout Bill Clinton's two terms as president. Most of the discussion focused on Hillary and the expanded opportunities and identities for women that had been catalyzed by modern feminism—as well as the profound ambivalence with which those new realities had been met. But another thread received far less attention: what did Hillary's talent and ambition say about Bill and, by extension, a generation of men who were partnered with strong feminist women? As Stephen Ducat reported, early in the president's first term the bulk of male political commentators organized their fears (of Hillary's power) around the notion of a castrated Bill Clinton. The right-wing magazine the *American Spectator* ran a cover story with a cartoon sketch of Hillary Clinton looming large over a small drawing of Bill under the headline "Boy Clinton's Big Mama." The emasculated president was a favorite theme of comedians as well. Arsenio Hall noted that President Clinton had not announced a Supreme Court choice because "Hillary hasn't made up his mind yet." David Letterman announced that Bill's Secret Service code was "Mr. Mom."[33] Former president Richard Nixon expressed the traditional view when he warned that Hillary's forceful intelligence was likely to make her husband "look like a wimp."[34]

But for many Baby Boomers, the Clinton partnership looked familiar. It was representative of a shift in marriage that had been underway for some years, as more women sought careers and two-income families proliferated. Far from being a liability for Bill, his marriage undoubtedly won him points with a growing number of women *and* men who agreed with the seventies bumper sticker: "A man of quality is not threatened by a woman for equality." Of course popular perceptions about the balance of power in the Clinton marriage were colored not only by the news of Bill's infidelity that surfaced during the 1992 campaign but also by subsequent revelations about his sexual relationship with White House intern Monica Lewinsky. As Ducat observed:

> It is interesting that after the revelations of the Monica Lewinsky scandal, Bill Clinton's image went from that of the neutered househusband of an emasculating harridan to that of a swaggering stud-muffin whose untrammeled lust for sexual conquest imperiled all females in his orbit...the formerly feminized president had been resurrected as a phallic leader.[35]

We also know that when the Monica Lewinsky scandal broke—and even after right-wing House Republicans succeeded in impeaching him—Clinton's job approval ratings actually improved, smoothing the way for his productive and largely acclaimed post-presidential career.

LEADING MEN

If Hillary Clinton's tenure as First Lady reflected the increasingly egalitarian gender politics in heterosexual marriages, her successor played a more retro, and much less controversial, role. Laura Bush was the anti-Hillary. Although she was a baby boomer, she was more of a traditional first lady than her mother-in-law. She was a sweet, friendly librarian who spoke softly and deferred to her husband in public, which not only provided a stark feminine counterpoint to his cartoonish performance of Texas cowboy masculinity but also reassured his followers that there are still women who are comfortable when men take the lead. "My life really began when I met my husband," she said. "...I give my husband some counsel, but I actually think counsel or advice from a spouse ends up being nagging."[36] Far from being seen as an anachronism, Laura Bush remained extremely popular throughout Bush's presidency and was widely acknowledged to be one of her husband's best political assets.

If Laura Bush's deferential femininity reinforced her husband's conservative manhood in the popular imagination, consider what Teresa Heinz Kerry's said about the virility of her husband John Kerry. The writer Christopher Buckley captured the contrast in this colorful description of the two party conventions in the summer of 2004.

> It is de rigueur to trot out the ladies to assure the electorate that the testosterone is diluted. Laura Bush is a Platonic ideal of Republican femininity; lovely, demure, reticent, the hair just so, exquisite but not too dressy in de la Renta blue. As she spoke, about her husband, daughters, family, literacy and all the rest, you could practically smell the pies cooling on the windowsill. In retrospect, the sexy-sultry Mozambican billionairess Teresa Heinz Kerry seemed hardly to mention her husband, coming off as rather more interested in, well, other things.[37]

It is routinely mentioned in postmortems of the 2004 election that Bush's wife enhanced his standing in the polls, while the impact of Kerry's wife on perceptions of him was mixed. Heinz Kerry, a highly intelligent and talented woman with cosmopolitan tastes and interests in health and philosophy, was typically referred to as both an asset and a liability to her husband. In the latter category, presumably, was her penchant for doing the opposite of what

CHAPTER 5: 1992: B. CLINTON VS. G. H. W. BUSH & R. PEROT

Nancy Reagan did when she stared up at her husband with those admiring doe eyes. Far from stroking his ego, Heinz Kerry seemed uninhibited about taking her husband down a peg, as when she told *Hardball*'s Chris Matthews that "I don't want to give (John) more (due) than he deserves."[38] Perhaps most telling was how often Heinz Kerry's independent spirit was described as a potential source of trouble for him. It wasn't just that she had the propensity to go off-script and say what she really believed. On a symbolic level her outspokenness reinforced doubts about Kerry's decisiveness, his abilities as a leader: how can a man be the CEO of the country if he can't even control his own wife?

Michelle Obama's burden in 2008 was unprecedented. Not only did she have to navigate the symbolic gender politics of potential first ladyhood; she had to do it while married to a black man with an African first name and a Muslim middle name, at the same time assuaging white anxieties about the prospects of a black family in the White House. This was an almost impossible task, especially when innumerable conservative TV pundits, talk radio hosts, and political columnists were looking for ways to dismiss her husband as unqualified for the job, and un-American to boot.

Not surprisingly, much of the 2008 discussion about Ms. Obama's impact on perceptions about her husband's masculinity was racialized. As the writer Rebecca Traister put it,

> Whether the anxiety Michelle produced in circles both black and white consciously or unconsciously had to do with her race, it was often expressed as concern that she might be hobbling her husband's presidential chances by making him either less of a man or too much of a black man.[39]

She was easily his strongest ambassador to those elements in the African American community who doubted the authenticity of his blackness. As Racewire's Malena Amusa wrote, Michelle was the typical "Strong Black Woman" who presented a "well-enginereed counter to Barack's black masculinity that has been attacked for being diluted,"[40] and the political scientist and media commentator Melissa Harris-Perry referenced Barack Obama's open adoration of his strong, smart, challenging wife as a reason many women decided to give him a chance.

LEADING MEN

If Michelle Obama's authentic south side of Chicago blackness helped her husband shore up his manhood with the black community, it raised anxieties among conservative whites for the very same reason. As a black woman, she was not even capable of being a conventional First Lady; she was rewriting the archetype from the moment she stepped into that role. Predictably, this prompted criticism from the guardians of tradition. Peggy Noonan, *Wall Street Journal* columnist and former speechwriter whose prose helped burnish the legend of Ronald Reagan, chided Ms. Obama for lacking "placidity." "All first ladies, first spouses, should be like Denis Thatcher," she wrote, "slightly dazed, mildly inscrutable, utterly supportive. It is the only job in the world where 'seems slightly drugged' is a positive job qualification."[41]

Noonan's description was part of what political communications strategist Ilyse Hogue referred to as "a growing backlash against real and perceived female empowerment that finds easy expression in criticism of our first lady."[42] One of the unfortunate effects of this backslash is that she is forced to play-act a kind of nonthreatening traditional femininity that downplays both her blackness and her feminism. As Hogue writes, "men are now lauded for choosing partners who are their intellectual match. But powerful first ladies are still portrayed as intrusive and their husbands as henpecked."[43] As a result of these kinds of pressures, the public is deprived not only of the benefit of seeing all of Michelle Obama's talents but also of observing how men and women—even at that rarefied level of power and privilege—navigate and negotiate the challenges of gender and partnership.

REPUBLICANS ARE FROM MARS, DEMOCRATS ARE FROM VENUS

Perhaps the defining feature of our political era is polarization and division. The divisions run deep and developed over a period of many decades. The presidency is one cultural institution in which these divisions are brought into stark relief every four years—and of course in the permanent campaign that precedes the official quadrennial campaign season. One of the central themes of this book is that presidential elections can be understood as contests between competing versions of masculinity, contests that take place largely in the media. Media constructions of presidential masculinity consist of both visual representations, especially those conveyed by television and more recently the Internet, and also rhetoric about what constitutes a "manly" leader. One polarizing aspect of this rhetoric is the invoking of binary categories that do much to shape political discourse and popular perceptions of what characteristics are considered "masculine" and "presidential."

Spoken and print rhetoric about candidates and parties is highly gendered. Scholars of gender have studied how political speech, including presidential campaign rhetoric, functions to reinforce the idea of the presidency as a masculine institution. Naturally, this has significant implications for women candidates, who are forced to navigate the complicated waters of a political process that is set up to their gender's obvious disadvantage. Kathleen Hall Jamieson identified a "double bind" for female candidates, in which they are judged either for being too feminine, or not feminine enough. The political scientist Georgia Duerst-Lahti explains the quandary for women presidential candidates:

> (Either) they do not match the expected gender performance for their sexed bodies, or they act in feminine ways and hence perform in a manner used to denigrate presidential candidates. This dynamic reflects a ... major consequence of gender dualism: women are expected to be feminine, but presidential candidates are judged by the quality of their masculinity. Therefore, women candidates must continually negotiate how to be womanly while projecting the manliness expected of presidents.[44]

The other major consequence of gender dualism outlined by Duerst-Lahti is that:

> Male candidates often have their credibility challenged through attacks on their masculinity, which are cast in terms of their being too feminine. This dynamic is one area in which press coverage of presidential candidates does seem to explicitly recognize masculinity, or the lack thereof. Coverage often focuses on whether a candidate is manly enough....in (various) instances, the feminine is deployed to denigrate the man and his masculinity.[45]

Duerst-Lahti and her research team conducted a study of "masculine" and "feminine" words in corporate print media coverage of presidential campaigns from 2003 to 2006. Not surprisingly, they found that masculine words (e.g., "attack," "command," "strong," "compete," "control") vastly outnumber feminine words ("cooperate," "sensitive," "soft," "sacrifice"). This language usage helps to construct a political discourse and universe that makes it very difficult for women candidates, because masculine qualities are more highly valued by both men and women voters. One 2003 study found that voters express preference for more masculine characteristics in their leaders, especially at the higher levels of government such as the presidency.[46]

Masculinity, of course, is not exclusively tethered to male biological sex. Recent research indicates that female candidates who display more "masculine" traits are more likely to be nominated for high political office. It seems certain that this played a factor in the meteoric rise of 2008 Republican vice-presidential candidate Sarah Palin, who was frequently described in political commentary as a "gun-toting hockey mom," a moose hunter who early in life had earned the nickname "Sarah Barracuda." These descriptions of Palin not only helped to masculinize the highly sexualized image of the former Miss Alaska runner-up. Because these terms attested to her reputation for controlled violence, they also served to reinforce the idea that if she ever ascended to the office of president, she would have the toughness that Americans expect of their (male) presidents.

Academic discussions over the past decade about gender and language have problematized the gender binary (masculine/feminine) as a constructed reality, but to this day binary thinking about gender continues to have enormous cultural influence. In the political realm, as Duerst-Lahti suggests, gender binary language disadvantages female candidates, in part because "Unlike any man, a female candidate is treated as a member of a category that is suspect and, hence, must first overcome the categorical suspicion before being judged on individual qualifications."[47] But by celebrating certain qualities as masculine and others as either feminine or less-than-fully masculine, this process also helps discursively to construct dominant masculinity. This is because (1) the influence of Western dichotomous thinking about gender is present even when two men are running against each other, and (2) misogyny remains a powerful cultural force. If complex issues like the reform of mandatory federal sentencing guidelines can be reduced to a discussion about who is "tough on crime" and who is "soft on crime," one (male) candidate will inevitably occupy the feminine ("soft") position, with predictably negative consequences, especially when it comes to the (white) male vote. In that sense,

CHAPTER 5: 1992: B. CLINTON VS. G. H. W. BUSH & R. PEROT

gender binaries affect not only which types of female candidates run for office and how they fare but which types of male candidates run—and which types win elections.

Furthermore, when you consider the unique pedagogical role of the presidency, the dualistic way we think and speak about gender and the presidency inevitably influences which "masculine" qualities are more broadly valued in our society. This dynamic is especially enhanced during presidential campaign cycles, with continuous media attention fixated on presidential races, when the airwaves, chat rooms, and blogosphere are filled with discussions about the qualities that are expected of the nation's chief executive. Media discourse about presidential masculinities has particular relevance in the socialization of boys and young men, who are constantly absorbing societal norms about masculinity, as well as the consequences of not conforming to them. It can be quite confusing for boys to make sense of the stream of information coming at them about how to be a man, especially when grown men themselves are unsure of what it all means. As William Pollack wrote in his 1997 bestseller *Real Boys:*

> Even as we continue to harden our boys the old-fashioned way, we expect them to live up to some very modern and contradictory expectations...we want them to be *new men* in the making, showing respect for their girl peers, sharing their feelings in emotionally charged circumstances, and shedding their 'macho' assumptions about male power, responsibility, and sexuality. In short, we want our boys to be sensitive New Age guys and still be cool dudes. Is it any wonder that a lot of boys are confused by this double standard?
>
> All of this gets absorbed by boys and promulgated by the society at large as an unwritten Boy Code...The code is a set of behaviors, rules of conduct, cultural shibboleths, and even a lexicon, that is inculcated into boys by our society—from the very beginning of a boy's life.[48]

The role of dialogue and debate in the gender socialization of boys is an understudied area. There has been some research into gender differences between boys and girls in terms of their political beliefs, around such questions as the role of women in politics. Researchers have identified a gender gap in attitudes toward policy and partisanship as early as eighth grade, with girls more likely to describe themselves as liberal and identify as Democrats, and boys more likely to describe themselves as conservative and identify as Republicans. This gender gap mirrors the adult gender gap and suggests that, according to one study, "the persistent gender gap in adult views about politics is rooted, at least partially, in gender differences during childhood socialization."[49]

But if the different ways that boys and girls are socialized is a factor in their ideological and political development, isn't it also possible that politics itself could play a role in their gender socialization? If, for example, media play an important role in the socialization of boys and girls, isn't it possible that political discourse in media might play a part in that socialization process? In the current 24/7 media environment, children and adolescents are exposed to political news and commentary in numerous and varied formats which include news stories, campaign ads on television, politically oriented websites aimed at kids, and satirical videos on YouTube. And surely the way adults talk about politics contributes to boys' understanding—or confusion—about what is considered masculine. This is an area that needs to be explored in future research. For example, what effect, if any, does it have on the gender identity development of young boys when they hear their fathers and uncles parrot the party line of white male hosts on cable TV and conservative talk radio who ridicule Democrats as "soft on terrorism" or "weak on defense," and correspondingly praise Republicans for their "toughness?" It is hardly far-fetched to suggest that the "Republicans are strong/Democrats are weak" frame that has been so influential in adult politics over the past thirty years might at least be partly responsible for the measurable gender gap among middle-school students, who are, after all, developmentally fixated on issues of gender and sexuality. In addition, what effect does it have on the development of empathy and compassion in boys when, in the simplistic gender dualisms that dominate political discourse, such qualities are considered "feminine"?

The sociolinguist Deborah Tannen maintains that at the heart of what she terms our "argument culture" is "our habit of seeing issues and ideas as absolute and irreconcilable principles continually at war."[50] She also makes note of a bias in media coverage of politics toward presenting issues and ideas in the form of a conflict between two diametrically opposed positions, a bias that is likely driven by producers' desire for controversy in the service of good ratings. In media the conflict "between two diametrically opposed positions"

CHAPTER 5: 1992: B. CLINTON VS. G. H. W. BUSH & R. PEROT

often takes the (unacknowledged) form of a conflict between contrasting styles or archetypes of masculinity, such as: a *Newsweek* magazine cover story during the 2008 campaign with a picture of Obama in blue and McCain in red, with the headline "Mr. Cool vs. Mr. Hot," or an *Atlantic* magazine cover with the heading "The Warrior vs. The Orator."

But conflict orientation is not merely a media phenomenon. Since the 1980s, many successful and high-profile political consultants—among them Lee Atwater, Dick Morris, and Karl Rove—have pursued a strategy of attempting to divide the electorate down the middle; they win as long as their candidate gets 50 percent of the votes plus one. This entire process is facilitated by the two-party system in US politics. There are other political parties, and some candidates flying their flags, such as Ross Perot in 1992, or Ralph Nader in 2000, manage occasionally to win enough votes to (arguably) influence electoral outcomes. But tens of millions of Americans vote every four years exclusively for either the Democratic or the Republican candidate. When you overlay the Democrat/Republican binary with the gender gap between Democrats and Republicans that first emerged in the 1980 presidential election, and you consider that no major party has ever nominated a woman for president, you have the perfect precondition for a struggle for primacy between two distinct types of men and the kinds of masculinity they represent. If US presidential races can be seen as quadrennially staged competitions between two (sometimes three) contrasting versions of masculinity, then it seems useful to examine some of the binary categories that artificially narrow the range of characteristics which are considered masculine, and thus help to shape mainstream political discourse about presidential—and hence societal—masculinities.

The words and phrases in *Figure 5.1* comprise many of the gendered binary categories within which much political discourse takes place. These binary categories typically have the effect of elevating the "masculine" while disparaging the "feminine" characteristics, a process mirrored in English language usage more generally. As noted above, this disadvantages not only female candidates but men who are tarnished by association with the devalued characteristics of femininity. This entire process contributes to the popular perception of the Republican Party as the party of masculine (white) men, and the Democrats the party of women (and feminized men).

Gender Binaries			
strong	weak	just folks	effete snobs
rational	emotional	Fox	CNN & MSNBC
man	woman	risk-taking	consensus-building
masculine	feminine	boots	flip-flops
straight	gay	daddy	mommy
tough on crime	soft on crime	NASCAR dads	soccer moms
hawks	doves	Right	Left
resolute	equivocating	conservative	liberal
straightforward	nuanced	red state	blue state
unilateral	multilateral	Republican	Democrat

Figure 5.1

What are some of the gendered implications of these binaries?

Unilateral/multilateral

Since at least the late 1970s, and culminating in the administration of George W. Bush, conservatives and neoconservatives have attacked and sought to discredit the legitimacy of multilateral organizations such as the United Nations, and international treaties such as the Kyoto Protocol on Climate Change. In brief, the conservative argument against multilateralism is that while international cooperation can be useful and beneficial, it is not in the interest of the US to sign on to agreements that restrict its ability to act in the world, especially when it comes to the use of military force. This is particularly the case in the post-Cold War environment, a "unipolar" moment of US strength and influence.

Political scientists and commentators can debate the merits of conservative arguments against multilateral approaches to global problems, or progressive arguments for their necessity in an increasingly interdependent world. But there is an underlying gendered dimension to the multilateral/unilateral binary, which can be read as a direct proxy for feminine/masculine. "Multilateralism" suggests a collaborative process of nations working together to craft solutions to common or shared problems. Because of its emphasis on partnership and cooperation, rather than competition, it is gendered feminine in the gender binary. By contrast, "unilateralism" embodies the rugged individualist ideal of a man—or country—who goes it alone, even in the face of daunting odds. When conservatives dismiss liberals' faith in international treaties and conventions, the unstated implication is that multilateralism is a "feminine" response to a problem—cutthroat competition between nations and nonstate actors—that requires a hardheaded "masculine" response. In his influential book about relations between the US and Europe, *Of Paradise and Power* (2003), the neoconservative theorist Robert Kagan outlined what he sees as a widely shared European perspective on the contrast between how the US and Europe conduct foreign policy:

> The United States... resorts to violence more quickly and, compared with Europe, is less patient with diplomacy. Americans generally see the world divided between good and evil, between friends and enemies, while Europeans see a more complex picture. When confronting real or potential adversaries, Americans generally favor policies of coercion rather than persuasion, emphasizing punitive sanctions over inducements to better behavior, the stick over the carrot. Americans tend to seek finality in international affairs: They want problems solved, threats eliminated. And, of course, Americans increasingly tend toward unilateralism in international affairs...
>
> Europeans insist they approach problems with greater nuance and sophistication. They try to influence others through subtlety and indirection. They are more tolerant of failure, more patient when solutions don't come quickly. They generally favor peaceful responses to problems, preferring negotiation, diplomacy, and persuasion to coercion. They are quicker to appeal to international law, international conventions, and international opinion to adjudicate disputes.[51]

While Kagan never uses terms like "masculinity" and "femininity," from beginning to end his entire analysis exemplifies the profound influence in conservative foreign policy debates of gender dualist thinking. For Kagan, as for so many theorists on the Right, aggressive, preferably military assertions of the "national interest" are masculinized, while negotiation and compromise are feminized. Simply stated: war is masculine, peace is feminine. In fact, Kagan sums up the gender politics of neoconservative foreign policy concisely—if unwittingly—when he states that "…on major strategic and international questions today, Americans are from Mars and Europeans are from Venus."[52] While the overarching framework of his study on relations between the US and Europe contains much insight and nuance, he might as well have said that Americans are real men and Europeans are a bunch of limp-wristed wimps. Thus it should be understood that when a presidential candidate or a sitting president is criticized by the Right for wanting to "consult with our allies" before taking military action, or he is derided as "naive" for believing that US interests would best be served by conforming to international human rights laws, it is his manhood—not merely his ideology and judgment—that is being called into question.

This dynamic surfaced repeatedly during the 2008 campaign, starting with the Republican presidential primaries, as a lineup of conservative white men competed for the right to succeed George W. Bush as the titular head of the Republican Party. Republican primaries in recent decades have provided a valuable resource for the investigation of some of the key themes of this chapter, because the Republican primary electorate is even more right-wing than the party as a whole. As a result, candidates regularly jockey to position themselves as the most willing to use military force—to be the "manliest" on issues of foreign and military policy, and hence the best able to assume the elusive leadership mantle of Ronald Reagan, to whom they all pay rhetorical homage, even as they conspicuously overlook elements of Reagan's record (such as arms control agreements with the Soviets) that undermine their martial mythification of him. Interestingly, many of the Republican candidates who take the hardest line on defense-related matters never served in the military; in fact some of them actively sought to avoid service during the Vietnam War era.

During one of the debates in early October 2007, former Massachusetts governor Mitt Romney was asked if he would seek congressional approval before taking action against Iran's suspected nuclear weapons program. He replied, cautiously, that he would "consult with lawyers" about this. Sensing weakness, his then-rival Rudolph Giuliani pounced. According to a news article in the *Boston Globe*:

The former New York mayor ridiculed Romney for saying during a

CHAPTER 5: 1992: B. CLINTON VS. G. H. W. BUSH & R. PEROT

debate…that he would consult with lawyers before deciding whether he would need congressional approval to take military action against Iran over its suspected nuclear weapons program.

Giuliani's campaign called it a "lawyer's test" for national security, and sought to saddle Romney with a comparison to a former presidential candidate from Massachusetts, Democrat John F. Kerry, who was roasted for saying during a 2004 debate that America must pass a "global test" before taking military action.[53]

In response to the criticism he received from Giuliani, which sparked furious arguments in conservative media about whether he was prepared to be commander in chief, Romney was forced to defend the idea that it made sense to act lawfully when responding to international challenges. Just days after this controversy, the Romney campaign aired a new thirty-second television ad in Iowa which cast the candidate as tough on terrorism and argued for an increase in the size of the military, a strengthening of US intelligence agencies, and the monitoring of calls made to the US by suspected terrorists.

Resolute/equivocating

On more than one occasion during his eight years as president, George W. Bush declared, "I don't do nuance." Instead of being greeted as an admission that should disqualify someone from high political office, for the first years of his presidency Bush was often praised by pundits and politicians— not just conservatives—for being the kind of confident, decisive leader we needed in a time of war and national crisis. This was no time to be distracted by philosophical debates or hampered by introspection—"navel gazing," according to dismissive critics. It was time to strike back at our enemies, and Bush was *The Right Man* for the job, in the title of a bestselling 2003 book by former Bush speechwriter and current conservative pundit David Frum. The book featured on its cover an iconic color photograph of Bush at ground zero, with a bullhorn in his hand, when the president forcefully promised a crowd of workers that they would "soon be heard" when, presumably, the US under his leadership would avenge the attacks on 9/11. Continuing the hagiography without any trace of irony or satire, the paperback version of Frum's book showed Bush dressed in an air force flight suit on the deck of the U.S.S. *Abra-*

ham Lincoln, where he delivered his notorious "Mission Accomplished" speech. As the 2004 election approached, the central message of the Bush campaign was clear: George W. Bush was a man of action who embodied the masculine virtues we need in a strong leader. Conservative commentators might have been willing to concede that his Democratic opponent, Senator John Kerry, was more knowledgeable about foreign policy (and almost everything else). But they mercilessly derided him as a waffler, an egghead who endlessly agonized over the finer points of an issue, even as our enemies plotted the next attack. It was an argument conservatives had used successfully for decades, such as in the 1950s, when the Democrats nominated the cerebral Adlai Stevenson to oppose the Republican war hero Dwight Eisenhower. Kerry himself provided plenty of fodder for his critics, such as the careless moment in 2004 that will go down in presidential campaign history as one of the classic gaffes by a candidate, when he said of a war funding resolution: "I voted for the $87 billion before I voted against it." Matthew Dowd, a former advisor to George W. Bush, assessed the surging popularity of the former history professor Newt Gingrich in the weeks leading up to the 2012 Iowa caucuses: "I don't think there's a de facto anti-intellectualism among Republicans," he said. "They just don't like intellectuals who seem weak and indecisive. They don't like nuance."[54]

The two most popular Republican politicians of the past thirty years—Ronald Reagan and George W. Bush—were inarticulate, incurious men, routinely described by their supporters as decisive, resolute leaders whose strength came not from their grasp of complex issues but from the elegant simplicity of their strongest convictions. As Bush was fond of saying, "I go with my gut." Supporters of Reagan and Bush might actually believe that the president of the United States—the leader of a highly complex and immensely powerful information-age society—need not possess at least a minimal degree of intellectual curiosity. But whether they actually believe it, or are motivated primarily by expedience, is largely irrelevant. They are merely articulating the latest version of an aggressive anti-intellectualism that is deeply rooted in American culture. In his 1964 classic *Anti-Intellectualism in American Life*, Richard Hofstadter traced the development of hostility to intellectualism in this country to a democratic impulse to reject the power of elites. But Hofstadter was ahead of his time in understanding that however populist in character, anti-intellectualism

CHAPTER 5: 1992: B. CLINTON VS. G. H. W. BUSH & R. PEROT

is also fundamentally about tensions and shifts in the gender order—especially as they relate to cultural ideas about manhood. In fact, Hofstadter places so much emphasis on the connection between class-based resentments and efforts to bolster the masculine credibility of working-class (white) men that *Anti-Intellectualism in American Life* can fairly be described as an early men's studies text. In the introduction, Hofstadter provides a description of the ideal assumptions of anti-intellectualism:

> Intellectuals, it may be held, are pretentious, conceited, effeminate, and snobbish; and very likely immoral, dangerous and subversive. The plain sense of the common man, especially if tested by success in some demanding line of practical work, is an altogether adequate substitute for, if not actually much superior to, formal knowledge and expertise acquired in the schools. Not surprisingly, institutions in which intellectuals tend to be influential, like universities and colleges, are rotten to the core."[55]

Hofstadter provides a detailed analysis of the role of anti-intellectualism in presidential politics through the early 1960s, but as the aforementioned passage demonstrates, the social forces he describes are still in play in the twenty-first century. It is hardly beside the point to note that since 1980, the two Democrats who have won the presidency have both been highly educated, intellectually precocious men who won the women's vote, but failed to achieve a majority among white men. During the same period, Republicans Ronald Reagan, George H. W. Bush, and George W. Bush—all of whom had college degrees but none of whom would ever be considered an intellectual—won the presidency by carrying huge majorities of the white male vote.

Rational/emotional

The rational/emotional binary is perhaps the classic gender division, one that men in patriarchal cultures have used for centuries to justify the perpetuation of their religious, economic, political, and familial control over women. Traditionally, men have been seen as more rational, and hence better equipped to handle public matters of politics and the economy; women, who are said to be more "emotional," were seen to be more suited to the private sphere of caregiving and maintaining relationships.

For a generation, feminist scholars in political science and sociology have critiqued the transparent sexism of the rational/emotional binary, because the sexist ideology that underpins the split between the public and private spheres provides an obvious advantage to men (over women) in terms of political leadership. Women's organizations that work to identify, support, and raise money for potential female presidential candidates have worked hard to discredit the lingering sexist belief that women's emotions somehow make them less capable of performing executive duties—especially those that involve authorizing the use of force. Among its many other negative effects, this sexism has likely forced some women candidates to overcompensate and adopt a more "masculine" public stance. As numerous commentators on the Right and Left argued, Hillary Clinton probably adopted some hard-line positions on foreign policy matters, and refused to renounce her 2003 senate vote to authorize President George W. Bush to invade Iraq, at least in part because she felt the need as a woman to demonstrate the requisite "toughness" to be commander in chief. Conservative *New York Times* columnist David Brooks put it this way: "The Clinton campaign seems to want to reduce the entire race (with Obama) to one element: the supposed masculinity gap. And so everything she does is all about assertion, combat and Alpha dog dominance."[56] Clinton's hawkish foreign policy positions were attractive to more conservative elements within the Democratic Party and muted some of the customary and reflexive criticism of her on the Right. But she likely lost support from progressives and others who saw her political persona as inauthentic, too willing to sacrifice higher principles for political expedience.

The experience of a generation of successful women in positions of formal military and civilian leadership, even more than any research study, provides ample evidence that women are no less capable than men of protecting the country. The rational/emotional binary nonetheless lingers in political discourse on media outlets such as *Fox News*, and particularly on conservative talk radio, one of the chief sources of news and political commentary for millions of white men. One has only to turn on AM talk radio for proof that the men-are-rational/women-are-emotional binary is still regularly referred to as immutable reality, if not biological fact. Almost daily, Rush Limbaugh issues thinly veiled attacks on liberal men based on the premise that liberalism itself represents a feminine way of seeing the world and that liberal men have been emasculated. Conservatism is logical and rational, he insists, a body of ideas and a governing philosophy that requires serious thought and study. On the other hand, liberalism is all about feelings and emotions, a yearning which many naïve women have that everyone be nice to each other. How, Limbaugh asks with mock exasperation, can you argue with someone's feelings? One wonders if Limbaugh—the self-appointed head of the fictional Limbaugh Institute for Advanced Conservative Studies—has ever studied the work of Richard Wirthlin, who as Ronald Reagan's chief strategist played a crucial role in Reagan's political success. Wirthlin not only contradicts Limbaugh's simplistic and sexist formulation; he also acknowledges that an important part of Reagan's success was an *emotional* connection he made with his supporters. Wirthlin explains,

> Issues are rational. But, I believe if you want to motivate people to vote, or take any kind of action, you've got to touch them not only rationally but emotionally…in developing the issues you've got to look toward how those issues impinge upon the values of safety, peace of mind, family, and so on. It took me a while to realize that Reagan did that almost naturally.[57]

It is almost comical how much some conservative men are invested in their own "rationality," and how far they'll go to prove that those who disagree with them—quite often on logical as well as moral grounds—have let their emotions cloud their reasoned judgments. On his nationally syndicated radio program, the Los Angeles-based conservative talk host Dennis Prager regularly declares that liberal thought is based on the heart, not on the mind. In his book *Still the Best Hope: Why the World Needs American Values to Triumph*, Prager outlines what he calls the "feelings-based nature" of liberalism and leftism (which he regularly, and absurdly, conflates). Notwithstanding the fact that the vast majority of intellectuals are left-of-center, a point that Prager concedes, "One must first recognize that the Left is animated largely by feelings."[58] Of course the "feeling" that Prager and other conservatives deride as incapable of competing with conservative "logic" is a feminine kind of feeling that has long been devalued in public discourse. In fact, conservative polemicists have so thoroughly feminized the word "liberal" that in recent years few Democratic candidates of either sex wanted to claim the label. Women candidates didn't want to be seen in narrow, stereotypical terms as a "woman's candidate," concerned about warm and fuzzy issues like health care and education, and incapable of handling the tough "masculine" realms of the economy and foreign policy. For their part, men have sought to avoid being derided and dismissed as "soft." The feminization of liberalism thus has major implications for the question of what kind of man gets to lead the state and its armed forces as commander in chief.

One of the most important jobs of a US president—both in a practical and a symbolic sense—is to protect Americans in a dangerous world. Thus the temperament of the individual who ascends to that position is always an important consideration. In the nuclear age, in theory, the president should not be too emotional, because after all, (he) has his finger on the nuclear button. If he is short-tempered and easily agitated, which is to say if he manifests in excess the traditionally masculine emotion of anger—he could be more likely to prematurely or mistakenly order aggressive military action, with potentially devastating consequences. There are some notable examples in presidential politics over the past generation where an emotional display of this type has cost a man politically. Perhaps the most well-known recent incident was the implosion of Howard Dean's run for the 2004 Democratic presidential nomination after Dean, the previous front-runner, grew overly excited and began shouting during a televised rally the night he lost the Iowa caucuses. But that case was exceptional. It is rarely more than a brief news item when a male politician publicly loses his temper. An excess of a "masculine" emotion might occasionally qualify as a political liability, but it does not call into question a man's manhood, and it rarely threatens his political career.

By contrast, if a man expresses too strongly such "feminine" emotions as empathy and compassion, or he cries in public outside of the ritualistic circumstances where it is permitted for men to do so, he "unmans" himself and risks sacrificing his credibility as a powerful leader. As Deborah David and Robert Brannon outlined in their groundbreaking study in the 1970s of traditional male stereotypes, the first imperative for being a "real man" is to be a "sturdy oak." Men should be stoic, stable, and independent, and they should never show weakness. The rationale for this in presidential politics is that if the president is too "emotional," meaning he thinks/feels too much like a woman, he might be afraid to use force when it is called for and as a

CHAPTER 5: 1992: B. CLINTON VS. G. H. W. BUSH & R. PEROT

result put the national interest at risk. As Harold Ford, Jr., former Tennessee congressman and head of the Democratic Leadership Council put it, "We forget that voters want a daddy and not a mama, and no matter how big the 'caring' issues are—education, health care—at the end of the day they want a president who is going to defend the country and not take too much of their money away from them."[59]

PUBLIC ROLES, PRIVATE LIVES

As I have argued, public perceptions about the masculinity of candidates is a critically important factor in presidential elections, especially in "national security" elections and others where violence at home or abroad is a key issue. These perceptions are especially (but not exclusively) salient when it comes to white male voters. As the leader of the country and its most powerful and visible man, the US president also fulfills an important role by measuring up to and exemplifying certain characteristics that are defined as masculine, thus contributing to the production and reproduction of social norms around what is considered "manly" behavior.

Among the key questions raised by this function of the presidency is the difference between the president's public role, which includes the political decisions (he) makes, and the example he sets in his "private" life. In the present era of 24/7 media, it is, of course, a bit misleading to talk of the "private" life of a person who is in arguably the biggest fishbowl in the world, with countless cameras and microphones trained on his every move. Nonetheless, to the extent that we can speak of the president's personal and family life, as well as his life experiences before his ascension to high office, it is necessary to examine some of the implications of the "private" side of the president's example.

Notably, conservatives in recent decades have seemed to express more concern than others about the example the president sets in his private life. This process began in earnest in 1992, when Republicans were eager to make Bill Clinton's character an issue in the election. During the Republican convention in August, Secretary of Labor Lynn Martin summed up the case against Clinton: "You can't be one kind of man and another kind of president."[60] Conservative Republicans in the US House of Representatives impeached President Bill Clinton in 1998 for conduct related to his private behavior, which they successfully forced into the public sphere when he lied under oath in a deposition in a sexual harassment lawsuit. Throughout Clinton's presidency, conservatives argued that the president's private behavior was a legitimate political issue, while many liberals maintained that a president's private life was only relevant if it impinged on his public duties. In terms of the pedagogical function of the presidency as it relates to social norms about masculinity, it seems clear that what a president does in his official role *and* what we know of his private life are relevant. If he is an exemplar of dominant masculinity, then he is influential in the example he sets in every area of his life. He might be able to *do his job* just fine even if his private life is messy. But the pedagogical power of his position does not stop where his professional responsibilities end.

Not only conservatives were angry at Clinton for degrading the office of the president and setting a poor example for the nation's children in the way he conducted an extramarital affair with an intern, Monica Lewinsky, and perhaps others. Because the White House is a workplace, there was also a question of whether he was guilty of sexual harassment, or at the very least of exploiting his considerable power in his relationship with a young woman who was his subordinate. In a culture where sexual harassment is widespread, it is, to say the least, worrisome if the highest status man engages in behavior that is at best ethically questionable, and at worst legally actionable, if not criminal. What was the message to boys and young men when they inevitably heard stories about Clinton's sometimes crude sexual overtures to women, and yet still received the support, adulation, and applause of millions of Americans? This is similar to the problem of elite athletes who are charged with crimes of violence against women, yet remain on their teams and receive standing ovations for their athletic exploits. This sends a powerful message both about the lower social status of women and about what is accepted, even expected, in terms of the behavior of "real men." Notwithstanding the fact that Republicans—most notably special prosecutor Kenneth Starr and the House Republican impeachment "managers"—forced the issue of Clinton's private behavior into the public realm and thus bear a significant share of the responsibility for the pedagogical lessons the episode provided for America's children, liberal feminists who supported Clinton politically were placed in a quandary: should they support him in the face of attacks from the Republicans, even when they believed his behavior to be indefensible? Is it better to have as president a man who sets a poor example for men and boys in his personal conduct with a small number of women if his policies, judicial appointments, and budgetary priorities are (arguably) much better for the health and well-being of millions of women than those of the reactionary, antifeminist Republicans? Which aspect of "how to be a man" is more important for a male president to provide: the example of his private sexual practices (to the extent that they become public knowledge), or the example he sets through his choice of political priorities and public commitments? While both might be important, in our political system at election time voters often have to choose one or the other.

While liberals and progressives need to wrestle with questions related to privacy and public pedagogy, conservatives frequently define "character" narrowly in terms of how a politician treats people around him, but fail to acknowledge that a person's political choices also reveal their character. Ronald Reagan generally received high marks from both partisans and pundits for conducting himself in office with dignity and honor. Peggy Noonan, one of Reagan's chief speechwriters, wrote a fawning book about him, entitled *When Character Was King*. One of the many things about Reagan that impressed Noonan was how he always made sure to put on a sport jacket before he entered the Oval Office, out of respect for the hallowed space. For the past twenty years, she and many others have repeatedly cited this anecdote as evidence of Reagan's admirable character, something, presumably, that young people and the rest of us should seek to emulate.

But how does one define character? Throughout much of the 1980s, Reagan's administration used profits from sales of arms to Iran to illegally fund a mercenary army in Nicaragua, composed of former elements of the armed forces of the fascist dictator Anastasio Somoza. The "Contra" army, whom Reagan ludicrously described as the "moral equivalent" of our Founding Fathers, routinely attacked health care facilities and schools, and committed countless murders and mass atrocities against unarmed peasants. During the same period, the Reagan administration provided funding, military advisors, and political support to the fascist regime in El Salvador, where government-funded, clandestine death squads murdered tens of thousands of labor organizers, workers in rural health and agricultural collectives, and religious leaders who spoke out in support of the poor, including the Catholic archbishop of San Salvador, Oscar Romero, who was shot and killed while saying Mass. Was President Reagan a man of character who set a good example for the nation's youth—especially its young men—because he always made sure to put on a jacket in the Oval Office?

At present, much of the public discourse about the influence a president has in the way he "leads by example" is degendered. Commentators talk about the president as the nation's leader, who sets a good example (or bad) for youth in the conduct of his personal and public life. Aside from notable exceptions such as the Clinton sex scandal, there is little discussion about the president's example *as a man* and what effect it has on the norms of masculine behavior. By contrast, when a woman is elected to the presidency, there will undoubtedly be an intense national debate not only about her style of leadership, but the example of femininity that she provides to girls and women—in private perhaps as much as in public. It will not simply involve what styles of clothing she chooses to wear, although that clearly will be the topic of endless debate. Much more so than her male predecessors, her entire persona will be scrutinized for the lessons it provides—and the messages it sends—about shifting norms of femininity in American history and culture.

CHAPTER 5: 1992: B. CLINTON VS. G. H. W. BUSH & R. PEROT

Chapter 6
2004: John F. Kerry vs. George W. Bush.

In 2004, the race between incumbent Republican President George W. Bush and his Democratic challenger Massachusetts Senator John F. Kerry brought to the forefront the ways in which constructed images of presidential masculinities fundamentally shape political discourse and impact voters' political identities and voting preferences. At times in 2004, the staged photo ops and public posturing of both candidates seemed more appropriate to comic opera than to the process by which voters are supposed to choose a leader of the "free world." But the 2004 race, carried out while the nation was at war in Iraq and Afghanistan, nonetheless provides a rich context for an examination of one of the central theses of this study: presidential races—primarily carried out in media—have long represented a staged contest for political and cultural supremacy at a given moment in history between two (or three) distinct types of white masculinity. An article by Roger Cohen in the *New York Times* two weeks before the 2004 election summed up the two contrasting versions of masculinity voters had to choose between, although characteristically the writer framed the difference between the two candidates with no explicit reference to gender.

Mr. Kerry's universe has faith in common sense, believes questions may sometimes be as important as answers, mistrusts conviction so absolute it can never be questioned, distrusts destiny, distinguishes between power and leadership and rocks to Bruce Springsteen.

Mr. Bush's universe has faith in faith, believes questioning empowers enemies, equates conviction with the strength that will spread freedom, is convinced there is no leadership without the projection of American power, and holds that American destiny is manifest and grooves to country music.[1]

The differences reflected in these views take on added significance when one considers that, according to a Gallup Poll in September of 2004, a mere 6 percent of Bush voters and 13 percent of Kerry voters picked the candidates' "agendas/ideas/platforms/goals" to be the most important reason for supporting them.[2] As Noam Chomsky explains, the political system prefers voters to focus on the personal qualities of candidates, or their images.

> The regular vocation of the industries that sell candidates every few years is to sell commodities. Everyone who has turned on a TV set is aware that business devotes enormous efforts to undermine the markets of abstract theory, in which informed consumers make rational choices. An ad does not convey information, as it would in a market system; rather it relies on deceit and illusions to create uninformed consumers who will make irrational choices. Much the same methods are used to undermine democracy by keeping the electorate uninformed and mired in delusion.[3]

As discussed previously, one of the functions of political ads is to catalyze discussions throughout the media about positive characteristics of a candidate, or more likely, to reinforce negative impressions about an incumbent or a challenger that might or might not have some basis in fact. While the effectiveness of individual ads is notoriously difficult to measure, it is fair to say that there is a consensus, or near-consensus, among campaign-tested political professionals that outside of candidate performance and unforeseen events, ad campaigns are perhaps the most critical component of modern presidential campaigns. This much is certain: for decades, television advertising has been by far the single biggest campaign expenditure.

The 2004 presidential race was at the time the most expensive in history. The *Los Angeles Times* estimated that the Bush and Kerry campaigns, along with "independent" groups, spent approximately $580 million dollars on TV ads in the 2004 race, contrasted with approximately $200 million in 2000. It is estimated that in the "battleground" states alone, there were 675,000 television commercials broadcast. The single most expensive ad of the 2004 race was a Bush TV commercial entitled "Ashley's Story" or "The Hug." It featured Bush embracing a 15-year-old girl who had lost her mother in the World Trade Center attacks on 9/11. The most memorable line of the piece was Ashley's: "He's the most powerful man in the world, and all he wants to do is make sure I'm safe, that I'm OK." In the hotly contested state of Ohio alone, this classic "president as protector" spot ran *seven thousand times*.[4] And this was only the "paid media." Incalculable amounts of TV and radio time were devoted to coverage of the campaign, including discussion of the paid media images. For example, the Swift Boat Veterans For Truth, an "independent" political action committee group with reputed informal ties to Karl Rove, ran ads in several battleground states, but the free media coverage of the controversy they created amounted to tens of millions of dollars in free anti-Kerry publicity for the (largely unproven) charges they raised.

With all of this money spent on political advertising, and a considerable amount of space in the nation's newspapers and in broadcast journalism devoted to a discussion of the role of advertising (and media more generally) in contemporary presidential politics, it is notable but perhaps not surprising that the conversation was generally superficial: Did Kerry help or hurt himself by doing a goose-hunting photo op in Ohio, crudely designed to show hunters that he would not take away their guns? As referenced in Chapter I, a substantial literature in political communication analyzes the impact of advertising, messaging, framing, etc. and can be used to examine aspects of Bush's and Kerry's masculinity as constructed by political ads and by the media.

GEORGE W. BUSH

A revealing story made its way around Washington political circles a few years ago about the first—and fateful—meeting of Karl Rove and George W. Bush. It was 1973 and Rove, a twenty-two-year-old aide at the Republican National Committee, was asked by chairman George H. W. Bush to go to Union Station to meet his son and give him the keys to the family car. As Rove described the encounter in *Newsweek* magazine,[5] he was blown away by his first impression of the then-twenty-seven-year-old Bush. "I'm there with the keys and this guy comes striding in wearing jeans, cowboy boots, and a bomber jacket. He had this aura," Rove remembered.

What Rove saw in Bush as he walked through a train station lobby was something the incipient conservative kingmaker later packaged and sold with great skill: an aristocratic white man with an affected blue collar Texas swagger who possessed in the force of his personality the raw material for electoral success. As a young Republican activist just out of college, Rove seemed to know intuitively what many professional political consultants—especially those who work for Democrats—have only recently begun to figure out: that the "aura" he felt from George W. Bush was the stuff of political power in the media era. With historically fateful consequences, he helped turn that insight, and aura, into nearly sixty million votes.

When George W. Bush launched his campaign for the Republican presidential nomination in 1999, he had several distinct advantages in addition to his "aura." As the son of a former president, a son who shared his father's name, he already had widespread name recognition. He had his father's, and his own, ties to wealthy oilmen and other rich Republican campaign contributors. He had served two terms as governor of one of the nation's largest states. But in terms of political currency in the realm of masculine iconography, he had the enormous advantage of his identification with the state of Texas. Although Bush is the scion of a blue-blooded aristocratic family from Connecticut and Maine who was educated at such bastions of the old Republican establishment as Andover, Yale, and Harvard Business School, the imagery surrounding him—carefully constructed by Rove and company—was largely about his "just folks" cowboy masculinity and his Texas roots. He and his wife Laura purchased their Crawford, Texas, ranch in 1999—just before the campaign began—presumably to provide a visual backdrop for thousands of subsequent photo ops that showed Bush as a down-home cowboy who, in the Ronald Reagan mode, liked to wear blue jeans, clear brush on his ranch, and ride in pickup trucks. Fundraisers for Bush's campaigns in 2000 and 2004 earned the designation of "Pioneers" if they raised $100,000, and "Rangers" for those who collected $200,000. Bush repeatedly sought to remind people of his identification with Texas and cowboys, and at the same time erase evidence of his aristocratic heritage. Once in 2004 on the campaign trail in southern Oregon, he opened a speech with the line "It's great to be in a place with more boots than suits."

In fact, George W. Bush's electoral success—especially his reelection in 2004—is inextricably interwoven with the constructed image of the cowboy as the embodiment of everything that is right with white American masculinity. European editorialists often mocked Bush's "cowboy" persona as immature, unsophisticated, and reckless, much as they used to criticize

Reagan. But as the 2004 election proved once again, for tens of millions of Americans the virtues of the cowboy continued in the new century to outweigh the shortcomings—especially in a dangerous world. In his introduction to a symposium on "The Return of Manhood" published by the right-wing website FrontPageMagazine, Jamie Glazov writes:

> After years of creeping feminization, manhood and masculinity appear to have made a significant comeback in American society. Since the national security crisis of 9/11, America has rediscovered the virtues of soldiers, firemen, policemen, and other traditionally male (and masculine) professions that require courage and physical strength. What explains this phenomenon? Why is manhood, once again, being held in high esteem?[6]

It might be a simple coincidence that Glazov refers to "years of creeping feminization" just after the end of the two-term presidency of Democrat Bill Clinton, but fears of cultural feminization and the need for hard (white) male leadership to counteract it is, as I have shown, a recurring theme in right-wing social commentary for more than a century. The terrorist attacks on 9/11 gave George W. Bush and the coterie of neoconservative strategists within the US political establishment a pretext to attack Iraq and carry out their imperial project in the Persian Gulf region. It also gave conservatives the perfect opportunity to revalorize heroic (white) masculinity after decades of decline. The rationale was as powerful as it was time-tested: external enemies represent an existential threat to the community, and the only language they respond to is force. In order to defend ourselves, we need to move away from cultivating metrosexuality and "sensitivity" in men, and return to a more conservative social order that respects men as protectors. As the Northwestern University psychologist David Guttman argued:

> Modern urban societies provide, via technology, the physical security—food, shelter and protection—that is the responsibility of tough men in rural settings. Young, urban men are free to remain psychologically 'soft' and to explore less physically demanding occupations. If this male relaxation was universal, then our boys could loiter forever undisturbed, in the Seinfeld condition.

CHAPTER 6: 2004: JOHN F. KERRY VS. GEORGE W. BUSH.

But unfortunately, the whole world does not go flabby all at once. When we go soft there remain plenty of 'Hard' peoples—the Nazis and Japanese in World War II, the Radical Islamists now—who will see us as decadent sybarites, and who will exploit, in war, our perceived weaknesses.[7]

Just twenty years after Reagan was elected with an overwhelming mandate from white male voters (and others) to remasculinize the country after Vietnam and the flaccid Carter years, another fake cowboy, George W. Bush, was poised to preside over a similar renaissance. It should not be surprising that westerns once again played a signal role in mapping the mythical terrain that drove US presidential politics. Jane Tomkins analyzes this cultural process in *West of Everything*, (1992), her study of the twentieth-century popularity of the western in both its novelistic and cinematic forms. According to Tomkins, the popularity of westerns can be understood in part as a response by men to the challenges posed to (white) male power and privilege by the emergence of a women's movement in the mid-to-late nineteenth-century. Westerns became a fictional space within which men could assert masculine power without apology, and where "feminine" traits such as empathy and compassion were seen as shortcomings in men who had to tame a wild frontier, fend off hostile natives, and enforce social codes of honor and decorum. Three of the key issues of women's reform were whiskey, gambling, and prostitution. Given the enormous publicity and fervor of the Women's Christian Temperance Union crusade, Tomkins asks, can it be an accident that the characteristic indoor setting for westerns—which were written almost exclusively by men for a largely male readership and audience—is the saloon?[8]

Tomkins examines another familiar plotline in westerns. A lone bad guy or a band of criminals is menacing the town. The authorities are ineffectual at responding to the threat. One classic scene is the outdoor funeral of someone killed by the bad guys, where the preacher is inveighing against sin and bemoaning the injustice of the killing. But of course all this talk means nothing to the criminals, who look on from a distance with contempt, and who understand only the language of violence. In this way religion is feminized, because it is equated with language and passivity. Nothing changes, nothing can change, until a man of action rides into town (John Wayne, Clint

Eastwood, etc), says little, but gets the job done with a burst of cathartic violence. In other words, while talk is feminized, action is masculinized.

The overarching issues in the 2004 presidential election were 9/11, the "war on terror," and the US attack on Iraq. The Bush team and many in the media successfully conflated the three, so that millions of Americans (especially viewers of *Fox News*) mistakenly believed that attacking Saddam Hussein, who led a violently repressive but secular government, was tantamount to striking back against Islamist terrorism. Many of Bush's photo ops and paid commercials aimed to burnish his credentials as a man of few words but decisive action—just the kind of man needed in a world where bad men speaking a strange language are trying to kill us (Osama bin Laden and al Qaeda). At the same time, Bush's negative ads, and those devised by his political allies, sought to describe John Kerry as an indecisive "flip-flopper," just the type of rudderless, nonmasculine pol whose "nuanced" style of leadership we could ill-afford to trust in dangerous times. Statements by prominent Republicans reinforced this theme and openly mocked Kerry's leadership ability, and his manhood. As Vice President Dick Cheney said at the Republican National Convention in New York City, "George W. Bush will never seek a permission slip to defend the American people." His administration also refused to acknowledge mistakes in the Iraq War because, as Stephen Ducat maintains, to do so meant risking their masculine identity. "To acknowledge a mistake," Ducat writes, "especially one that involves failure to listen to advice—the proverbial refusal to ask for directions—imperils their manhood. And so, instead of this kind of behavior being pigheaded arrogance, it's framed as manly resoluteness."[9]

The sociologist Arlie Hochschild suggests that Bush was able to win working-class white male support because he—and his political/media advisors such as Karl Rove—was able to skillfully manage and manipulate their anxieties.

> Whether strutting across a flight deck or mocking the enemy, Bush with his seemingly fearless bravado—ironically born of class entitlement—offers an aura of confidence. And this confidence dampens, even if temporarily, the feelings of insecurity and fear exacerbated by virtually every major domestic and foreign policy initiative of the Bush administration. Maybe it comes down to this: George W. Bush is deregulating American global capitalism with one hand

CHAPTER 6: 2004: JOHN F. KERRY VS. GEORGE W. BUSH.

while regulating the feelings it produces with the other. Or, to put it another way, he is doing nothing to change the causes of fear and everything to channel the feeling and expression of it. He speaks to a working man's lost pride and his fear of the future by offering an image of fearlessness. He poses here in his union jacket, there in his pilot's jumpsuit, taunting the Iraqis to "bring 'em on" — all of it meant to feed something in the heart of a frightened man. In this light, even Bush's "bad boy" past is a plus. He steals a wreath off a Macy's door for his Yale fraternity and careens around drunk in Daddy's car. But in the politics of anger and fear, the Republican politics of feelings, this is a plus.[10]

By the time he left office, Bush had few defenders in media. But when he was still riding high, before the Iraq War began to go poorly, prior to Abu Ghraib, and before it became common knowledge that his administration had attempted to mislead the public, silence critics, and bully Congress into supporting the invasion under false pretenses, it is important to remember that he had plenty of cheerleaders. During Bush's reelection campaign, Chris Matthews of MSNBC, later to become a fierce critic of the president, had this to say about Bush:

> We're proud of our president. Americans love having a guy as president, a guy who has a little swagger, who's physical, who's not a complicated guy like Clinton or even like Dukakis or Mondale, all those guys, McGovern. They want a guy who's president. Women like a guy who's president. Check it out. The women like this war. I think we like having a hero as our president. It's simple. We're not like the Brits.[11]

JOHN F. KERRY

Initially, John Kerry posed at least a theoretical problem for the Bush reelection team, because he had the formal masculine credentials—as a decorated veteran of military combat—that could give working-class and middle-class white men who had deserted the party in recent decades cover to vote once again for a Democrat. These credentials were the most important factor when the Democratic primary electorate judged him to be the most "electable" candidate in a general election against Bush, who after all was a wartime president and leader of a party that had marketed itself for the past thirty years as the "masculine" party. The Kerry campaign played up his military-man bona fides, most famously when he accepted his party's nomination in Boston by declaring with a salute, "I'm John Kerry, and I'm reporting for duty."

Because one of the pillars of Republican electoral strategy since the 1980 election of Reagan had been to secure a large percentage of white male voters, Rove and company somehow had to discredit Kerry's masculinity. They were surely aware that Kerry, in his several successful campaigns for the US Senate in Massachusetts, had received a strong majority of white working-class male votes in blue collar cities across Massachusetts. The aristocratic Kerry was able to escape the fate of other Democrats who had been smeared by Republican operatives and right-wing media voices as "elitist snobs," largely because of his Vietnam War service. Kerry often appeared in campaign photo ops with fellow Vietnam veterans, blue collar as well as white collar, and he also appeared in public frequently with members of the firefighters union, further reinforcing his identification with traditionally masculine blue-collar white men.

The birth of the 527 "independent" group Swift Boat Veterans for Truth in 2003 was a direct response to these aspects of Kerry's political strength. Karl Rove had long been known for his electoral strategy of undermining his opponent's strongest suit. Since Kerry's greatest political asset in the 2004 presidential race was (arguably) his military service, Rove knew that the Bush campaign had to counteract this by somehow casting doubt on the credibility of Kerry's war hero status. (Rove was reputed to have strong Texas ties to one or more of the key architects of the Swift Boat Veterans for Truth group). It is important to restate that in a campaign that can be characterized as a competition between two distinct "brands" of presidential masculinity, the "issues"—such as the candidates' and their parties' contrasting visions of how to fight terrorism, manage the economy, or address the health-care crisis—matter much less than such factors as whether potential voters feel the candidates "understand" the problems of "people like me," whether they can be "trusted," or, the perennial favorite, which candidate the voters would "rather have a beer with." In the intellectually degraded environment of the modern presidential campaign, special advantage goes not to a candidate like Kerry who was described in *The New York Times* as "a meticulous, deliberative decision maker, always demanding more information, calling around for advice, reading another document," but to the candidate who is perceived to be "genuine," who cuts the most impressive figure on television in the starring role of commander in

CHAPTER 6: 2004: JOHN F. KERRY VS. GEORGE W. BUSH.

chief, the man who looks most impressive getting off Air Force One and waving to the crowds, and who can project an aura of personal toughness that can—supposedly—keep our violent enemies on the run.

The Swift Boat ads hit hard at Kerry's carefully constructed image as a warrior whose battle credentials earned him the respect of his "band of brothers." Although almost all of the men with whom he served directly strongly supported him, the hundreds of Navy veterans the Republicans found who served on swift boats near or contemporaneous with Kerry successfully planted the idea that he was a poseur who exaggerated his own credentials and would say or do anything—including compromise his principles—to get elected. Kerry himself contributed to this image by waiting weeks to respond forcefully to the ads, and by employing a cautious campaign strategy and failing to delineate sharp differences with Bush's policy in Iraq until the late stages of the campaign.

Kerry did make numerous attempts to remasculinize his image, such as riding a motorcycle onto the set of *The Tonight Show*, or being photographed hunting. But it was too little, too late. Since the conservative media was determined to feminize him, right-wing cable TV and talk radio hosts mercilessly ridiculed what they recognized as Kerry's staged and insincere pandering to working and middle-class white guys. The Democratic strategist Donna Brazile said of Kerry's entreaties to these men, "The only thing he hasn't done is sit down with a six-pack and chew tobacco with them." An editor of a prominent Wisconsin state politics website summed up Kerry's dilemma. Comparing Kerry's problem connecting to working-class voters with Al Gore's, Jeff Mayers said Mr. Kerry "can be inflicted with senatoritis, and he has had trouble connecting with people in a state where pretension does not play well and likeability often trumps policy."[12]

There are clearly a number of reasons why George W. Bush—who some commentators have labeled the worst president in modern times, and whose first term earned him the title of "A Failed Presidency" by the *Los Angeles Times* in an editorial endorsing his opponent—nonetheless won reelection by a popular vote margin of some three million votes. While there were numerous allegations of voter disenfranchisement, and thus the true winning margin might never be known, it is also true that Bush got the most votes of any presidential candidate in US history. (Kerry received the second most). There will be debates for years to come about how this happened, but Frank Rich's conclusion seems apt: "Only in an election year ruled by fiction could a sissy who used Daddy's connections to escape Vietnam turn an actual war hero into a girlie-man."[13]

GOD, GUNS, AND GAYS

During the 2004 presidential primary season, former Vermont Democratic Governor Howard Dean said in his typical stump speech that he was tired of coming to the South and fighting elections on "God, guns, and gays." "We're going to fight this election on our turf," he said, "which is going to be jobs, education, and health care." The Republicans, of course, had other plans, and their record of success in presidential races for thirty years suggested that they knew better which type of "turf" attracted a majority of voters.

Dean's use of the phrase "God, guns, and gays" suggested that he understood one of the central premises of this study: that since the 1960s, presidential elections have turned to a disturbing extent on the identity politics of gender and sexual identity—areas where the Democrats were more in tune with long-term cultural shifts even while they were losing electoral majorities. Like its alliterative antecedent "abortion, amnesty, and acid," the phrase "God, guns, and gays" can be understood as a coded reference for a set of challenges to white male power. Dean might as well have said that he wasn't going to allow the GOP to turn this election into yet another culture war struggle about the embattled state of traditional white masculinity. What follows is a brief discussion of the gendered nature of Dean's clever phrase, specifically how the issues of God, guns, and gays are linked to struggles around male power and white masculine identity.

God

Contemporary discussions about the role of religion in US politics, or the proper role of the state in supporting religious institutions, are more often than not debates about the status of conservative Christianity and its influence in the public sphere. Conservative Christians espouse a deeply patriarchal theology and set of religious beliefs and practices. This is evident in the writings and public pronouncements of leaders on the Christian Right, who often explicitly state that among their central goals is the reassertion of men's authority in the traditional nuclear family.

CHAPTER 6: 2004: JOHN F. KERRY VS. GEORGE W. BUSH.

Reassertion of patriarchal authority is one of the chief goals of the evangelical men's organization, Promise Keepers, which was founded in 1990 by Bill McCartney, then the football coach of the University of Colorado. Promise Keepers calls itself a "Christ-centered organization dedicated to introducing men to Jesus Christ as their Savior and Lord, and then helping them to grow as Christians." Once referred to as the leading voice in the "Christian men's movement," the Promise Keepers are best known for holding large rallies in football stadiums throughout the 1990s, where tens of thousands of men professed their belief in Jesus and their dedication to keeping promises to God, their families, and their community. While many of these promises were positive assertions of adult responsibility and appeared relatively benign, *Seven Promises of a Promise Keeper* by Pastor Tony Evans, a senior official in the organization, revealed a key aspect of the underlying ideology of the organization when he wrote: "I am convinced that the primary cause of (our) national crisis is the feminization of the American male...I'm trying to describe a misunderstanding of manhood that has produced a nation of sissified men who abdicate their role as spiritually pure leaders, thus forcing women to fill the vacuum." He went on to give advice to men:

> The first thing you do is sit down with your wife and say something like this: "Honey, I've made a terrible mistake. I've given you my role. I gave up leading this family, and I forced you to take my place. Now I must reclaim that role." Don't misunderstand what I'm saying here. I'm not suggesting that you ask for your role back, I'm urging you to take it back... Unfortunately...there can be no compromise here. If you're going to lead, you must lead. Be sensitive, listen. Treat the lady gently and lovingly. But lead![14]

The male supremacist ideology of Promise Keepers is similar to what is articulated in the Baptist Faith and Message, which summarizes Southern Baptist thought and was adopted in 2000 by the Southern Baptist Convention. It includes the following:

> A husband is to love his wife as Christ loved the church. He has the God-given responsibility to provide for, to protect, and to lead his family. A wife

is to submit herself graciously to the servant leadership of her husband even as the church willingly submits to the headship of Christ.

The coalition that elected Ronald Reagan in 1980 included a significant percentage of white evangelical Christians, who backed him over Jimmy Carter 61 percent to 34 percent. Those same voters had supported Carter, one of their own, in 1976, but then abandoned him in 1980 in favor of the divorced and relatively unreligious former Hollywood actor. Reagan might not have been personally devout, but his political project was clearly a vehicle for the antifeminist and antigay rights agenda of the emerging Moral Majority organization, founded by the Reverend Jerry Falwell in 1981, and later the Christian Coalition, founded in 1987 by the Pentecostal preacher, media mogul, and 1988 presidential candidate Pat Robertson. The commentator E. J. Dionne has noted that white evangelicals had been moving toward the Republicans since at least 1972, and the primary reason was race, not gender and sexuality.

While right-wing Christians profess to embrace the loving and compassionate teachings of Jesus, for many of them "God" is perceived as more of an Old Testament-style deity: a stern, authoritarian ruler—God the father—without whose commandments and divine interventions men's authority in the family and beyond is jeopardized, and the society comes unraveled. In fact, in what could be interpreted as a repudiation of turn-the-other-cheek Christianity, certain strains of right-wing Christian evangelicalism embrace what the writer Chris Hedges describes as a "cult of masculinity" in which

> Jesus is portrayed as a man of action, casting out demons, battling the Anti-Christ, attacking hypocrites and castigating the corrupt. This cult of masculinity brings with it the glorification of strength, violence and vengeance. It turns Christ into a Rambo-like figure; indeed depictions of Jesus within the movement often show a powerfully built man wielding a huge sword.[15]

Elections that are ostensibly about "God," therefore, are often really about men. Each election season, thousands of conservative Christian pastors urge men to support candidates who advocate ultraconservative social, economic,

CHAPTER 6: 2004: JOHN F. KERRY VS. GEORGE W. BUSH.

and foreign policy positions not simply because they are ideologically committed to them but because the "liberal" alternative is both ungodly and unmanly. George W. Bush, who proclaimed during a Republican primary debate in 2000 that Jesus was his favorite philosopher, not surprisingly derived a great deal of his political support from conservative Christians. He received 68 percent of the white evangelical vote in 2000, and a dramatic 78 percent in 2004, which constituted 36 percent of his voters.[16]

Guns

Less than a month before the 2004 election, John Kerry went hunting for geese in the battleground state of Ohio, armed with a twelve-gauge shotgun. According to Roger Cohen in the *New York Times*, Kerry went hunting "because in critical swing states, including Ohio and Pennsylvania, shooting birds and buck is a big deal. He doesn't want to repeat the mistake of Al Gore, whose antigun positions during the 2000 campaign cost him votes in a country where more than 40 percent of adults live in households with guns."[17] Kerry's staged photo op, which emulated Bill Clinton's similar one in 1992, was roundly criticized on talk radio and gun rights websites as a patronizing insult to gun owners, especially considering that Kerry had cast votes for sensible gun control measures for nearly two decades in the United States Senate, a record that was widely publicized by gun advocacy groups such as the NRA. But Kerry's hunting performance was not only about sending a message to "sportsmen" that he wouldn't threaten their pastime. As Stephen Ducat wrote, "Apparently, Mr. Kerry wanted to reassure the male electorate that even though he supports a ban on assault weapon sales, he still likes to kill things."[18]

While the issue of gun control raises legitimate constitutional questions about the right of the individual to self-defense versus the rights of the community to fashion social policy on matters related to public safety, ongoing debates about the Second Amendment and "gun rights" versus "gun control" can also be read as proxy debates about masculinity. Advocates of so-called gun rights often invoke the right of citizens to protect themselves from violent threats, presumably emanating from their fellow citizens, as well as from what are perceived as the tyrannical decisions of an authoritarian government. While approximately 10 percent to 15 percent of National Rifle Association members are women, and millions of conservative women support Republicans and Democrats who routinely block gun control legislation, men comprise the vast majority of gun owners and gun rights activists. For decades, polls have shown that women are far more supportive of strict gun control laws than are men. In fact, a major survey by the National Opinion Research Center in 1999 concluded:

> Men and women have fundamentally different viewpoints on firearms and their regulation....Across all 36 topics women are more concerned about guns and more in favor of their regulation, and 34 of the differences are statistically significant. The differences are often quite pronounced. In fifteen cases they range from 10 to 20 points and in 10 instances, 20 percentage points.[19]

One clue as to why there is such a gender gap on the politics of gun control is provided by Drew Westen, who draws a contrast between a typical urban dweller's emotional reaction to the word "gun" and that of a typical rural resident. The urban dweller hears "gun" and that taps into an associative chain that includes *handguns, murder, muggings, robbery, inner-city violence,* etc. He/she thinks of their vulnerability in an urban landscape awash in firearms and crime, and is more likely to regard gun control measures as sane social policy. The rural resident hears "gun" and the words that come to mind include *hunt, my Daddy, my son, gun shows, gun collection, rifle, protecting my family, deer, buddies, beer,* and a host of memories that connect them to their fathers and grandfathers. In other words, gun rights versus gun control is an emotional issue for millions of men. For many men, urban and rural, the word *control* itself is a hot-button issue. Westen argues that many of them don't like the term *gun control* because it suggests a curtailment of their freedom. But it also implies a direct challenge to the power and control that so many men associate with masculinity itself.

Conservatives intuitively understand that cultural tensions around the meanings of manhood lie at the symbolic core of gun policy debates, which is why they often equate sensible gun control measures with emasculation, such as when the rabidly right-wing radio talk host Michael Savage described the assault weapons ban President Bill Clinton signed into law as the

CHAPTER 6: 2004: JOHN F. KERRY VS. GEORGE W. BUSH.

"de-balling" of America.[20] The Republican Party itself realizes that guns are loaded with emotional resonance for millions of men, which is why they oppose most restrictions on gun ownership. The Democrats, on the other hand, have conflicted sentiments about the issue, reflecting not only the class and geographic diversity of the party but also the fact that many Democratic men who have come of age over the past generation have rejected the "John Wayne" model of manhood in favor of a nonviolent and more emotionally complex masculinity. And of course the Democrats also have to be responsive to the concerns of their large female voter base, which overwhelmingly supports stricter gun laws.

Gays

From the moment Jeane Kirkpatrick coined the phrase "San Francisco Democrats" in her speech at the 1984 Republican National Convention, it has been used by conservative pundits and assorted figures as a code phrase that equates Democrats—especially Democratic men—with gays. Gay-baiting has long been practiced in American politics, and as the culture continues to move in the direction of openness and acceptance of sexual diversity, it will become increasingly anachronistic. Nonetheless heterosexist conservatives in mainstream media continue to attack the masculinity of Democratic men by playing on the false equation between gender and sexual orientation. In other words, when men in public life—including politics—refuse to conform to the rigid standards of traditional masculinity, they take the chance that they will be tagged as gay, thus exposing themselves to ridicule, potential ostracism or discrimination. Whether done by adolescent boys on the playground, or by Ann Coulter on C-Span, calling men "faggots" if they fail to display proper deference to received notions of appropriate masculine behavior has the same effect: it polices heterosexual men (as well as gays and bisexuals) into silent conformity.

Along with the civil rights and women's movements, the gay rights movement that launched with the Stonewall riots in New York City in 1969 represents a major challenge to white heterosexual male power and privilege. Gay men especially represent an implicit threat to heterosexual men, and not simply on religious grounds. The degree to which many heterosexual men are afraid of gay men, a fear that is often mislabeled as "hate," is best described in psychological terms. As Stephen Ducat explains, homophobia has its roots in femophobia, or men's fear of their own femininity. It is not surprising, therefore, that researchers have repeatedly found that homophobia has been correlated with authoritarianism, cognitive rigidity, opposition to gender equality, and an intolerance of ambiguity.[21] Because issues related to homosexuality tap so powerfully into issues of sexual and gender identity—especially for men—whenever there are legislative issues related to homosexuality, or if a right-wing group successfully places a referendum on gay marriage on the ballot, it is relatively easy to mobilize conservative men's (and women's) fears, defensive energies, and votes to oppose what they then misleadingly call the "gay agenda."

TERRORISM AND TOUGH GUYS POST-9/11

The Iranian Hostage Crisis in 1979 was a major media spectacle that served as a harbinger of the rise of Islamist terrorism as a decisive factor in subsequent US presidential politics and electoral campaigns. It also represented a milestone event in the growing vulnerability of American citizens to violence from Islamist radicals arising out of US policy in the Middle East.

The threat of terrorism occupied a fairly low-level presence in media culture and politics even after the first World Trade Center bombing in New York City in 1993, but it became a frontline political issue in the US after 9/11. Although he came into office after a disputed vote count in 2000 that Douglas Kellner (2001) and others have characterized as a "stolen election," George W. Bush's leadership in the days and months following the unprecedented attacks gave him a huge boost in public approval ratings and allowed him to amass significant political capital that he used to enact a radical program to roll back civil liberties protections, dramatically increase military spending, and cut taxes on the wealthy. Much of George W. Bush's political success in his first term came about as the country rallied behind him in the wake of the attacks on September 11, 2001, but some of his own televised performances enhanced his aura as a take-charge guy who could be counted on in a crisis. Notably, one of the first media moments where Bush asserted his manly "street cred" was an unscripted event just after the attacks that became one of the defining

CHAPTER 6: 2004: JOHN F. KERRY VS. GEORGE W. BUSH.

moments of his leadership after 9/11. On September 13, Bush arrived at ground zero and was soon surrounded by a crowd of workers. Someone handed him a bullhorn, but when he began to speak, his mouth was too close to the mouthpiece, and his words were muffled. A worker shouted "We can't hear you!"

Bush replied, "Well I can hear you. The rest of the world hears you. And the people who knocked these buildings down will hear all of us soon." It was a bravura public performance of masculine assertiveness delivered along with a thinly veiled threat of an impending revenge-taking, and the largely blue-collar male crowd responded enthusiastically. They thundered "USA! USA! USA!" and countless commentators in the media announced that Bush, a son of wealth and privilege who had been searching for his political identity on September 10, had found in the tragedy an answer to his destiny and purpose in life. (How his professed Christianity might have complicated his role as revenger-in-chief was rarely mentioned in polite conversation).

Before the fall of the Soviet Union, right-wing critics routinely accused liberal Democrats (and Republicans) of being "soft on communism." After the attacks on 9/11, terrorism immediately became a central foreign policy concern and ubiquitous topic of media conversation. Reprising the strategy they employed for so long during the Cold War, conservatives seized on the opportunity to ridicule as "soft on terrorism" liberals, progressives and anyone who dissented from the George W. Bush administration's conduct of the "war on terror," as well as the invasion and occupation of Iraq. Their intent was to identify Bush's strategy against "terror" as the clear-eyed, aggressive, and implicitly masculine approach, and to link liberal Democrats with a policy of capitulation and appeasement, the latter term meant to conjure up negative associations with British Prime Minister Neville Chamberlain's appeasement of Adolf Hitler in 1939. Some influential conservative leaders were even more explicit in their attempts to feminize the opposition. During the 2004 campaign, Vice President Dick Cheney ridiculed Senator John Kerry for saying, at a conference of minority journalists, "I believe we can fight a more effective, more thoughtful, more strategic, more proactive, more sensitive war on terror that reaches out to other nations and brings them to our side." Seizing on the Democratic nominee's use of the word "sensitive," Cheney mocked Kerry in a summer speech before an Ohio crowd of veterans, law enforcement officers, firefighters, and current service members in a sound-bite that played repeatedly on cable TV programs and talk radio. "America has been in too many wars for any of our wishes," he said as members of the audience chuckled, "but not a one of them was won by being sensitive."[22] A few weeks later, in his speech at the Republican National Convention in New York City, Cheney revisited this theme by further distorting and mis-characterizing Kerry's views, to the laughter and cheers of the hyperpartisan Republican audience: "Even in this post-9/11 period, Senator Kerry doesn't appear to understand how the world has changed. He talks about leading a 'more sensitive war on terror'...as though al Qaeda will be impressed with our softer side."[23]

Cheney knew that Kerry had a detailed plan for fighting al Qaeda, one that included improving intelligence gathering, increasing counter-terrorism resources, and strengthening law enforcement cooperation with other countries. But his goal was not to debate Kerry in an exchange of contrasting policy statements; it was to ridicule and feminize the senator's position and thus send a message to white men in the Republican base that the only choice for "real men" was to support the president's policy. Glenn Greenwald argues that the Bush campaign's overall aim in 2004 was to preclude serious debate about different approaches to fighting terrorism, a strategy for which he received a great deal of assistance from sycophantic and impressionable figures in mainstream media. Greenwald captures perfectly the mocking tone of the criticism Kerry endured:

> Kerry's advocacy of an alternative course to Bush's failing militarism provoked wild controversy and great derision, from the Bush campaign as well as journalists and pundits across the ideological spectrum. Kerry's approach lacked—indeed, it rejected—the fulfilling, reassuring simplicity of cheering on wars. The Bush campaign and the tough-guy media pundits wildly distorted, then caricatured, and then scornfully laughed away Kerry's point; it provoked everything except a substantive response and meaningful debate about how best to handle terrorism: Oh, how hilarious—weak little John Kerry wants to treat terrorism like a law enforcement problem! He wants to protect against al Qaeda attacks with police methods! He would

CHAPTER 6: 2004: JOHN F. KERRY VS. GEORGE W. BUSH.

'protect us' by serving subpoenas on Osama bin Laden! He wants to surrender to the terrorists and give them therapy! He only wants to defend America if he first gets a permission slip from the U.N. That is so funny.[24]

Several months after Bush's reelection, Bush's senior political adviser Karl Rove delivered a speech that was putatively about the politics of antiterrorism, but which could be read as a primer for how Republican candidates in coming elections should position themselves in order to win the votes of white men. Rove sought (once again) to associate conservatism with hardheaded masculine realism, as against the mushy and emasculated liberal virtues of empathy and compassion, when he said:

Conservatives saw the savagery of 9/11 and the attacks and prepared for war; liberals saw the savagery of the 9/11 attacks and wanted to prepare indictments and offer therapy and understanding for our attackers. In the wake of 9/11, conservatives believed it was time to unleash the might and power of the United States military against the Taliban; in the wake of 9/11, liberals believed it was time to submit a petition.... Conservatives saw what happened to us on 9/11 and said: We will defeat our enemies. Liberals saw what happened to us and said: We must understand our enemies.[25]

What Cheney's and Rove's public pronouncements reveal is that the debate about how to respond to Islamist terrorism post-9/11 is less about competing political or military doctrines than it is about a struggle between two (or more) competing definitions of (white) masculinity. As long as conservatives are the only ones who get this, they will continue to attack the masculinity of liberal and progressive men, a bullying tactic that has successfully kept millions of white men from identifying with and supporting their own best interests in domestic or foreign policy.

But it wasn't just men who were taken in with right-wing rhetoric about getting tough in a dangerous world. The phenomenon of so-called "security moms" surfaced in the 2004 election, with many polls showing that women who were chiefly concerned with terrorism and the safety of their children were more likely to vote for George W. Bush. One such woman, Elizabeth Cromer, wrote the following letter to the editor in the *Boston Globe* in the spring of 2004:

I'm writing to you in support of our president, George W. Bush. His leadership through a trying time in American history has renewed my faith in the safety of our country. When 9/11 occurred, I prayed to God in thanks that George W. Bush was our president instead of Al Gore. He was like a father comforting a crying child, and I knew that he would make everything safe again, and I was right. With John Kerry, I'm afraid for the safety of our nation.[26]

It is not clear to what extent political ads, talk radio, or other media discourse about which candidate or party would be "tougher on terrorism" influenced the votes of women such as Ms. Cromer, although a wealth of polling data over the past three decades shows that women voters in general, including white women, are less likely than men to make voting choices based primarily on issues of national security. Of course it is necessary to acknowledge that many other factors influence women's votes, such as the fact that many white married women with children vote Republican for perceived tax advantages, as well as other economic reasons.

POPULISM AND SPORTS METAPHORS
Bush and Kerry were both patrician politicians, and in some ways the race between them boiled down to the question of which one could convince working-class white men that they understood and identified with them. Since the early 1970s, as we have seen, Republicans have had the distinct advantage in this process, as they have skillfully used cultural appeals to mask their indifference to the economic interests of the working class. There are few platforms more effective than sports in forging ties across class distinctions, especially for men. But the gender and class politics of candidates' sports participation and fandom have their own internal logic and codes that can be a challenge to decipher, especially when they intersect with race, as we've seen with Barack Obama's experiences with bowling and basketball.

With some variation, certain sports are identified not only with men, but with men from specific social classes. For example, racquetball in the US is largely viewed as a sport primarily for middle-and upper-class men in health and fitness clubs, whereas boxing and football are considered more blue-collar (although their fan base draws heavily from the middle and upper class as well). The "masculinity" of a given sport thus has a class dimension. As

Nicholas Howe (1988) points out, American politicians "especially those of patrician background, have long appreciated that the use of sports metaphors allows them to affect a common touch or forge a bond with average voters."[27] By calling on shared passions or team loyalties the wealthy have in common with working-class men, sports metaphors and other references are surefire ways to demonstrate populist appeal. A famous example from the pre-television era is the aristocrat Teddy Roosevelt's use of boxing metaphors. More recent examples include Richard Nixon's frequent references to baseball and football, or Ronald Reagan's close identification with football.

Reagan's football credentials were enhanced by his having been a college football player, and from his movie role as George Gipp in the 1940 film about a famous football coach, *Knute Rockne: All-American* (the source of the famous line, "Win one for the Gipper," which became part of Reagan lore). Reagan also effortlessly employed gridiron metaphors, such as when he stated in 1981 that European opponents of the neutron bomb were "carrying the propaganda ball for the Soviet Union,"[28] or when he said, in 1984, "Isn't it good to see the American team, instead of punting on third down, scoring touchdowns again?"[29] Reagan's ability to talk the populist language of football while cutting programs that served working-class families and pursuing an economic policy that redistributed income upward is one of the reasons he earned the nickname the "Great Communicator."

On the other hand, politicians who get the class politics wrong—or who are characterized by their opponents as getting them wrong—run the risk of revealing themselves as elitist, out of touch, or aristocratic in a way that is not read as manly by millions of working and middle-class male voters. For example, during former Massachusetts governor Michael Dukakis's run for the White House in 1988, he repeatedly referred to his campaign as a "marathon," invoking his Greek heritage. The political effectiveness of this was questionable, because while many Americans admire and are often in awe of marathon runners, marathon running is not seen in the dominant US culture as a "masculine" endeavor. Additionally, Dukakis's penchant for "power-walking" with the TV cameras rolling did not help bolster his masculine image, as this form of exercise is more often the object of ridicule than emulation.

In the 2004 presidential campaign, news commentators and conservative media personalities had a field day with footage of John Kerry skiing and snowboarding in Sun Valley, Idaho, and windsurfing off Nantucket Island. While these visuals showed him to be athletic and adventurous, and symbolically reinforced Kerry's similarities and identification with fellow Massachusetts senator and former president John F. Kennedy, they also accentuated the idea that his sports passions were rooted in upper-class traditions of leisure and recreation. Kennedy was frequently photographed playing touch football, a "populist" sport, but also sailing on expensive boats. Nonetheless the class and cultural imagery surrounding the Democratic and Republican parties in the early twenty-first century have changed dramatically since the Kennedy era. Hence widely circulated images of Kennedy sailing large schooners in the early 1960s played out very differently—and much less negatively—for him and his political persona.

Kerry's skiing, snowboarding, and windsurfing conveyed a masculine image that sharply contrasted with his opponent and fellow aristocrat George W. Bush's carefully stage-managed image as an average guy who rides in pickup trucks and loves baseball, as someone with whom plain folks could identify. The windsurfing photos also served as another kind of sports metaphor: they were the perfect visual illustration of the Republican theme of John Kerry as a "flip-flopper" who did not stand for anything and would just blow with the prevailing winds. During the 2012 Republican primaries, Mitt Romney reinforced the class chasm between him and the blue-collar base of the GOP while attending the Daytona 500, a prototypical Southern white working-class motorsports event. When asked by a reporter if he follows NASCAR, Romney responded, "Not as closely as some of the most ardent fans. But I have some great friends who are NASCAR team owners."

During those same 2012 primaries, Rick Santorum played the cultural and class politics of sport much more adeptly in his use of bowling as a campaign strategy. Leading up to the Wisconsin primary, Santorum made regular appearances at bowling alleys, where his familiarity with the social scene and his bowling ability drew favorable reviews from some of the locals. "I feel a common denominator with him," a forty-year-old homemaker, Carrie Pritchard, told the *New York Times*. "If anyone can come to a bowling alley and hang out with everyone, I like that a lot," she said. For the Santorum campaign, the bowling alley appearances highlighted the candidate's comfort with working-class people, in stark contrast to the upper-class Romney's awkwardness and distance. Of course in such encounters and the media

CHAPTER 6: 2004: JOHN F. KERRY VS. GEORGE W. BUSH.

stories about them, there was rarely any mention of Santorum's voting record in the United States Senate, where he voted consistently for tax breaks for the wealthy and cuts to programs serving the kinds of low-and middle-income families with whom he was bowling. What was highlighted was Santorum's personal "connection" to those voters. "It [bowling] is really meant to be a cultural story, who Rick really is," John Brabender, his chief strategist, told the *New York Times*.

The nexus of sports and politics also involves complex questions of culture and ethnicity. Few universal sports metaphors work equally well to define manhood across national or cultural boundaries, in part because different cultures have varying definitions of what is considered "masculine." For example, in most parts of the world, soccer is considered a manly sport (even if women also play it), and male soccer stars are often national icons. This is not true in the US. Although soccer is our most popular youth sport in terms of athletic participation, it is not even close to American football in its cultural influence, masculine identification, or metaphorical power. It is rare to find a national-level politician in the US who uses soccer metaphors, precisely because to do so would call into question the strength of their American identity, as well as their masculine credibility. Thus it is important for people who use sports metaphors in their speech or writing to know which sports are identified with the dominant kind of manhood in a given society, and to use references to those sports and avoid others. For politicians or political commentators in media, failure to do one's "homework" in this instance would be to expose oneself as either oblivious to local norms and customs, or in the case of a man, as not masculine enough because he discusses, plays, or enjoys feminized—or otherwise "wrong"—sports. Political professionals are well aware of this trap, which accounts for the fact that in 2004 John Kerry's presidential campaign downplayed his collegiate soccer record and emphasized his hockey credentials.

It is possible to interpret this de-emphasis on Kerry's soccer past as an attempt by his handlers to steer clear of biographical information that reinforced his European—especially French—sensibilities, as this was a line of attack that right-wing activists and media pundits used to paint him as elitist and out of touch with average (working class) American voters. Right-wing critics of Kerry are undoubtedly aware of the gender and class politics that surround soccer in mainstream US culture. As Franklin Foer points out in his book *How Soccer Explains the World*, (2004), in most of the world, soccer is both broadly popular and the province of the working class. But in the US, with the exception of Latinos, and recent immigrants from Asia and Africa, "the professional classes follow the game most avidly and the working class couldn't give a toss about it...half the nation's soccer participants come from households earning over $50,000...the solid middle-class and above."[30] Moreover, Foer argues that when a "generation of elites" adopted soccer in the 1960s and 1970s, it gave the impression that they had "turned their backs on the stultifying conformity of what it perceived as traditional America,"[31] yet another example of how Democrats and liberals were supposedly out of touch with average folks in the "red states" and elsewhere. But even these ethnic/class politics are in flux. For example, as the Latino population increases as a percentage of the US electorate, it is interesting to speculate whether Latino politicians—and Anglo politicians seeking Latino votes— choose to use soccer metaphors in their speeches or press conference banter. How will that play out in Anglo culture, especially among sports talk radio hosts and other media personalities who have historically condescended to soccer and ridiculed it as "wimpy" in relation to American football?

FAKE NEWS SATIRIZES REAL MEN

By the late twentieth century, it was widely acknowledged in mainstream political commentary that entertainment values had thoroughly infused US politics, especially in the context of a media culture where the lines between entertainment, news, and opinion had blurred long ago. This is, after all, an era in which a cinematic killing machine, Arnold Schwarzenegger (*The Terminator*) was twice elected governor of the nation's largest state, and in which the former lead political columnist for the *New York Times*, Frank Rich, got his training to write about politics from his years as that paper's theater critic. But while the role of entertainment media in shaping popular percep- tions about politics and politicians has been discussed, there has been little, if any, analysis about if and how entertainment culture has influenced attitudes and expectations specifically about presidential masculinity.

Prior to George W. Bush's terms in office, other presidents in the mass media era have had their masculinity lampooned in media, such as Bush's father, who was portrayed by Dana Carvey in *Saturday Night Live* skits as an effete, feminized aristocrat. But from the late 1980s to the early 1990s, those skits were broadcast only once and then repeated later that year, and unlike today, they didn't achieve a second life on YouTube. During the years of George W. Bush's presidency, the availability of broadband technology increased exponentially, enabling millions of homes to receive streaming video. In addition, advances in digital editing have made it possible in today's 24/7 media environment for satirists and partisans to use video in unprecedented ways to reveal the constructed nature of political candidates' gendered appeals. In the past decade, liberal cable TV programs that make frequent use of video clips have proliferated; not only Comedy Central's *The Daily Show with Jon Stewart* and *The Colbert Report* but also HBO's *Real Time with Bill Maher* and MSNBC's defunct *Countdown with Keith Olberman*. Conservative shows like Fox News Channel's *Hannity* and *The O'Reilly Factor* employ similar tactics to discredit liberals and flatter conservatives. But whether these tactics were wielded by liberal or conservative media outlets, during the first decade of the twenty-first century a confluence of technological developments and an increasingly aggressive infotainment culture on cable TV caused George W. Bush to become the object of an unprecedented outpouring of ridicule that used his own staged performances against him.

One of Bush's key characteristics that satirists exploited was his faux-cowboy act. Countless editorial cartoons, as well as video skits, played off Bush's presentation of himself as a plain-spoken Texan who embodies the cowboy virtues of straight talk and forthright action. A popular YouTube video that lampooned this aspect of Bush's performance appeared during the 2004 presidential campaign, sponsored by the nonprofit political advocacy organization Americans Coming Together (ACT). It was a short comedy piece featuring the popular actor Will Ferrell playing George W. Bush. Ferrell had been playing Bush on *Saturday Night Live* skits for several years, so his Bush caricature was already well-known. In fact, Ferrell developed his Bush satire into a successful Broadway show, *You're Welcome America*, which sold out a several-month run in the winter of 2008–2009, and which aired as a special on HBO in March 2009. In the YouTube short video, Ferrell plays Bush outside on a ranch dressed in jeans and a western-style shirt. The clip opens with him walking toward the camera, holding a pitchfork. A voiceover recited by Ferrell-as-Bush says, "I am George W. Bush, and I approve of this message. In fact I think it is awesome," which signaled to the viewer that the skit was a parody of a political ad. For most of the short video, Ferrell-as-Bush is positioned leaning up against a split-rail wooden fence, speaking to the camera as if he's being filmed for a campaign commercial. But the goofy, verbally challenged Bush constantly misspeaks, or says something unintentionally self-critical.

"Hello there. How you doin' America? I hope you're enjoying the freedom and liberties that we as Americans enjoy. As you well know, ever since I took office, well things have been really bad."

A male director's voice off-camera yells, "Cut!"

Ferrell-as-Bush says, "That seemed like a good one. I'm just finding my groove, I'm getting my groove on."

He starts "playing" guitar on a rake he's holding, as a production assistant snaps a "Take 133" sign. After a couple more failed takes, he says, "There's people out there that would have you believe the economy isn't doing so well. Well to that I answer hey, for the two million jobs that we've lost, that means there's two million people sitting at home watching repeats of quality television, such as *The Jeffersons* and *Facts of Life*, and that equals more ad revenue to radio and TV stations."

The director yells "Cut!" and Bush responds "What do you mean, cut?"

By March 2009, the four-minute video had been viewed close to seven million times.

One area of the politics-entertainment nexus that has been the subject of academic and journalistic inquiry is the role of so-called "fake news" programs in bringing news and politics to television viewers, particularly younger Americans who watch *The Daily Show* or *The Colbert Report* and who get most of their information about current events from those sources. But even those analyses rarely examine the gendered aspects of the biting satire offered there or speculate about how they might undermine or reinforce cultural norms about masculinity and leadership. Satirical treatment of political leaders has a long and colorful history in the United States, but George W. Bush's tenure in office offers some especially poignant examples of how comedy can provide insights into how male politicians use, or misuse, cultural ideas about manliness to sell themselves to the voting public.

CHAPTER 6: 2004: JOHN F. KERRY VS. GEORGE W. BUSH.

THE DAILY SHOW

Throughout his presidency, but particularly after the Iraq War began to go poorly, repeated satirical treatment on *The Daily Show* punctured Bush's hypermasculine bravado, and arguably did serious damage—especially with young viewers—to his masculine credibility. Although Bush provided plenty of material to hold himself up as an object of ridicule, such as his ill-fated "Mission Accomplished" speech on the aircraft carrier U.S.S. *Abraham Lincoln* in May 2003, *The Daily Show* regularly trained a spotlight on Bush's seemingly insatiable need to prove his manhood. One recurring skit on the show was a cartoon video entitled "The Decider," which had its origins in a televised statement Bush made in 2006 to the effect that he was "the decider." The video is a superhero spoof with Bush in the lead role. The cartoon, which only aired a few times but gained a life of its own online, ridicules the simplicity of Bush's Manichean worldview as it mocks his narcissism and his seeming need to be—or appear to be—in control at all times.

During George W. Bush's presidency *The Daily Show* became one of the most politically influential programs on television. A 2008 study by the Pew Research Center's Project for Excellence in Journalism concluded that "*The Daily Show* is clearly impacting American dialogue" and "getting people to think critically about the public square."[32] But while few discussions of *The Daily Show*'s impact on presidential politics offer any sort of explicit gender analysis, arguably one of the show's signature features is its host's embodiment of a kind of "oppositional masculinity" that questions traditional authority and skewers the pretensions of powerful men. Satirists have long played this role, but digital editing processes and the ubiquitousness of media have helped take their effectiveness to a new level. For example, Jon Stewart might show a clip of a male candidate in some kind of campaign photo op or making a forceful public declaration that is intended to bolster his image as a take-charge leader. Then Stewart, with a knowing smile and a well-timed sarcastic comment, runs a clip of the same man contradicting himself on the same subject in a different setting, which has the effect of completely undermining the power of the staged performance. The juxtaposition, shown to raucous laughter by the New York studio audience, uncovers the performative and phony aspects of presidential posturing with unprecedented speed and transforms a staged photo op into an object of satirical humor. Stewart calls this digital-era satiric device the one-to-one: "If you can get a one-to-one with a guy saying the exact opposite of what he said today, then you don't even have to do anything. You just lay them back-to-back and sit back and giggle."[33]

For the past decade Stewart and *The Daily Show* have helped to define a certain kind of generational sensibility for millions of college students and other young viewers. Individual skits from the popular Comedy Central program are perennial favorites online; at this writing there were more than two million videos related to *The Daily Show* posted on YouTube.

THE COLBERT REPORT

If Jon Stewart undermines the masculine mythification of the presidency in part by using video to carefully deconstruct the words and actions of sitting presidents as well as would-be challengers, Stephen Colbert directly satirizes right-wing masculinity more generally on *The Colbert Report.* On the show Colbert plays a right-wing talk show host patterned self-consciously after the top-rated Fox News Channel personality Bill O'Reilly. Colbert describes the character he plays as a "well-intentioned, poorly informed, high-status idiot."[34]

Colbert's show first aired in 2006, during the presidency of George W. Bush, who used the presidential bully pulpit to valorize anti-intellectualism and champion, as a guide to policy, (conservative) religious faith over reasoned argument or scientific evidence. Likewise Colbert's character frequently invokes gut feelings and tortured logic to justify his beliefs, despite the obvious absurdity of the conclusions he often reaches. On the show's debut, Colbert's character declared that "I am not a fan of facts. You see, the facts can change, but my opinion will never change, no matter what the facts are."

Out of character, Colbert explained,

"Language has always been important in politics, but language is incredibly important to the present political struggle. Because if you can establish an atmosphere in which information doesn't mean anything, then there is no objective reality...what you wish to be true is all that matters, regardless of the facts."[35]

CHAPTER 6: 2004: JOHN F. KERRY VS. GEORGE W. BUSH.

He added the term "truthiness" to the contemporary lexicon, to express the idea of something that seems to be true, the "truth we want to exist."[36]

While O'Reilly's fans tune into Fox to hear the snarling host angrily battle secular humanist elites who are waging a "war on Christmas" and other cherished traditions in white middle-America, Colbert's audience on Comedy Central is treated to a nightly parody of O'Reilly and the angry white men he represents. O'Reilly rose to the head of the pack in the cable talk universe by playing the part of the beleaguered everyman whose most cherished beliefs have been under relentless assault for decades—and who is not about to go down without a fight.

Colbert's signature satiric contribution is his running parody of anti-intellectualism among conservative white men, which is a running feature in American politics but which has seemed to accelerate over the past couple of decades as the Republican Party has shifted ever further to the right. The right-wing populist disdain for facts when they don't conform to right-wing ideology, or science when it doesn't support conservative dogma, has placed Republicans who accept the settled science of evolution or human-caused climate change in a precarious position, especially Republican men who reject the absurd notion that adherence to logic and science is somehow unmanly. One political result of that know-nothing environment is that Republicans who want to be elected president, such as John McCain in 2008 and Mitt Romney in 2012, are forced to pretend that they have doubts about or don't accept the scientific consensus on these and other issues. Colbert thus portrays contemporary conservative white masculinity as threatened not just by the rise of women, gays, or multiculturalism but by the very thing that used to define traditional masculinity outside of certain strands of conservative Christianity: the belief in logic and the pursuit of knowledge.

Colbert's show arose at a cultural-political moment when the president of the United States was desperately seeking to establish and trumpet his manly authority in a way that often bordered on self-caricature. As David Gutterman and Danielle Regan maintain, Bush's

> great and tragic determination to act like a man highlights the resonance and the fragility of the normative performance of gender in America. The lost cause of 'defending' a (crumbling) gender order is portrayed as a valiant

fight, and when it fails, those who wish to see the myth will understand it as a grand battle for traditional values. Despite the reality that conventional markers of manhood are increasingly fleeting, crafting identification with the mythical man to excite potential male voters has been a vital tactic for the Bush administration.[37]

Colbert's character might be anti-intellectual and often clueless, but he, along with the audience, is keenly aware that white men's cultural authority is in decline. His fumbling defiance of this decline is the source of much of the show's humor: audiences laugh at Colbert's attempts to explain events in a way that makes sense to a man who sees threats everywhere to his way of life and tries to "fix the facts" to fit his narrow worldview. In Colbert's character there is even an element of pathos, or romantic yearning for a long-gone golden era. As Colbert wrote—in character—in his best-selling book *I Am America (and so can you)*, "America used to live by the motto 'Father Knows Best.' Now we're lucky if 'Father Knows He Has Children.' We've become a nation of sperm donors and baby daddies. But there's more to being a father than taking kids to Chuck E. Cheese and supplying the occasional Y-chromosome. A father has to be a provider, a teacher, a role model, but most importantly, a distant authority figure who can never be pleased. Otherwise, how will children ever understand the concept of God?"[38]

CHAPTER 6: 2004: JOHN F. KERRY VS. GEORGE W. BUSH.

Chapter 7
2008: McCain vs. Obama

The 2008 race between John McCain and Barack Obama lent itself to descriptions that utilized simple binary categories: old vs. new, experience vs. change, the warrior vs. the orator, conservative vs. liberal. But the 2008 presidential campaign was also a competition between two styles (and ideologies) of masculinity, and in that sense this election was like every other one. The key and dramatic difference was that Obama is not white, which meant that for the first time in US history a presidential race featured a competition between one version of white and another version of black masculinity.

Because Obama was the first African American to be nominated for president by a major party, it was inevitable that race became a major topic of discussion during the campaign. But the focus on race served to ensure that the gendered components of the equation remained invisible, or else hidden in plain sight. For example, a *New York Times* magazine cover story by Matt Bai ran three weeks before the 2008 election entitled "Can Obama Close the Deal With Those White Guys?" The subhead asked, "Will gun-toting, church-going white guys pull the lever for Obama?" The article focused on Obama's attempt to connect with working-class white men in rural Pennsylvania and Virginia. But the entire discussion centered on whether Obama could transcend issues of racial difference, and, because of his education and accomplishments, the class-coded "elitist" tag that Democrats had been tarnished with for the past forty years. The article did not contain even one mention of the "guys" aspect of the "white guys" referred to in the article's title. The only hint that Bai grasped the gendered nature of rural white men's disaffection with Democratic presidential candidates was the centrality he gave to issues related to guns. As I have maintained, debates about "gun rights" versus "gun control" are often proxies for the playing out of tensions between static and changing definitions of manhood.

After Obama defeated Hillary Clinton in the Democratic primaries, commentary about gender tended to skip over the men in order to focus on Sarah Palin, the only woman on a major party ticket. But masculinity remained a crucial subtext of the political discourse in the Obama vs. McCain matchup—even if few in mainstream media identified a contest between two men explicitly as a struggle about gender. One revealing headline on the cover of *Time* magazine read "Why Obama Is Tougher Than He Looks." Perhaps responding to relentless right-wing criticism of Obama's readiness to lead the armed forces as commander in chief, the authors of the article stated that "you don't rise in Chicago politics or come this far this fast in a national race by being soft, naïve, or scared of a fight." They claimed that Obama's "…mild manner belies fierce self-control. The frequent self-mocking conceals a stubborn self-confidence. He not only plays hard; he plays to win, rubs it in sometimes if he does and takes losses hard."[1]

Media commentary about Obama as a presidential candidate repeatedly featured sports metaphors that were used to assess his campaign strategy *and* to size him up as a man; as per usual, boxing references abounded. During the primary season, one *New York Times* article entitled "Taking blows from all sides and weighing when to punch back," contained a representative paragraph.

> Counter-punching, as Mr. Obama's advisers are quick to say, is a tricky business. If Mr. Obama goes toe-to-toe too often, he risks appearing edgy and even defensive, not to mention turning off those supporters who harbor affection for his rival. But let too many blows go unmatched, and he risks appearing passive, not to mention ending up unconscious.[2]

One of Obama's right-wing critics, talk radio host Hugh Hewitt, managed to combine boxing and football metaphors with this caustic dismissal: "Rolling the dice with an untried rookie might be something a desperate NFL franchise might try with a quarterback, but the world cannot afford to have its only superpower turned over to a completely unqualified and wholly inexperienced lightweight."[3] Hewitt's reference to NFL quarterbacks was perhaps unintentionally apropos, because there are unavoidable similarities between the historic exclusion of black quarterbacks from professional football and the unease that still grips many white Americans about the idea of a black president of the United States. But just as a new generation of NFL fans has grown up accustomed to seeing black men in the preeminent leadership role of quarterback, so too have Americans of all races now been conditioned to see as unremarkable a black man as the chief executive of the federal government—and symbolic face of the nation.

As referenced in a previous discussion, sports can help candidates forge a bond with voters—but they can also exacerbate racial and class differences. Bowling might have played that role for Obama in 2008. On a campaign swing in Pennsylvania prior to the primary, on one stop Obama was supposed to shake hands with bowlers, but instead got out on the floor and played a few frames. He threw a number of gutter balls and scored a thirty-seven in seven frames. His campaign manager David Plouffe later wrote that he thought the episode was "refreshing" to voters because it showed Obama's willingness to try something he was not good at.[4] But it's hard not to see that the bowling incident played right into the hands of the right-wing media, which referenced it repeatedly in the next few months as evidence that the city-slick black Senator was not "one of us."

Obama also had to fend off criticism that he was an elitist, by now a familiar charge by the Right against all liberals and most Democrats, but one whose veracity he foolishly abetted with a statement at a campaign fundraiser in San Francisco. Talking about why he was having trouble connecting with white working-class voters in Pennsylvania, Obama tried to downplay the implication that racism was at the root of it and instead talked thoughtfully about the loss of manufacturing jobs and other macroeconomic forces that spanned many decades. But then he got to the sentence that made headlines and provided fodder for years worth of talk radio rants: "It's not surprising," Obama said, "when (rural, working-class white) people get bitter, they cling to guns or religion or antipathy to people who aren't like them or anti-immigrant sentiment or anti-trade sentiment as a way to explain their frustrations." The comment was manna from heaven for the right-wing

CHAPTER 7: 2008: MCCAIN VS. OBAMA

media, who repeated the quote endlessly in an effort to drive as big a wedge as possible between the Democrat Obama and the white working class. A few months later, Karl Rove provided a fresh opportunity to revisit the elitism charge when he called Obama "coolly arrogant" at a breakfast with Republican insiders at the Capitol Hill Club. "Even if you never met him, you know this guy," Rove said. "He's the guy at the country club with the beautiful date, holding a martini and a cigarette that stands against the wall and makes snide comments about everyone who passes by." It was a stunning display of right-wing chutzpah: dubbing as a country club snob a black man who was raised by a white single mother and who was married to a working-class black woman from the south side of Chicago—exactly the kind of people who would never be admitted to the kinds of country clubs historically (and to this day) linked with Republicans.

But Rove knew his business. He was a College Republican activist when Richard Nixon discovered that the elitist tag was an effective smear tactic conservatives could use to attract working-class white voters—especially men—in part by using class-coded language to impugn the manhood of Democrats and liberals, and even moderate Republicans. The idea was that "real men" work with their hands (and vote Republican), not like those wimpy upper-class types who drive Volvos, sip lattes, and listen to National Public Radio.

Initially, John McCain hoped that his war hero status and image as a "maverick" politician would be enough to win a wide margin among white male voters against the cerebral (and Black) Obama, who had no military record and scant foreign policy credentials. But unlike the election of 2004, when the Bush campaign exploited the fear of terrorism to help win an electoral majority, in 2008 the election's focus was squarely back on the domestic economy—where millions of white men (and women) feared for the loss of their jobs and the shrinkage of their retirement accounts. And after the subprime mortgage crisis precipitated a Wall Street collapse in the early part of the general election campaign, and the economy became the dominant campaign issue, Obama was able to project an image of competence and stability in the face of crisis, as the terms of debate shifted about the "masculine" qualities necessary in a president.

One of the more remarkable developments in American political history was the emergence of a black man as a reassuring presidential presence at a time of great national anxiety. As the economic picture darkened, the traditionally masculine quality of presidential "toughness" in the face of a dangerous world receded in importance, and fiscal stewardship became more important. In this regard, Obama benefited both from Bush's failures and McCain's missteps in statements he made about the economy during the campaign. The endless and endlessly bloody occupation of Iraq, the scandal of Abu Ghraib, and the failure of Bush's broader Middle East policies had to a certain extent discredited the idea that in twenty-first century global politics, it was important to have a president who was willing to use brutal force—even torture—to advance US interests. And when John McCain in mid-September said that the "fundamentals of our economy are strong," he more or less destroyed any credibility he might have had as a leader who understood enough about what was wrong to offer a realistic path out. By contrast, Obama was not only highly intelligent but also well-informed and rhetorically persuasive, both about the causes of the financial crisis and about what action needed to be taken by the federal government.

Barack Obama built and energized an electoral coalition of young voters, first-time voters, and an overwhelming majority of voters of color, especially African Americans. Like every Democratic presidential candidate for the past three decades, he lost the white vote. Still, he won a landslide victory among all women. And while he failed to capture the white male vote, he did much better with white men than John Kerry did in 2004. Kerry lost among white males by twenty-five points; Obama lost by only sixteen. As a result, he won the overall men's vote by one percentage point, which together with his margin of victory among women was enough for him to achieve a comfortable electoral majority. While this election will be analyzed for many years, at this point it is reasonable to infer that Obama did so well among white men (and thus all men) in part because of the effectiveness of his performance of a new kind of presidential masculinity in an intensely high pressure environment. An editorial endorsing Obama in the centrist-liberal political journal *The New Republic* summed up his appeal to political elites—along with the broad middle class—with the following statement:

We... have hopes that Obama will govern as the person who revealed himself in this campaign. On the whole, he has turned in one of the more

CHAPTER 7: 2008: MCCAIN VS. OBAMA

impressive performances in recent political history—demonstrating an ability to explain complex ideas in plainspoken English, impeccable managerial skills, evenness of temper, avoidance of sloppy errors, and pragmatism, not to mention that he can really deliver a speech.[5]

BARACK OBAMA

What was even more impressive about Obama's performance during the 2008 presidential campaign is that as a black man he was able to project a kind of cool masculine competence in a way that attracted not only the overwhelming majority of black voters, but also the largest number of white male voters for a Democratic presidential candidate in over thirty years. The fact that Obama won the most white male votes (41 percent) of any Democrat since Jimmy Carter in 1976 prompts its own set of questions: what was it about Obama's masculinity—not simply his blackness—that proved attractive to millions of white male voters? What are the differences as well as similarities between how African American men and white men see Obama *as a man*? Obama's charisma played an important role in this, but prior trends in entertainment media contributed as well. As the movie critics Manohla Dargis and A. O. Scott wrote, Americans were ready to see a black man as president because in the virtual America of movies and television, they had already seen several: "The presidencies of James Earl Jones in 'The Man,' Morgan Freeman in 'Deep Impact,' Chris Rock in 'Head of State,' and Dennis Haysbert in '24' helped us imagine Mr. Obama's transformative breakthrough before it occurred. In a modest way, they also hastened its arrival."[6]

At the beginning of the long campaign, the question of whether Obama was "black enough" was debated repeatedly on TV and radio programs and in print journalism. It is not possible to do justice here to the complexity of issues related to "African American" versus "black" identity that informed this debate. But a crucial part of Obama's background—the implications of which he discussed at length in his memoir *Dreams From My Father*—is that his mother was white and his father was an African and thus not a product of American society and its racist heritage. Obama also grew up in Hawaii and Indonesia, giving him a kind of "outsider" status in US black culture. Some of the early skepticism about Obama's "authentic blackness" (which faded as the campaign progressed) might also have been a reaction to how comfortable whites seemed to be with him, which, interestingly, was one of his greatest political assets in a country where African Americans comprise a little more than ten percent of the electorate. Remarkably, Obama was able to convey strength and masculine confidence *as a black man* while minimizing the anxiety this produced among white men. In so doing, it is possible that he ushered in a new archetype of presidential manhood. He did this not with blustery displays of anger or martial fervor but with a more cerebral confidence, which he managed to carry without coming off as condescending, as Al Gore did in 2000, or as emasculated, in the way populist conservatives have for decades sought to portray intellectuals. As Jewel Woods (2008) wrote near the start of the general election campaign:

> …The key to Senator Obama's appeal among men is not solely his intelligence or his elocution, but his smooth and unflappable character, or simply his 'coolness.' Obama has become the embodiment of smooth. He is like one of the agents in the Matrix trilogy who moves so fast you can't tell he's dodging bullets. He possesses a 'grace under fire' that men have always found intoxicating. Similar to a "Black Frank Sinatra," Obama possesses a Billy Dee Williams type of cool. The result is that he…has accomplished what men like John Kerry and the former Al Gore were not able to accomplish—he has brought sexy back to white-collar masculinity.[7]

In the end, Obama won the presidency after a grueling and historic primary and general election campaign where, according to most pundits, he kept his cool in the face of relentless attacks against his character, personal associations, and readiness to lead, earning him the nickname of "No Drama Obama." His campaign was also quick to respond to attacks from Hillary Clinton's campaign and then John McCain's, which reinforced the idea that Obama could not only "take a punch" but would not respond passively when his "manhood" was rhetorically tested.

THE FIRST FEMALE PRESIDENT

Of course campaigning is very different from governing, as Obama and his many passionate supporters discovered soon after the thrill of victory began to wear off. In Obama's second year the Pulitzer Prize-winning conservative columnist Kathleen Parker wrote a column entitled "Obama: Our First Female President," where she praised Obama for doing things "a woman's way," but reasoned it had hurt the president politically. It seemed that people weren't quite ready for a male leader who exhibited feminine leadership traits.

> While men seek out ways to measure themselves against others, women are more likely to talk out problems. Barack Obama is a chatterbox who makes Alan Alda look like Genghis Khan…We still do have certain cultural expectations, especially related to leadership. When we ask questions about a politician's beliefs, family or hobbies, we're looking for familiarity, what we can cite as "normal" and therefore reassuring.

After decades of feminist activism, the rise of the "new man" in the 1970s, and other progressive cultural phenomena, it seems that many Americans continue to need reassurance that a president can successfully perform a certain kind of traditional masculinity. Or as the comedian Bill Maher said in reference to Obama, "The American people don't really care what side of an issue you're on. They just don't want you to act like a pussy."

Parker suggested that Obama had the opportunity in 2010 to demonstrate his capacity for a more familiar masculine style of leadership with the oil spill in the Gulf of Mexico. Instead,

> The BP oil crisis offered a textbook case of how Obama's rhetorical style has impeded his effectiveness. The president may not have had the ability to "plug the damn hole," as he put it in one of his manlier outbursts. No one expected him to don his wetsuit and dive into the gulf, but he did have the authority to intervene immediately and he didn't. Instead, he deferred to BP, weighing, considering, even delivering jokes to the White House Correspondents' Association dinner when he should have been on Air Force One to the Louisiana coast. His lack of immediate, commanding action was perceived as a lack of leadership because, well, it was.[8]

At a certain point into his presidency, the cool detachment that had worked so well to convey competence during the campaign started to become a liability, especially with white middle and working-class men who were out of jobs or worried about losing them. Many progressive supporters of the president watched in dismay as *Fox News* and right-wing talk radio led the way in championing Republicans—the party of never-ending tax cuts for the wealthy—as the party who cared about jobs for working people. While it might be true that the crash of the housing market and the broader economic collapse dramatically constrained the Obama administration's ability to maneuver, Obama's temperamental predilection for compromise was a tough sell in a cultural climate where viewers/voters—especially men—had been conditioned to see compromise as weakness. They wanted someone who would fight for them—and come across as passionate in doing so. Charles Blow put it like this in September of 2011 in the *New York Times*, after a strong speech by Obama to a joint session of Congress: "Has he finally realized that you can't rub the belly of the beast that wants to eat you, that you have to fight your way off the plate and bring the monster to heel? Has he come to understand that Americans value valiant struggle over bloodless surrender?"[9]

From his astounding primary run to the early days of his presidency, Obama had been praised in mainstream media—and on the Left—for his ability to project an audacious self-confidence without unduly rattling the anxieties of middle-aged white men. As a black male leader who was unafraid to talk about "empathy" and the need to have dialogue with America's enemies, he represented a potentially new masculine presidential archetype. But as his well-publicized compromises mounted, most notably on health care but also on issues related to national security and civil liberties, the narrative changed. Criticism of Obama's masculinity was no longer confined to the Right. In the *Washington Post*, Dana Milbank wrote that Obama is "the victim of bullying. He is bullied by Republicans on health care…by congressional Democrats on everything. He is bullied by his own cabinet….the world's most powerful man too often plays the 98-pound weakling; he gets sand kicked in his face and responds with moot court zinger."[10] MSNBC's Matt Miller developed a list of synonyms for journalists to use when talking about Obama: "Buckle, fold, concede, bend, defer, submit, give in, knuckle under, kowtow, surrender, yield, comply, capitulate."[11]

By the halfway point of Obama's first term, liberals and progressives—once enamored of the charismatic young politician and impressed by his brio—had taken to chastising the president for his "spineless" inability to

CHAPTER 7: 2008: MCCAIN VS. OBAMA

"stand up" to Republican bullies and pass tough banking reform and repeal tax cuts for the wealthy. Something of a consensus had emerged on progressive radio and cable TV shows and the Left blogosphere after his second year in office that Obama was indeed "soft," as his right-wing detractors had long maintained—but for different reasons. He was too eager to compromise with intransigent Republicans, not willing enough to "draw a line in the sand" and hold his ground. As William Greider wrote in *The Nation* magazine, "There is a cloying Boy Scout quality in his style of leadership—the troop leader urging boys to work together on their merit badges—and none of the pigheaded stubbornness of his 'I am the decider' predecessor, nor the hard steel of Lyndon Johnson or the guile of Richard Nixon."[12] As Blow wrote in the *New York Times*,

> Americans want him to identify his core beliefs. It's simple, they want to fully understand his values and how they apply to us as individuals and as a country....Americans respect authenticity and conviction even when they don't fully agree with it. Conviction bespeaks strength; strength bespeaks power; and for better or worse, this is a culture that applauds and is comforted by power.[13]

Former CBS anchor Dan Rather spoke for many when he said

> Obama got into office having run a bold, audacious, campaign and...in the public perception, he began to play it safe. He got a reputation for playing a little soft...What happened is that the perception got out that President Obama was not willing to really stand up in Harry Truman fashion.

After the excitement of his rapid rise and triumph in 2008, he was turning out to be yet another disappointing (male) liberal who lacked the courage to "take off the gloves" and fight for progressive principles.

But if his fighting instincts were suspect in his approach to domestic policy, they were fully on display in his conduct of foreign policy. President Obama's decision to organize and authorize an elite team of Navy Seals to carry out a daring raid in Abbottabad, Pakistan, on May 1, 2011, in which the commandos killed Osama bin Laden while suffering no casualties changed the narrative about his manhood yet again. The targeted assassination dealt a stunning blow to a central tenet of modern right-wing propaganda—that Democrats are inherently timid about the use of force, and thus insufficiently manly to lead the world's most powerful nation. In an exuberant column praising Obama for his leadership on the bin Laden mission, the political journalist and author Peter Beinart wrote that:

> The killing of Osama bin Laden has greater potential to change the Democratic Party's reputation on national security than any single event since Vietnam. It almost perfectly rewrites the narrative of Democratic weakness that Republicans have labored decades to build.... Obama...is now fused in the public imagination with the most successful American military operation since Inchon. Symbolically, it's the opposite of the Carter Iran mission; in fact, it's America's Entebbe.
>
> ...That's what Obama has now given them. He's provided a "U.S.A., U.S.A." moment at a time when Americans hadn't had one for a long time. Three days ago, Republicans were getting ready to run against him for supposedly pursuing a foreign policy doctrine of "leading from behind." Now all those generalities have evaporated. Obama has inoculated himself against charges that he's soft on national security in a more visceral way than any Democrat in decades.[14]

One caller to the (liberal) Stephanie Miller Radio Program summed it up like this: by killing the most wanted man in the world, "Obama went from Urkel to Shaft."

HILLARY CLINTON: ACT LIKE A MAN?

Hillary Clinton's bid for the 2008 Democratic presidential nomination was the most successful run by a woman in the history of US presidential politics. While she did not make it as far as the general election, she won numerous primaries and eighteen million votes, and continued to battle for the nomination until shortly before the Democratic National Convention. Along the way, her candidacy raised numerous questions about the gendered nature of presidential politics, questions that were rarely if ever asked in previous years, when exclusively (white) men vied for power: What does it mean for women presidential candidates that the presidency plays a powerful cultural role in producing and reinforcing masculine norms? Do women have to "act like men" even to be considered, especially to the extent that acting like men means taking tougher stances on issues related to violence, such as those that have been the subject of this book? For example, is it even conceivable that a woman could be elected president if she opposes the death penalty, favors serious cuts in military spending, and/or places greater priority on traditional women's concerns, such as health care and education, rather than issues of foreign policy? Is it possible that a man could be elected on such a platform? In a two-party system that will continue to limit the range of acceptable political alternatives for the foreseeable future, what is the likelihood that the first woman president will be a liberal Democrat, as opposed to a conservative Republican? As *New York Times* columnist Nicholas Kristof wrote in 2005, "Ambitious, high-achieving women are still a turnoff in many areas, particularly if they're liberal and feminist. And that's not just in America: Margaret Thatcher would never have been elected prime minister if she'd been in the Labor Party."[15]

As Yogi Berra says, it is impossible to make predictions—especially about the future. In politics there are simply too many unknown variables, such as the strength of specific candidates, the state of the economy, unforeseen international developments, and a host of other factors. But if the experiences of Hillary Clinton and, to a certain extent, Sarah Palin in 2008 are indicative of what is to come in electoral struggles in the future, a number of relevant questions emerge about the gendered nature of presidential campaigns. For example, in the Democratic primaries, Hillary Clinton, by many accounts, sought to appear tougher than Barack Obama, especially by staking out more aggressive and militaristic positions on issues of foreign policy. James Carville, a Clinton partisan, famously said of Clinton, "If she gave Obama one of her (cojones), they'd both have two." For his part, Obama projected an aura of unflappable cool, refusing to ante up to Clinton's challenges by adopting more aggressive rhetoric.

In a sense, each candidate had adopted a style—whether it came naturally or not—that their gender and race seemed to require, as they embarked on terrain that had previously been reserved for white men. As a woman, Clinton and her campaign team felt she had to prove her masculinity even to be considered. The easiest way to do that was to posture aggressively and signal that she was willing to use the violent power of the state to achieve her foreign policy objectives. As a black man, Obama had to appear in a way more feminine, or at least not as stereotypically masculine, to ease the anxieties of white voters who over the decades had been conditioned to fear the anger and potential violence of black men.

In a 2008 front-page *New York Times* story with the provocative title of "Seeing Grit and Ruthlessness in Clinton's Love of the Fight," Mark Leibovich and Kate Zernike wrote that Clinton was casting herself as a "warrior" for ordinary Americans who need jobs, health care, and cheaper gasoline, while at the same time establishing a contrast with her opponent, suggesting he is an "untested lightweight." Leibovich and Zernike reported that Clinton "mocks Mr. Obama's rhetoric as naïve and challenges him to debate on the back of a flat-bed truck."[16] Further highlighting the boxing metaphor, one of her supporters, North Carolina Governor Michael Easley, said "She makes Rocky Balboa look like a pansy," and an Indiana union leader praised her "testicular fortitude." All of this contributed to an image of Hillary Clinton as a fighter, which contrasted her with Democratic male candidates who have been seen as deficient in that respect by voters in recent decades, to their great electoral disadvantage. Yet, as a woman, Clinton walked a fine line, in part because her aggressiveness reflected a break with traditional femininity. Speaking of all the boxing language that people were using to describe Clinton's candidacy, Leibovich and Zernike (2008) wrote:

> This kind of language and pugilistic imagery…also evokes the baggage that makes Mrs. Clinton such a provocative political figure. For as much as a willingness to 'do what it takes' and 'die hard' are marketable commodities in politics, they can also yield to less flattering qualities, plenty of which have been ascribed to her over the years.[17]

Susan Faludi, meanwhile, pointed out that the aggressive qualities demonstrated by Clinton that some in media were "tut-tutting" were actually the source of her growing popularity with white male voters. While some commentators attributed the erosion of Barack Obama's white male support during the primary battle with Hillary Clinton to racism, Faludi suggested

CHAPTER 7: 2008: MCCAIN VS. OBAMA

that what they failed to see was that Clinton was forcing them "to rethink precepts they've long held about women in politics."[18] Senator Clinton, Faludi wrote,

> Has been converting white males, assuring them that she's come into their tavern not to smash the bottles, but to join the brawl. Deep in the American grain, particularly in the grain of white male working-class voters, *that* is the more trusted archetype. Whether Senator Clinton's pugilism has elevated the current race for the nomination is debatable. But the strategy has certainly remade the political world for future female politicians, who may now cast off the assumption that when the going gets tough, the tough girl will resort to unilateral rectitude. When a woman does ascend through the glass ceiling into the White House, it will be, in part, because of the race of 2008, when Hillary Clinton broke through the glass floor and got down with the boys.[19]

By demonstrating that a woman could earn the respect of millions of men by being a fighter, Hillary Clinton might also have proven that the qualities Americans expect in their president do not depend as much on the biological sex of the person as on the gendered features of their persona. This would be a significant victory for feminism, with one huge qualification: many liberal and more radical feminists have long worked to promote new archetypes of femininity that don't emulate the characteristics of traditional masculinity, but instead define strength in less aggressive and militaristic terms. Many feminists and progressives had thus been disappointed with Clinton, dating back to her early years as a US Senator, when she voted to authorize President George W. Bush's plan to invade Iraq. "Without women's support, her (senate) campaign wouldn't have made it off the ground in the first place," said Carolyn Eisenberg, cofounder of Brooklyn Parents for Peace, a group that petitioned Clinton to speak out against the use of cluster bombs in Iraq. "She wrote the little book about the little village full of sanctimonious statements about the responsibility to protect the young, but when it came down to it, her position is not much better than Bush's. I thought she'd be better."[20]

Across the political spectrum, there seems to be a consensus that the demands placed on women candidates—especially those with presidential aspirations—are much different than those expected of men. This confirms a thesis of this book, because it suggests that the president is not only the nation's chief executive but that he/she plays a powerful symbolic role in the gender order. When a woman runs for president, she carries the dreams of millions of women. But she also inevitably embodies many of the contradictions inherent in a culture that remains conflicted about women's leadership. Marie Wilson, founder of the White House Project, which, according to its website, "aims to advance women's leadership in all communities and sectors—up to the US presidency—by filling the leadership pipeline with a richly diverse, critical mass of women," explained some of the challenges women politicians have with *female* voters in the US "Women want a cross between Mother Theresa, Joan of Arc, Eleanor Roosevelt, and Madonna" in their female officeholders," she said. At the same time, as the journalist Sharon Lerner pointed out, if they appear too strong—or don't, say, temper their competence with personal tidbits about mothering and piggish romantic partners—they get written off as icy and inhuman. Male politicians don't have to walk the same tightrope. "After 9/11, when Giuliani added a dash of caring, they worshipped at his throne," Wilson said. "But women have to do that all the time."[21]

Women also have to pass the commander in chief threshold, since in addition to fighting wars, the US is engaged in global counterterrorism operations with no end in sight. Thus it is important to consider the prospects in coming elections of any candidate for president—woman or man—who does not successfully "measure up" in traditional masculine terms. Are they electable? It might be hard to know if or to what extent concerns about *appearing* strong guide any politician's actions, whether in office or aspiring to one. But questions remain. For example, during the 2008 campaign, to what extent did Senator Obama's promise to increase the US military presence in Afghanistan provide (masculine) cover for his (feminine) opposition to war and occupation in Iraq? Did these campaign commitments, shaped in part by the politics of presidential masculinity, then contribute to policy decisions that have life and death implications for US servicemen and women? Did Obama's aggressive stance on Afghanistan, like his later counterterrorism policies as president, allay concerns by some—especially white men—that he might not be tough enough for the job? Even if he believed firmly that the policy direction he set in Afghanistan was the best way forward in an extremely difficult and possibly hopeless situation, campaigns—in the best of circumstances—weigh a multitude of factors before taking a position. Sometimes decisions are rushed, sometimes they are the well-considered products of deliberative debate. But every decision a presidential candidate makes is political.

Questions about the use of military force—always difficult to begin with—have special significance for potential female presidential candidates. Their burden—especially if they are Democrats—is even greater than it is for men, because *as women* they suffer from categorical discrimination: until they prove otherwise, they are likely to be *perceived* by a significant percentage of the electorate—men and women—as not "masculine" enough to credibly "lead the troops" and keep Americans safe. It is naive to think that such political considerations will play no part in the policy decisions and public statements made by the next woman running for president. It is equally naive to think that such considerations have not always affected men.

Hillary Clinton's historic 2008 campaign unleashed a fury of sexist invective from men who were unsettled by the prospect that a woman might finally succeed at becoming the most powerful person in the country. Her victory would have struck a giant blow for gender equality by undermining the sexist idea that men's proper role was to be in charge—in public as well as private. "Here is the subject of the opposition to women's equality in the state," Elizabeth Cady Stanton wrote. "Men are not ready to recognize it in the home."[22] As the political theorist Corey Robin put it, "Behind the riot in the street or debate in Parliament is the maid talking back to her mistress, the worker disobeying her boss. That is why our political arguments about the family, the welfare state, civil rights and much else touch upon the most personal relations of power."[23] Hillary Clinton came closer than a woman ever has to disrupting the symbolic role of the president as the embodiment of American manhood; pushback was inevitable.

But not all of it came from conservative Republicans. In her first-person narrative about the gender politics of the 2008 campaign, *Big Girls Don't Cry*, Rebecca Traister wrote about ostensibly progressive men whose reaction to Clinton can only be described as misogynous: one man told her friend that whenever he heard the New York senator's voice he had the urge to punch her in the face; another told Traister that when he heard her speak he had the urge to punch her in the uterus.

> I was made uncomfortable by the persistent note of aggression that marked (some progressive men's) reactions to Clinton…Hating Hillary had for decades been the provenance of Republican blowhards, but now men on the left were spewing vitriol about her voice, her views, her presumption—and without realizing it were radicalizing me in my support for Clinton more than the candidate herself ever could have.[24]

What these men's reactions to Hillary Clinton suggest is that many men who support gender equality out of a philosophical commitment to democratic principles are not necessarily comfortable with powerful women on a visceral level. This is one of the key cultural impediments to women's success in politics—and elsewhere. Sheryl Sandberg, the chief operating officer of Facebook, put it this way in a speech to graduating seniors at Barnard College.

> You should also know that there are external forces out there that are holding you back from really owning your success. Studies have shown…that success and likeability are positively correlated for men and negatively correlated for women. This means that as men get more successful and powerful, both men and women like them better. As women get more powerful and successful, everyone, including women, likes them less.[25]

Despite the gender equity gains in recent decades catalyzed by women's movements, men who are liberal and progressive were raised in the same deeply patriarchal society as conservative men. As a result, many of them benefit—as men—from sexism, even those who work actively for equality and social justice. Just the same, it is unfair to characterize some "progressive men's" reactions to Clinton as representative of all progressive men; millions of men vote for women candidates and would vote for a woman as president if given the chance. Many of the eighteen million people who voted for Hillary Clinton were men. The tipping point for the election of a woman president will come when a critical mass of men decides that their commitment to fairness and democratic values—or a specific woman candidate—

overrides any personal discomfort they might feel, and they join with women to elect a woman as the nation's leader.

It's not going to come easily. In coming years, as (presumably) more women enter presidential politics, some of the personal sexism that surfaced in the campaign of 2008 will continue to rear its head, as will some of the gendered obstacles that women candidates face. Take the role of sports in politics, including the role of sports metaphors. Will women candidates need to perfect the language and style of male sportspeak in order to succeed in a political world that is still dominated by men, much as female sportscasters and sportswriters have had to adjust to the male-dominated sports/media complex? It might be too early to tell. As one journalist stated in an article about Hillary Clinton's athletic credentials, "There is no playbook for a woman running for president."[26] Clearly, this is treacherous terrain for women candidates, in part because they are expected to be comfortable with what has been a predominantly (but not exclusively) masculine sports discourse. But they can't be too comfortable, lest they commit the unforgivable sin in politics of appearing "inauthentic." One conundrum for women seeking the presidency is whether or not it is possible to talk—and be talked about—in the violent language of boxing and football metaphors, thus bolstering their image as "tough" enough to be commander in chief, without appearing to be a wanna-be in the jockocratic world of male politics. One woman politician who seems to have worked out some middle ground on this is New York Democratic Senator Kirsten Gillebrand, who started an organization to encourage women to get involved in the decisions that shape their lives in school, the community, and politics. The name of the organization: Off the Sidelines.

One thing is certain: male pundits will use sports metaphors to try to put women candidates in their place, especially if those women have the chutzpah to compete in the "all-boys' club of presidential politics," as Hillary Clinton put it in a speech at her alma mater, Wellesley College. *Fox News* personality Mort Kondracke chided Clinton in the fall of 2007 for supposedly playing the gender card simply for mentioning that it was time for women to roll up their sleeves and get to work in shattering the glass ceiling. "I think it is very unattractive," Kondracke said, "for a general election candidate, who wants to be the commander in chief of the free world, to be saying 'They're ganging up on me!' I mean, this is the NFL. This is not Wellesley versus Smith in field hockey."[27] One woman with relevant knowledge about football and men is Condoleezza Rice, secretary of state in the George W. Bush administration. Rice has stated publicly numerous times that she would like to be commissioner of the National Football League. In a *New York Times* article early in Bush's first term, she asserted that she is a "student of the game," but that despite her knowledge of football and her passion for it, men often underestimate what she knows because she is a woman.[28] Would male voters be comfortable with a woman running for president who knows more about football than many of them? Would women? It remains to be seen. Hillary Clinton is not a football fan. And as an appointed official, Rice has never faced the electorate as a candidate for office.

THE CURIOUS CASE OF SARAH PALIN

Sarah Palin was a guest of Bill O'Reilly's on *The O'Reilly Factor* on her first night as a paid commentator for *Fox News* in 2010. At the end of the show, O'Reilly asked the former governor of Alaska and Republican vice-presidential nominee how she felt the interview had gone. Palin seized the moment. "I was with the Big Man on Campus!" she gushed. Commentary about the Palin *Fox* debut in the blogosphere and elsewhere mentioned this, but few bloggers and pundits seemed to attach any significance to the statement, or to the cultural meanings it conveyed. By contrast, it is precisely those cultural meanings surrounding Palin's flattery, and the gender politics they suggest and advance, which concern me here.

From the moment she was announced as John McCain's vice-presidential pick, Sarah Palin's rapid rise as a cultural-political phenomenon in the reality-TV era has been dissected and debated at length. For example, her emergence as a formidable force in American politics has occasioned a copious amount of hand-wringing among feminists, for whom the elevation of women to positions of public and political authority has been a priority for many decades. Palin presents an obvious problem for people who work for women's advancement, because although she embraces her identity as both a mother and a working woman, she works politically to limit women's rights and freedoms, and generally opposes public policy initiatives that benefit women as a group. But even some of the many women who loathe her nasty and divisive rhetoric and consider her right-wing populism dangerous to democracy nonetheless admire certain of her qualities. As the feminist/progressive writer Amy Alexander put it: "Palin's raw ambition is very close to the self-confidence we want to encourage in our daughters."

But if for many women Palin represents a fascinating twenty-first century fusion of Annie Oakley, June Cleaver, and Caribou Barbie, what does she represent for men? For them, Sarah Palin's popularity even as a *potential* presidential candidate presents a special problem for my central thesis. If the presidency is fundamentally a masculine institution, and many white men's sense of manly identity is bolstered by having a "real man" in the White House, how could they possibly be okay with a woman president? Regardless of what they may tell pollsters, isn't it understandable that many men would have a hard time with a woman standing metaphorically in the shoes of Washington and Lincoln and usurping the historic role of a man as "protector" of the nation? And wouldn't the election of a woman to the highest office in the land strike a massive blow for the goals of feminism, a movement for gender equality that conservatives have fought almost every step of the way?

Moreover, what is the source of Sarah Palin's political appeal specifically to conservative white men—a segment of the electorate one might reasonably assume would be conflicted about the prospect of *any* woman as president of the United States, not to mention one who is regarded as a major sex symbol on the Right? What gendered historical currents converged in her vice-presidential campaign to lead one man at a Palin rally in Indiana to wear a button that said: "Proud to be voting for a hot chick"? Is her political popularity with right-wing men reducible to the fact that she is, in the words of Leslie Savan, a "spokesmodel for conservatism?" But thinking she's good for the movement is not the same thing as supporting her as a candidate for president of the United States, as taking her brains and political views seriously. Listen to *National Review* editor Rich Lowry, after watching Palin's 2008 vice-presidential debate with Joe Biden.

A very wise TV executive once told me that the key to TV is projecting through the screen… Palin… projects through the screen like crazy. I'm sure I'm not the only male in America who, when Palin dropped her first wink, sat up a little straighter on the couch and said 'Hey, I think she just winked at me.' And her smile. By the end, when she clearly knew she was doing well, it was so sparkling it was almost mesmerizing. It sent little starbursts through the screen and ricocheting around the living rooms of America. This is a quality that can't be learned; it's either something you have or you don't, and man, she's got it.[29]

This sounds less like a pundit's assessment of a candidate's charisma than it does an adolescent boy's hopelessly unrequited crush on a hot model or movie star. While Palin is an emblematic reality-TV star for our times, it is important to do our own reality check. Sarah Palin is not just an attractive woman who happens to be a conservative. She was the first woman to be chosen as the vice-presidential nominee of the Republican Party. And from Election Day in 2008 until the candidate filing deadline came and went in 2011, she was on every pundit's short list of the top competitors for the 2012 GOP presidential nomination.

Presumably, something about Sarah Palin as a woman and as a political figure compensates for, or neutralizes, the aversion many conservative white men have for independent women as leaders. Or maybe those men don't have an aversion to all independent women—only to moderately liberal women like Hillary Clinton, who refuse to assuage men's egos and make them feel as if they're still in charge. Many conservative men experience that kind of woman as emasculating, a fear that was (in)famously articulated by TV personality Tucker Carlson, who said that when Hillary comes on television, he involuntarily crosses his legs. Which brings us back to Palin's "Big Man on Campus" comment.

Palin's use of that term evokes the idealized white suburban world of the 1950s that plays such a powerful role in the right-wing cultural imagination. It especially conjures up images of the prefeminist gender order, where the most popular boys were jocks and the most popular girls aspired to be cheer-leaders—and there was no confusion about which sex was on the field and which was on the sidelines cheering. Feminism and the 1960s challenged those social norms, both by objecting to the unquestioned subservience of women in that sexist arrangement and by emphasizing women's right to engage in their own athletic contests. One of the many ironies of Palin's political career is that she developed the self-confidence to bash liberals in

CHAPTER 7: 2008: MCCAIN VS. OBAMA

part by playing sports that were opened to women as a result of the passionate activism of liberal feminists.

Right-wing women such as Palin and Michelle Bachmann manage to be strong and assertive without raising the hackles of conservative men because they don't ask anything of men, except of course for their votes. For her part, Bachmann—who was the only woman to compete in the Republican primaries in 2012 and even briefly enjoyed front-runner status—made it clear that while she openly sought political power, in the private realm she willingly submitted to her husband. Katherine Marsh explained in The *New Republic* that Palin ran for vice president as "a spunky can-do Republican-style feminist mom who meets challenges head-on instead of whining about them," a type of femininity that appeals to antifeminist men who see organized efforts to promote gender equity as "whining." Rush Limbaugh often refers to the National Organization for Women as the National Association of Gals, or "NAG." Limbaugh is a big fan of Palin's, even though he has continued to undermine her attempts to achieve something approaching political gravitas by repeatedly sexualizing her. The enormously influential talker refers to Palin as a "babe," and compares her favorably with other "annoying" female politicians whom he likens to men's first wives. By contrast, he said of Palin that "she's not going to remind anybody of their ex-wife, she's going to remind men 'Gee, I wish she was single.'" During the 2008 campaign, she also gave him one of his favorite lines, which allowed him to masquerade as a supporter of women even as he played his familiar bullying role toward Democratic men. After Obama won the Democratic nomination, Limbaugh stated repeatedly on his radio program, "I don't think Barack Obama is half the man Sarah Palin is."

But Palin's attractiveness to conservative white men goes beyond the obvious fact that she is skilled at advocating right-wing positions which never threaten men's power or prerogatives. Precisely because she is a charismatic, photogenic woman who holds conservative views, she simultaneously serves two critical functions: (1) she reinforces the right-wing myth—advanced by Ann Coulter and trumpeted perhaps most loudly in mass media by Rush Limbaugh—that conservative women are attractive, sexy, and presumably know how to please men, in contrast to liberal feminist women, who are supposedly physically unattractive and likely to be hostile to men, and (2) she routinely attacks the masculinity of liberal and progressive men, which serves to stroke the egos of conservative men, whose manhood she implicitly and explicitly praises. Consider Palin's national coming-out speech at the 2008 Republican National Convention, where 98 percent of the delegates were white, and 68 percent were men. In that speech, from which she emerged as a major figure on the Right and in the Republican Party, she managed to both ridicule and subtly feminize Obama: "I guess—I guess a small-town mayor is sort of like a community organizer, except that you have actual responsibilities," or "My fellow citizens, the American presidency is not supposed to be a journey of personal discovery." As the philosopher Slavoj Zizek wrote, Palin "has a 'castrating' effect on her male opponents not by way of being more manly than them, but by using the ultimate feminine weapon, the sarcastic put-down of puffed-up male authority—she knows that male 'phallic' authority is a posture, a semblance to be exploited and mocked."[30]

At the same time that she demeaned Obama, she made it clear that John McCain was the true man in the race.

> ...though both Senator Obama and Senator Biden have been going on lately about how they're always, quote, "fighting for you," let us face the matter squarely: There is only one man in this election who has ever really fought for you. There is only one man in this election who has ever really fought for you in places where winning means survival and defeat means death. And that man is John McCain.

Since Palin was not at the top of the ticket in 2008, it remains to be seen—if she ever runs for president—if the benefits she offers conservative men as an attack dog for the Right will trump their reticence to upend tradition by nominating a woman to do what many still consider a man's job.

POSTSCRIPT TO THE 2008 ELECTION

Race and gender have long played a powerful subtextual role in US politics, but until the 2008 election, their importance had not been fully acknowledged in popular commentary or academic discourse. Because every election until 2008 featured a contest between two (or three) representatives of the dominant white male culture, issues of race and gender in the political struggle remained largely invisible. The 2008 campaign represented a break with that historic pattern for two reasons. The first was that Hillary Clinton's bid for the Democratic presidential nomination was the most successful run by a woman in the history of US presidential politics. While she did not make it as far as the general election, she won numerous primaries and eighteen million votes, and continued to battle for the nomination until shortly before the Democratic National Convention. Along the way, her candidacy raised numerous questions about the gendered nature of presidential politics, questions that were rarely, if ever, asked in previous years when exclusively (white) men vied for power.

The second difference demarcating the 2008 presidential campaign was the emergence of an African American, Barack Obama, as the standard bearer for the Democratic Party. Obama's campaign for the Democratic nomination, and his subsequent run against Republican John McCain, forced the issue of race into the foreground of political discourse. Race had long been a subtextual factor in US presidential politics, and the Reverend Jesse L. Jackson's Democratic primary runs in 1984 and 1988 brought the presidential politics of race right up to the surface. But Obama's success elevated it to an unprecedented centrality. The success of Clinton and Obama made visible what historically had been hidden in plain sight. In every previous presidential campaign, voters had the choice between two (or three) white men, a homogeneity that was a predictable consequence of the longstanding dominance of white Protestant Christian masculinity in the US political elite.

Throughout the 2008 primary season and into the general election, conservative commentators, talk radio hosts, and assorted right-wing ideologues chastised the Democratic electorate for considering race and gender when deciding whom to support. Their intent was to shame Democratic voters for voting (at least in part) on the basis of something as superficial as the color of someone's skin or their biology. Not coincidentally, this strategy helped to keep people's attention off the Right's obsession with the whiteness and masculinity of their own candidates. As Rudy Giuliani is fond of saying about terrorism, when you stay on offense, it's a lot easier to play defense. Meanwhile on the Left, the concern was not the focus on race and gender, but the historic tensions *between* them. Would the first black (male) president precede the first (white) woman?

LEADING MEN

But as noted throughout this book, race and gender have always mattered in presidential elections. The big difference was the "race" that always mattered was whiteness, and the gender was men. Without those credentials, potential candidates didn't stand a chance. Voters did not get to choose among the widest possible range of qualified candidates; they got to choose between two (or three) white men. No matter how smart or capable they might have been, women have never made it to the "final round" of consideration for the top job in government, because their gender prevented people from seeing them as "presidential." If there was one thing that truly represented "change" in the historic election season of 2008 it was the change in what it means to appear "presidential." In the past, whether a candidate was a Republican or Democrat, conservative, centrist, or liberal, their race and gender were predetermined. They were inevitably—and invariably— white and a man. But the pathbreaking candidacies of Barack Obama and Hillary Clinton forced a shift in the definition of "presidential." Tens of millions of Democratic primary voters cast ballots for these candidates, thus casting aside the limitations inherent in the old idea of the American president as the embodiment of white patriarchal authority. Obama, of course, was elected president. And as Clinton herself said in her historic 2008 concession speech,

> I know there are still barriers and biases out there, often unconscious. You can be so proud that, from now on, it will be unremarkable to have a woman in a close race to be our nominee, unremarkable to think that a woman can be the president of the United States. And that is truly remarkable.

Chapter 8
2012 and Beyond

Throughout this book I have argued that in order to understand American presidential politics, one has to be aware of how gender operates not only in the candidacies and voting behavior of women but also in the psyches and political preferences of men. Presidential scholars and journalists alike have identified a number of variables that predict electoral outcomes—the economy, foreign policy crises, money—but they've missed one of the biggest. As I have recounted, much contemporary political analysis fails to account adequately for the powerful influence that cultural ideas about manhood exert on who becomes president and what they can accomplish once they get there.

It has been forty years since Richard Nixon found, in Rick Perlstein's words, the "magic incantation" that helped drive millions of white working-class men to the right in a time of rapid cultural change. Perlstein didn't name it as such, but the "magic" was manhood—white manhood. The civil rights, women's, and gay rights movements might have represented a major step forward for participatory democracy, but they also constituted a serious threat to the cultural position of white men—especially, in a time of growing economic uncertainty, those who were not insulated by class privilege. By no means were all white men threatened by these movements; many Baby Boomer and Gen Xer men embraced the changes as an opportunity to move beyond the limitations of the old John Wayne template for "real manhood." For example, over the past generation millions of men have forged new models of partnership with women in their personal and professional lives; struggled to develop and sustain emotionally connected relationships with their children; and adjusted to—and sometimes embraced—sexual diversity among their family members, friends, and colleagues.

But cultural openings often prompt closings as well, and there has been a well-documented backlash to the epochal progressive social movements of the 1960s and 1970s. Many white men have responded angrily to their loss of status and what they perceive to be a rejection of their values. Throughout the seventies they fought back with the assistance of a burgeoning conservative movement that gave voice and political expression to their grievances and resentments. The election of Ronald Reagan in 1980 marked the political return to power of a certain kind of old-school white masculinity, wedded to the past and to a romanticized vision of benevolent patriarchy. Starting in the nineties this culturally backward-looking movement has had the benefit of a vast conservative media empire based in cable TV, talk radio, and publishing. To this day, the conservative cultural backlash can be felt across American society, including in presidential politics, where the "culture wars" flare virtually every election cycle, and where struggles over the meaning of (white) manhood have played out for more than a generation.

Since 1968, when Richard Nixon was first elected president in the midst of cataclysmic events at home and abroad, there have been eleven presidential elections. For those keeping score, the Republicans are leading the Democrats seven to four. But like a sports event where the final score is misleading because it doesn't adequately convey the reality that one team was in control throughout, that tally does not do justice to how much the Republican Party, and the conservative movement in general, has been able to slow, derail, and sometimes reverse the progress toward racial, gender, and sexual equality—however uneven and messy that progress might have been—which grew out of the 1960s. It is no great secret or surprise that white men have been the driving force behind this resistance to change.

This is not just historical analysis. The appeals to white racial identity and traditional manhood that Nixon employed so skillfully in the early seventies are still potent factors today. While the backdrop is economic anxiety, in the cultural realm masculinity is still the litmus. Candidates for the presidency are still judged as to whether they "measure up" to certain standards of manliness, and presidential campaigns are still fertile ground for cultural dialogue and debate about the leadership roles and identities of men and women.

Consider the strange political career of Willard "Mitt" Romney, who ran for the Republican nomination in 2008 and was the "last man standing" after a bruising primary battle in 2012. The lengths to which Romney went to prove his manhood to the Republican base reveal just how potent a force gender remains in American politics. In his relentless quest for the White House, Romney not only flip-flopped repeatedly on policy issues related to women's and gay rights; he also changed basic elements of his personal narrative—the stories he told about himself that provide insight into who he is as a person and as a man. One of the more remarkable features of the 2012 GOP presidential nominating process was how much effort their presumptive nominee went through to reassure the party's populist conservative base that he was man enough for the job, which for reasons of class and culture many of them simply refused to accept.

The upper-class Romney had trouble connecting with working-class elements in the Republican Party at least as much for personal as for ideological reasons. On the personal side, the sixty-five-year-old father of five is a very wealthy businessman with an elite educational pedigree, including not one but two graduate degrees from Harvard. He grew up in a rich and well-connected Mormon family, didn't serve in the military, and has never held a blue-collar job. Unfortunately for him, he is not identified as a fan or participant in any blue-collar sports, which could help build a cultural bridge to working-class voters. He was elected governor of liberal Massachusetts in 2002 as a moderate Republican. In other words, with the exception of his somewhat exotic Mormonism, he is seen by some as an effete country club Republican, the kind that the conservative movement has been trying to purge from the party's leadership for the past thirty years.

Romney's record as a moderate who once supported abortion rights and gay rights makes him ideologically suspect to the Far Right, as does his technocratic approach to problem solving. Moreover, when he's taken a hard right turn on cultural or policy issues to placate rabid conservatives, he can't seem to convey authentic passion for those positions. This is perhaps most glaringly evident when it comes to the politics of gun ownership and the gender politics of hunting. As Massachusetts governor, Romney supported the Brady gun control law and signed a tough assault weapons ban. "That's not going to make me the hero of the NRA," he said at the time.[1] But when he decided to run for president, Romney knew that he would need the votes of white men (and women) in the Republican base for whom extremist interpretations of the Second Amendment *and* a robust endorsement of hunting were unofficial litmus tests, not only of an establishment candidate's antielitist credentials but also of his manhood. So he switched his positions on gun control measures and tried to sell himself as a hunter. Even for a politician as famously unprincipled as Romney, his attempts to use guns to toughen up his image were especially awkward and transparent.

Take his evolving stories about hunting. Out on the campaign trail during his race for the 2008 Republican nomination, he said "I purchased a gun when I was a young man. I've been a hunter pretty much all my life." Soon after he made that statement, an aide acknowledged that Romney had hunted only twice in his life, once with his cousins at age fifteen, and the second nearly forty-five years later on an outing with major donors to the Republican Governors Association in 2006. In addition, he was ridiculed by late night comedians and across the blogosphere when he talked about the kinds of animals he liked to kill: "I'm not a big-game hunter," he said. "I've made it very clear, I've always been a… rodent and rabbit hunter, all right? Small, small varmints. I also hunted quail in Georgia, so…it's not really big-game hunting…it's not deer and large animals. But I've hunted a number of times …various types of small rodents." Since killing small rodents is not the stuff of heroic manhood, in preparation for his 2012 run, Romney clearly knew he would need to add large animals to his repertoire. In 2012, Romney acknowledged that he's still "not the great hunter," but he was happy to say he had added "elk hunting" in Montana.

Misrepresenting himself as an enthusiastic hunter is only one of Mitt Romney's tactics for reaching out to working- and middle-class white male voters. For years, Romney has been trying to convince Republicans that he is his generation's Ronald Reagan: an older white man with movie star looks who can sell sunny optimism and project a can-do spirit to Americans who want to believe that our best days lie ahead. On the purely superficial level of televisual image, there is a case to be made. But sunny optimism was never the sole source of Reagan's electoral appeal to the Republican base. What they loved was his performance of old-school authoritarian masculinity—and his willingness to attack liberalism and central tenets of the New Deal consensus head on. From the moment he delivered his famous speech in the waning days of Barry Goldwater's failed but ultimately catalytic campaign in

1964, the right wing loved Ronald Reagan not because he was so nice but because he effectively—and sometimes aggressively—expressed their hostility to social unrest and disorder, and to the democratic changes that were transforming American culture. In addition, Reagan drew a great measure of his political strength through the 1960s and 1970s from whites—in the South and beyond—who harbored deep-seated racial resentments as a result of the stunning successes of the civil rights movement. In fact, Reagan's first speech after accepting the nomination for president in 1980 was in Philadelphia, Mississippi, the site of the infamous murders of three civil rights workers in 1964, and in that speech he proclaimed his support for states' rights.

What made Reagan so effective politically beyond the fevered precincts of the Right was that he was able to provide cover for that right-wing and racist animus through his actor's ability to play the role of the nation's leading man in a way that articulated conservative resistance to gains made by blacks, women, and gays without coming across as overtly racist, sexist, or homophobic. But Reagan's anger shone through when he needed it to. Although it is barely mentioned in the glut of revisionist romanticism about him that has appeared in the media since his death in 2004, Reagan was a "law and order" politician who talked tough and favored harsh treatment not only for criminals but for antiwar protesters. Consider as well that one of the most memorable and quoted lines of Reagan's presidency was at the Brandenburg Gate in Berlin in 1987 when he told Soviet General Secretary Mikhail Gorbachev to "tear down this wall!" This was Reagan the aggressive cold warrior at his best, not the genial old man of blessed memory. Whether one admired or was repulsed by the positions he took on matters foreign and domestic, it is undeniable that Reagan's ability to project anger was highly attractive to his most passionate supporters on the Far Right—and crucial to his political success.

During his runs for the GOP presidential nomination, Mitt Romney has done a good job of mimicking Reagan's antigovernment diatribes and "better days ahead" rhetoric. But unlike Reagan, whose anger by all accounts was authentic, Romney is utterly unbelievable when he adopts a more aggressive tone. He's too Ned Flanders to come off as Winston Churchill. In the 2012 primary season, this was especially easy to see in contrast to one of his main rivals, Newt Gingrich. At one GOP debate in Iowa there was a back and forth between Romney and Gingrich that exemplified this critical difference between them and that accentuated one of Romney's greatest political weaknesses. The topic was Gingrich's statement that the Palestinians were an "invented people." Sensing that he could exploit Gingrich's lack of rhetorical discipline on a foreign policy issue that called for diplomatic subtlety, Romney said that if he were president, he would exercise "sobriety, care, stability" in his handling of the Israeli-Palestinian conflict. "I'm not a bomb thrower," he continued, "rhetorically or literally."

Gingrich pounced on the opportunity to outman Romney. "I think sometimes that it's helpful to have a president of the United States who has the courage to tell the truth," he said. He then made reference to Reagan's once-controversial statement that the Soviet Union was an "evil empire," and pointed out how Reagan had overruled his own State Department to make his famous "tear down that wall" comment. "I'm proud to be a Reaganite," Gingrich declared. "I will tell the truth, even if it's at the risk of causing some confusion sometimes with the timid."

According to conventional wisdom, Gingrich temporarily surged in the polls because conservatives were looking for an alternative to Mitt Romney. First it was Donald Trump, then Michelle Bachmann, then Rick Perry, then Herman Cain, then the former Speaker, and finally Rick Santorum having his turn in the spotlight. According to this view, Romney was too much of a flip-flopper to be ideologically trustworthy, and the Tea Party was in no mood to compromise on "conservative" principles. But something more elemental and visceral was at work. The last men standing, Gingrich and Santorum, were often described as "throwing red meat" to the Republican base. Unlike Romney, who made a point of saying he was not a "bombthrower," Gingrich was popular with the Republican base precisely because he was. The violence of these metaphors is not coincidental. The right wing of the Republican Party is restive and angry; they get this way whenever a Democrat is in the White House. But this time, fueled by the apocalyptic rhetoric on conservative talk radio ("America as we know it is finished if Obama is reelected") a frightening number of white conservatives actually imagine themselves to be warriors in a battle to save Western civilization. For conservatives who saw the 2012 election as a cultural war, Romney's aw-shucks Mormonism was always a hard sell, not because he wasn't saying the "right" thing on issues but because he wasn't a credible enough "man's man," and temperamentally he could never adequately give voice to their rage.

THE TWILIGHT OF WHITE MEN'S RULE?

If demography is truly destiny, it is quite possible that debates about how to win the votes of white men will eventually become obsolete, and the role of presidential elections as referenda on manhood correspondingly diminished. In fact, the journalist Thomas Schaller argued in 2007 that the white male vote, while still important, has become increasingly less of a factor in electoral outcomes. "The Democratic obsession with the down-home, blue-collar, white male voter, that heartbreaker who crossed the aisle to the Republicans many decades ago, may finally be coming to a merciful end," Schaller wrote.

> The underlying reason may be demographics. In 1952…white males were nearly half the American electorate. Thanks to the recent growth in the Latino population, however, the white male share is now dropping about a percentage point a year… accelerating a decline that began with the increased enfranchisement of African-Americans in the civil rights era. In next year's election, white males may account for fewer than one out of three voters. Bubba is no longer a kingmaker.[2]

In the long run, Schaller's prediction might prove true. Not only are white males gradually losing political influence relative to other segments of the electorate, but if current demographic patterns continue, in the future the presidency itself will not be such a flashpoint for cultural clashes around the meaning of manhood. In a symbolic sense, the election of the first African American president was a major milestone in this historic process; the next gigantic step will be the election of the first woman. But the gendered forces in presidential elections that I have described in this book will be with us for decades. This presents liberals and progressives with a choice: try to win presidential elections with only a small percentage of the white male vote by building a coalition of women, people of color, and young people, as Obama managed to do in 2008. Or try to learn from the Right's success with white men in presidential elections over the past generation, and fashion a politics with an accompanying narrative that speaks compassionately to the concerns and unsettled identities of white men—especially those who have been downwardly mobile.

For forty years conservatives have won presidential elections in part by marketing themselves as the party of white men who are fighting to hold onto an idealized and mythologized past, when people like them felt they were at the center of the universe, and no one questioned how or why they deserved to be in that position. That earlier, simpler time was exemplified and embodied in the person of Ronald Reagan, to whom all subsequent Republican nominees are inevitably, and unfavorably, compared. This is the kind of identity politics that drives progressives crazy, especially because it provides cover for attacks by the ownership class on workers' wages and benefits—and deflects attention away from the Right's efforts to dramatically cut programs that serve the needs of working families, in a time of growing wealth inequality and widespread economic insecurity. But smokescreen or not, the Right presents white men with a coherent narrative that explains their lost glory and diminished status, and voting Republican gives them a way to vent their anger and resentment.

It is important to emphasize that the twenty-first century Republican Party does not deploy its reactionary ideology solely as an electoral marketing strategy; it is also a critical part of the party's extremist social issues agenda. Since the triumph of the conservative movement in the 1980 election of Reagan, the GOP has led the fight against women's rights in the legislative and judicial realms. For more than thirty years feminist organizations have had to fight merely to retain rights that American women had already won. The Iranian human rights activist and Nobel Peace Prize winner Shirin Ebadi said that "although the 1979 revolution in Iran is often called an Islamic revolution, it can actually be said to be a revolution of men against women."[3] An analogous dynamic is present here in the Republican "war on women." While the GOP may not be as extreme as the mullahs, the success of the rabidly antifeminist Rick Santorum in the 2012 primaries is a chilling reminder that the modern Republican Party is the electoral home of a movement that wants to roll back the feminist gains of the twentieth century and reestablish men's collective power over women through laws that would strip women not only of their reproductive rights but of many other state supports and legal protections as well.

Mitt Romney's selection of far-right wing Wisconsin Congressman Paul Ryan as his vice-presidential running-mate confirmed this backward slide. Ryan, an unapologetic apostle of rugged individualism and unfettered capitalism who required his staff to read the novels of the right-wing writer Ayn Rand, is best-known for his budget-cutting zeal and plans to replace the popular Medicare program with a system of vouchers. But Ryan's adherence to outdated notions of manhood go beyond his Randian belief in "every man for himself" and extend to his rejection of women's rights to control their reproduction. Ryan not only opposes abortion in cases of rape, incest, and in some cases even threats to the life of the mother, but he also co-sponsored a "fetal personhood" amendment with Missouri Republican Congressman Todd Akin, the 2012 US senate candidate who caused an uproar when he said that women couldn't get pregnant by a "legitimate rape."

For women *and* men who take certain fundamental precepts of gender and sexual equality for granted, the radicalism of Republican attempts to repeal hard-won rights and at the same time unravel the social safety net is breathtaking and alarming. But there are many ways, both in and outside of the Democratic Party, to fight back.

PRESIDENTIAL MANHOOD: NEW MEDIA, NEW NARRATIVES

The first step is to shine a bright critical spotlight on the role of gender in politics. That does not mean simply calling out the sexist ways that women candidates are targeted for criticism about their looks, what they wear, how they make insecure men feel uncomfortable, etc. Challenging sexist commentary about women in politics—from the Right or the Left—is important. But it is not the only place gender needs to be on the agenda. Focusing on gender also means making masculinity visible by exposing the mechanisms—structural and symbolic—through which (white) men maintain such disproportionate power in national politics. It also means identifying and countering cultural biases not only against women in positions of leadership but against certain types of men.

For example, in the same way that sexist commentary about women in politics needs to be criticized and stigmatized as socially unacceptable, pundits and other opinion-makers need to identify attacks on a candidate's manhood as off-limits as well. This goes for both sides, but as I have recounted throughout this book, the Republicans have been doing it much longer, and more effectively, than the Democrats. Repeated right-wing criticism of President Obama as a "weak and timid" president might fall within the bounds of acceptable political discourse in the contemporary period, but in their broader societal context they are a form of bullying through the mass media. It is one thing for candidates and others engaged in electoral contests to accentuate policy differences and engage in robust debate about them. Strong differences of opinion and heated arguments are intrinsic to the practice of democracy. It is even understandable and perhaps inevitable that with the stakes so high, attacks (on both sides) can often get personal. But personal attacks degrade the democratic process and send a powerful message beyond the political realm that it's okay to taunt and make fun of the gender, and sexuality, of people with whom you disagree. Bullying tactics should be as unacceptable in politics as they are on the playground. What kind of moral standing do we have to teach children not to ridicule or shame boys or girls who do not measure up to some idealized standard of "manhood" or "womanhood" when leading politicians regularly do that very thing?

Right-wing bullying and name-calling are not just damaging because of the message they send to children. They also give conservatives a tactical advantage by driving presidential politics to the right, as candidates from both major parties try to prove they're "tough" enough for the job, usually by advocating increasingly more conservative solutions to domestic and foreign policy problems. To the extent that millions of white male voters continue to equate liberal policies with emasculation and weakness, it will always be difficult to attract their support for a wide range of progressive initiatives related to fair taxation, education, health care, the prison industrial complex, reductions in military spending to a level commensurate with our actual security needs in the world; and a host of other issues.

An indispensable component of any effort to make gender visible in presidential campaigns—even when, as I have pointed out, it's a race between two men—is to have more women writing and talking politics in print and on TV and radio. Currently the media deck is stacked heavily against women. Women comprise only from 10 to 20 percent of op-ed writers at major media outlets; a spring 2012 survey showed women were 20 percent of writers at Salon.com, and even at the woman-owned and led *Huffington Post* the female percentage was only 31 percent. It's even worse on television. One study of Sunday morning TV talk shows during one month in 2012 found that out of a total of fifty-six guests booked to discuss national affairs, fifty-two were men. And this was during a month when the issues of birth control and women's access to health care became major topics of debate on the presidential campaign trail![4] Of course there are women and people of color who espouse conservative perspectives on gender and politics and are "cheerleaders for the patriarchy." But generally speaking women bring a different lens to politics than men. The feminist philosopher Sandra Harding offers this explanation: as outsiders to dominant institutions such as politics and media, women have insight into the gendered ways those institutions function. Women are more likely, for example, to recognize the "masculine" character of the institution of the presidency, which often remains invisible to male journalists and political thinkers, "whose life patterns and ways of thinking fit all too closely the dominant institutions and conceptual schemes."[5] At the very least, women are more likely than men to raise matters of gender, in much the same way that people of color would be more likely to raise the topic of race. Women of color are uniquely positioned in this regard, but they're even less likely than white women to have a platform from which to be heard in the cultural mainstream.

In the academic field of political science, the subfield of presidential scholarship is heavily dominated by men, for whom gender is rarely a central line of inquiry. As we have seen in previous chapters, men who write, speak or produce scholarly works about presidential politics typically avoid questions of gender even as they highlight the importance of other variables related to identity: class, race, ethnicity, religion—as if such factors do not themselves contain gendered elements worth exploring. Even when they do talk about gender, most people in the mainstream cultural/political commentariat, as well as in academia, fail to grasp the necessity of looking at the presidency as a "masculine" institution and men as gendered beings, and instead confine their analyses to women. It is notable, if not surprising, that the intellectual foundations for much of the journalistic and scholarly work about masculinity and politics that is beginning to emerge has been done by women.

Feminist perspectives have historically been marginalized in political discourse inside and outside academia, but the growth in political importance of the Internet, Web, and blogosphere has already begun to change this. Feminist bloggers have a vibrant and expanding presence in online political discourse, and as a result increasing political influence. A case in point was the moment early in 2012 when Republican Committee Chairman Darrel Issa refused to let Georgetown University law student Sandra Fluke testify on a panel in a congressional hearing on "religious liberty" and the Obama administration's proposed mandate on insurance coverage of birth control. The panel was all-male, reinforcing the idea that conservatives who oppose women's reproductive freedom are also contemptuous of women's input. But instead of this being a one-day story that got lost in the shuffle of a crowded 24/7 news cycle, the photo of the all-male panel went viral, and the story of Fluke's exclusion lit up in the feminist blogosphere. When Fluke ended up testifying at a hearing organized by congressional Democrats, Rush Limbaugh went on a misogynous tirade against her for three consecutive days, calling her, among other things, a slut and a prostitute. Limbaugh's rant became a major news story itself, fueling the Republican "war on women" theme that Democrats hoped would draw female voters away from the GOP. It is conceivable that this story would have been big news in the days before the feminist blogosphere, but it's unlikely it would have exploded in the way it did without the online activism of women who were no longer hampered by their lack of access to forums in mainstream media.

For all of the reasons listed above, it is important to amplify women's voices in political journalism, commentary, and scholarship. But campaign ads are still by far the most influential media force shaping presidential races, and the gendered discourse about the candidates and parties they represent. It is a central article of faith in progressive circles that without radical campaign finance reform, little can really change in presidential politics. In a process that is dominated by media-driven narratives, private interests simply have too much money and power to influence the stories that are told, and thus shape not only the terms of debate for millions of voters but the very configuration of reality. This is especially true since the Supreme Court's 2009 *Citizens United* decision gave wealthy corporations and individuals nearly carte blanche to influence the political process. It bears mentioning that the vast sums of money that are spent on modern elections go largely to purchase TV and increasingly web-based advertising, which, as discussed earlier, typically appeal to voters' emotions, as well as their cultural and tribal identities. As noted in chapter one, paid political advertising by campaigns and their surrogates constitutes one of the chief vehicles through which contests about presidential manhood take place. A prime example are political ads that play on people's fears. These ads directly manipulate voters' gender identifications and anxieties and thus are especially ripe for exploitation; mountains of research in political communication demonstrates that audiences that are made to feel afraid are more likely to respond by supporting politicians who appear tough or are more willing to pursue aggressive, get-tough tactics or militaristic policies. Systemic and far-reaching campaign finance reform is a necessary step to change this system that fundamentally distorts democracy by deemphasizing substantive debate and turning elections into little more than brand wars between armies of wealthy individuals and corporate interests.

Many promising strategies and initiatives are percolating for the reform and limitation of the corrupting role of money in politics. Until sweeping campaign finance reform is achieved, activists, educators and others who are concerned about the degradation of democracy can initiate a call for media literacy education to be integrated into all levels of civic education—from grade school to graduate school, and anywhere else people learn about the political system. In a political culture that is dominated by media, it is simply unthinkable that students or others could be educated about politics or American government without developing the analytic tools with which to identify how conventions of political coverage, as well as established practices in paid media, help to frame narratives and shape the identities of candidates and voters. Powerful tools of critical media literacy have been developed over the past thirty years; many of them analyze cultural messages about gender that are encoded into popular media and entertainment, such as the work of Jean Kilbourne on the representation of women in advertising. My own work looks at images of masculinity in media, and how mainstream portrayals help to normalize violence and tough guy posing. *Political* media literacy education would need, of course, to include explicit attention to the ways that gender is represented in the images and rhetoric of presidential politics.

Any serious attempt to analyze how presidential masculinity is represented in media must grapple with the sweeping changes in the technologies and economics of media that have come about in recent decades. The old

CHAPTER 8: 2012 AND BEYOND

model is long obsolete of an all-powerful corporate news-delivery system that consisted of a few major television broadcast networks, along with newspapers and radio networks, controlling the images and representations available to citizen-voters. The proliferation of cable TV, and then in the past two decades the rise of the Internet, have contributed to a significant decline in viewership for the major television networks, and significant decreases in the readership of traditional newspapers. Corporate downsizing in news divisions and economic restructuring in traditional broadcast and print journalism, together with the rise of talk radio and the increased cultural presence of "infotainment" have combined to create a new media landscape that is changing how presidents are represented and talked about in media. Perhaps most importantly, the interactivity of new media and information technologies through the Internet, such as blogs, bulletin boards, wikis, YouTube, and social networking sites such as Facebook and Twitter are providing new opportunities for online political organizing and fundraising, and rendering obsolete more traditional ways of doing, as well as analyzing, politics.

One result of this shift toward more interactivity in media and information technology is there are now more means available to resist and counteract dominant narratives of presidentiality. For example, feminist netroots activists can challenge and contest the masculine mythification processes that often characterize coverage of US presidents in mainstream media, especially during wartime. There is also more space on the Internet for positive representations of "alternative" masculinities, such as anti-war, profeminist, and queer masculinities, all of which are marginalized and confined—if not openly ridiculed and dismissed—in the mainstream. But if new media enables feminist voices that would have been excluded by the gatekeepers of the old media, they also give a platform to antifeminist men (and women) who can anonymously attack candidates on blogs, Listservs, and elsewhere with aggressively misogynistic rhetoric that can be abusive and harassing. A relatively new obstacle to women's advancement in politics is the open misogyny that female candidates regularly encounter online. Furthermore, in an online culture that is saturated with both the stylistic and rhetorical excesses of pornography, women candidates are often not only objectified in the crudest ways imaginable but are also barraged with messages of sexualized aggression, which creates yet another disincentive for women to challenge men in the public arena of politics.

LEADING MEN

Howard Dean's 2004 campaign pioneered the use of new media in presidential elections, but Barack Obama's campaign in 2008 took the new communications technologies to new heights of influence. Obama raised an unprecedented amount of money on the Internet, generated over two million friends on Facebook and 866,887 friends on MySpace and reportedly had a campaign Listserv of over ten million email addresses, enabling his campaign to mobilize youth and others through text messaging and emails.[6] In 2012 his campaign and Mitt Romney's are likely to far surpass those numbers. It is sobering to note that the enhanced democratic image-making enabled by new media technologies will not necessarily result in the triumph of dramatically alternative types of presidential masculinities. Alas, as the late Andrew Breitbart and a new generation of right-wing media activists have demonstrated, individuals and groups with an ideological investment in maintaining traditional white male power have access to the same technologies and are getting more and more adept at using them.

BUILD IT AND THEY WILL COME

For years, conventional wisdom in the Democratic political establishment and mainstream media held that the party needed to moderate its policy agenda and move to the center in order to capture the votes of independents and nonideological centrists. This advice stood in stark contrast to the complaint by many on the left that the Democrats needed to advocate more aggressively for the interests of working and middle-class families, against the party of the 1 percent. This criticism often took the form of bodily metaphors that signified strength and virility: they need to *show some backbone*, they need to *grow a pair!*

Since the 1960s the Right has tried to feminize liberalism as a mushy, emotionally driven ideology, in stark contrast to the hard-headed realism of conservative thought. From the days of anti-Vietnam War senator George McGovern's presidential candidacy, men who lean left have been ridiculed by conservatives as "wimpy liberals," a phrase that many on the Right regard as redundant. At the same time, progressive activists and others to the left of the Democratic establishment have long lamented the rightward drift of the party, and the capitulation of many of its leading figures on issues of concern to the base, and in some cases to majorities of voters. To many on the left,

Democrats don't need to be cautious; they need to nominate candidates—men and women—who are willing to provide bold leadership in the service of social justice, human rights at home and abroad, and basic ideas of equality and fairness. In other words, they don't need more moderation; they need to move *to the left*. Many progressives who supported Barack Obama in 2008 had just this in mind, which is why so many were disappointed by the compromises and capitulations in his first term, on everything from labor issues, to health insurance reform, to the stimulus bill and the debt ceiling showdown, as well as all of his broken promises on matters of civil liberties and the expansion of the national security state.

At first glimpse these contrasting critiques present what might appear to be a paradox: how can the Right attack the manhood of liberals, while at the same time the Left accuses them of weakness and cowardice—for not being liberal enough? One explanation is that liberals are being judged—by both the Right and Left—less for the content of their beliefs than for their lack of passion and sincerity in defending them. When liberals run from the label, are temperamentally defensive, and seem overly eager to compromise with their ideological adversaries, they convey to voters that they don't have the courage of their convictions. Unfortunately, in recent decades the Democratic Party has abetted right-wing propaganda about the Left through its political timidity in a way that reinforces the premise of its right-wing critics. This timidity, in turn, fuels the charge that Democrats—especially the liberal wing of the party—are weak and politically spineless, which over the years has turned off many white male voters, and presumably many white women, as well.

Take the symbolically potent issue of gun control. Gun violence continues to take the lives of more than 30,000 Americans each year, including thousands of children, teenagers, and other innocent victims. Since 1979, more than twice as many American children and teens have been killed by guns than died in the Vietnam War.[7] The Republican Party consistently opposes any new regulations, insisting we have too many already, and in fact has been leading efforts at the state and federal level to roll back existing restrictions on gun ownership. Where have the Democrats been on this issue? In recent years Democratic politicians more often reassure gun owners that they're not going to "take away their guns" than press for stricter laws, such as reinstituting the assault weapons ban that Clinton was able to push through in 1994, but which expired a decade later. In fact Barack Obama, whose reelection National Rifle Association president Wayne LaPierre fantastically claimed would "completely and forever" eradicate the Second Amendment and roll back three decades of progress on gun rights, has been nearly silent on gun policy, even after a string of highly publicized mass murders perpetrated by heavily armed gunmen in the past couple of years, such as the Aurora, Colorado, movie theater massacre in the summer of 2012. According to journalist Richard Kim, Obama's only reform of gun policy to date has been *expanding* gun owner rights by allowing guns into national parks, which led the Brady Campaign to Prevent Gun Violence to give him an F rating in 2010.[8]

The typical explanation for the Democrats' passivity is the fear of reprisal by the NRA, as well as the tenuous position of moderate and conservative Democrats in culturally conservative areas of the country. The gun lobby has proven its ability to mobilize its members and punish candidates who don't conform to its dictates; Al Gore's loss of his home state of Tennessee in 2000 is often attributed to the efforts of the NRA to defeat him. But the Democrats' unwillingness to fight the NRA ends up reinforcing what the Right already says about liberals and progressives—that they're passive in the face of conflict and quick to back down. In other words, they're unmanly, and therefore unfit to lead—especially at the presidential level.

In fairness, it is easy for armchair commentators to say that a politician *should* take a stand that could cost them their job at election time. Politics, after all, is the art of compromise, and many savvy progressives have compromised on issues in order to stay in office to fight even bigger battles down the road. But it is also true that people like fighters, and respect those who stand up for their beliefs even when they're not likely to win a majority. I would not argue that the Democrats need to make a major push to reform the gun laws; at this point in history, they don't have the votes, and it would be politically foolish, perhaps even suicidal. Nonetheless they have paid a price for their silence in terms of voters' respect for their leadership and courage. A similar dynamic emerged recently with same sex marriage. President Obama's statement that he had "evolved" in his views and now supported the right of same sex couples to marry was met by waves of celebration on the cultural Left, but the respect he earned came with a caveat due to the politically cautious way he handled it. Fairly or not, many people believed that the president had long favored gay marriage on ethical and constitutional grounds, but lacked the courage to lead on such a hot-button issue. That's how millions of voters feel about liberal Democrats in general—in private they hold positions that they fear might not be popular in "middle America," so in public they hedge, qualify, and prevaricate. Pat Buchanan captured this sentiment when he railed in his infamous "culture war" speech at the 1992 Republican National Convention that the recently held Democratic Convention was "a giant masquerade ball...where 20,000 liberals and radicals came dressed up as moderates and centrists in the greatest single exhibition of cross-dressing in American political history."[9]

For more than a generation progressive writers and activists have criticized the national Democratic Party leadership for focusing on technocratic solutions to complex economic and fiscal problems while neglecting the cultural realm of values and identity—and for failing to ignite people's passion for fairness and justice. The argument is that most people don't vote, or become involved in politics, based on a narrow reading of their economic self-interest. In 2009, writing about the Democrats' tepid response to GOP disinformation about the Affordable Care Act, Rick Perlstein wrote,

> You can't demand that people be more logical. Emotion is part of the human animal. What I would have liked to have seen, as an advocate of healthcare reform, is for Obama and the rhetoric to combine rational appeals with emotional ones—like FDR and Truman and LBJ did so effectively in their own attempts to pass progressive legislation. They roused people in their lizard-brains, too, just for progressive ends...Truman made arguments in a very blunt, emotional style.[10]

People care about the health and safety of their communities, the quality of their kids' education, the values of the society that are transmitted through religious teaching, entertainment culture, sports, and so on. As Geoffrey Nunberg writes, "We make electoral decisions on the basis of a hodgepodge of conflicting metaphors (and) symbols ...weighing group solidarity, self-interest, and moral principles in different proportions."[11] When people vote for president they have more at stake than that which is simply quantifiable, like which candidate is going to vote to raise or reduce their taxes. They also have an identity investment: Can I relate to this person and (his) values? Does he speak for me? Would I be proud to say that I support him as the leader of my country? In addition, as I have argued in this book, many Americans continue to have an ideological and psychic investment in the president *as a man*.

Some on the left, such as Michael Lerner, Cornel West, and Jim Wallis, have sought to counter the narrow economism of mainstream Democratic Party marketing appeals (e.g., "It's the economy, stupid") by injecting spiritual values or prophetic Christianity into secular calls for social justice. Lerner has long maintained that there is a spiritual crisis in American society, and that what he refers to as the Left's knee-jerk antagonism to religious and spiritual concerns allows the Right to articulate the pain people feel "living in a society dominated by consumerism, materialism, selfishness, narcissism and a utilitarian/instrumental way of looking at other human beings and at nature."[12] Cognitive scientist George Lakoff and others have sought to push Democrats to use the language of ethics and morality and not simply argue for their positions on the basis of reason and rationality. For his part, the linguist Nunberg says that the Left needs to remake not just the language of politics and social change but the larger stories and meanings within which the words are situated. One story with great political consequence is about (white) American men, and the changing times in which they've come of age.

The Right tells its own version of this story, in which a main thread of the narrative is that the diminution of white men's cultural authority over the past few decades tracks closely with the economic and moral decline of America. One of the more revealing comments in recent decades about the centrality of gender and sexuality to this trope of decline in conservative social commentary came after 9/11 from the late Reverend Jerry Falwell, a Southern Baptist preacher and founder of Virginia's Liberty University, who helped usher fundamentalist and evangelical Christian voters into the Republican Party and thus was a pivotal figure in American politics in the latter part of the twentieth century. In what became one of the most widely quoted commentaries about the causes of the terrorist attacks on the World Trade Center and Pentagon, Falwell said,

I really believe that the pagans, and the abortionists, and the feminists, and the gays and the lesbians who are actively trying to make that an alternative lifestyle, the ACLU, People for the American Way, all of them who have tried to secularize America, I point the finger in their face and say, "You helped this happen."

In other words, the decline of America for which we were being punished by God was linked not to the continuing triumph in our society of private profit over human needs, the fact that millions of children live in poverty, or that we are the only one among the world's developed nations that does not provide free health care to all of its citizens. We were being punished, according to Falwell, because women, gays, and secularists had successfully undermined traditional patriarchal power in the family and society.

What Falwell expressed in religious terms was a belief that is widely held on the secular Right as well, which is that liberalism and progressivism are weak-kneed and flaccid ideologies that have done grave damage to this country and threaten to corrode it from within. Conservatives have long monopolized the mantle of real manhood and sought to link the "manly" virtues of hard work, loyalty, and patriotism with support for conservative policies on both domestic and foreign affairs. Of course, progressives and feminists need to challenge the very premise that virtues like hard work and patriotism are somehow "masculine," as opposed to human, virtues. But they also need to reject the idea that those are inherently, or exclusively, conservative values. It is specious to define liberalism or progressivism as "un-American," when many of the most impressive features of American society are products of those proud, if embattled, traditions. It is equally misleading to suggest that in order for American men to be strong, they need to keep women, and gays and lesbians, in their place, along with anyone else who might challenge traditional manliness. This conclusion rests on the false assumption that lifting men up requires keeping women down.

It has been clear since the 1980 election of Ronald Reagan that a decisive majority of Republican voters want to elect a president who will defend (heterosexual) men's political, economic, and cultural dominance by attempting to roll back the gains of social movements for sexual and gender equality that took root in the 1960s. Would-be Republican candidates understand this, which is why 2012 Republican presidential nominee Mitt Romney—a one-time "moderate" who supported gay rights and who, when campaigning to be governor of Massachusetts in 2002, promised to "preserve and protect" abortion rights—moved swiftly to the right on gay rights and reproductive rights as he prepared to compete on the national stage in 2008. It is also notable that the candidate who received the second most votes in the 2012 Republican primaries, Rick Santorum, not only opposes women's right to abortion in all circumstances but has warned about the "dangers of contraception," which is "a license to do things in a sexual realm that is counter to how things are supposed to be." Santorum, whose electoral performance in 2012 has positioned him to be a major leader in the conservative movement and a potential presidential nominee in future elections, has taken the politics of anti-feminist backlash even further than the bedroom, blaming cultural acceptance of the phenomenon of working mothers on "radical feminism."[13]

If adherence to conservative orthodoxy in American politics in the early twenty-first century requires Republican presidential candidates to oppose some of women's most basic rights in the area of sex and reproduction, it also requires them to take positions on issues that are not typically seen as gendered but which nonetheless contain crucial gendered elements. For example, any conservative who wants to rise in Republican Party politics faces enormous pressure to dismiss mountains of evidence and defy international scientific consensus by opposing legislation aimed at stricter regulation of greenhouse gas emissions, even though the vast majority of climate scientists worldwide believe these emissions are contributing to potentially catastrophic climate change. Because conservative white men are at the forefront of climate change denial, and because leading figures like Rush Limbaugh openly mock the manhood of male environmental activists while calling human-caused climate change a giant "hoax," it is worth asking whether that denial might go beyond predictable right-wing opposition to regulatory constraints on business and have its roots in the much more personal realm of gender politics. In their article on climate change denial, "Cool Dudes," Aaron McCright and Riley Dunlap maintain that "climate change denial seems to have become almost an essential component of conservative white male identity,"[14] and speculate that this denial might be rooted in some white men's need to maintain order and the stability of a system that has served many of them well.

For more than a generation, Republican presidential candidates have attracted the support of large majorities of white men who were unhappy with progressive challenges to their cultural status and power, and who were led to believe that strength in men resided in opposing and resisting these challenges. They were abetted in this misconception by a Democratic Party that failed to provide a bold alternative, torn by fealty to racial and gender equality and by internal divisions between its corporate benefactors and its historic base in labor and the white working class. But the fecklessness of the Democrats notwithstanding, there is another way for men both in and outside of politics to be strong. Liberals and progressives need to make this clear by telling a different kind of story about men's lives—and by changing the terms of the debate. While the Right is trapped in defending old and arguably obsolete notions of manhood, those on the Left need to emphasize that resistance to change is not always a virtue, nor is it inherently "manly." Conservatives rightly argue for the moral imperative and practical necessity of holding onto traditions that serve human needs. But it is also important, and necessary for survival, to adapt to changing circumstances. For male political leaders, this means having the courage both to envision and put into practice new ways of being men that rely less on authoritarian methods of maintaining control and more on collaborative and cooperative forms of decision making. The conundrum in presidential politics for progressives and feminists—as Barack Obama has learned—is that sometimes transformative political action requires an old-school exercise of power that is more traditionally "masculine" and thus does not model a new kind of manhood or leadership style.

Nonetheless, at this point in history adaptability is one of the most important qualities that men who aspire to leadership can possess. Being adaptable should not be confused with lacking a moral core or lacking the will to fight with gusto for one's beliefs. To the contrary, in this context adaptability simply means redefining—and updating—what it means to be strong. It means identifying strength in men as the willingness to fight *for* gender and sexual equality, not against it in some ill-fated attempt to hold back the democratic tides of history. It means standing with women and not against them as they seek to become full and equal partners with men in all areas of private and public life. For heterosexual men, it means standing with LGBT people in their struggle for full civil and human rights. For all men it means defining strength not as knee-jerk support for military action but as a willingness to take a stand against war when it is unnecessary or unjust, without fearing that chicken-hawk talk radio shouters will attack them. It means having the courage to fight *against* the idea that real men are all rugged individualists who believe in a dog-eat-dog world and *for* policies and programs that serve the needy and vulnerable, children, the sick, and the elderly—without apology, and only making political compromises when it's absolutely necessary. It means standing up to right-wing bullies and not appeasing them.

This is not just the right thing to do; it can also be a winning political strategy. Millions of voters—men and women—are clearly attracted to political leaders who are willing to fight for progressive principles, regardless of what their pollsters tell them to say. These voters might not agree with every position a candidate takes, but there is reason to believe that in an era of complex and seemingly insoluble economic and political problems they will gravitate to political leaders who have—at a minimum—the courage of their convictions and are not simply functionaries for the corporate state. If the Democrats produce candidates for president who are willing to go out on a limb and truly fight for economic and social justice, as well as engage in more cooperative and less confrontational methods of addressing global problems in an increasingly interdependent world, the voters will come. And many of them will be men.

I have argued throughout this book that presidential elections are, for all their other virtues and vices, the site of an ongoing struggle over the meanings of American manhood. This struggle is destined to continue into the foreseeable future, and it is a struggle with greater implications than which person or party wins a given election. Nonetheless, the gendered analysis of elections that I have outlined raises a number of questions which anyone who is concerned about the complex interplay among gender, sexuality, social change, and politics should engage. For example, the classic tension between rugged individualism and community that is central to the American story can be understood as a gendered struggle between masculine and feminine approaches to life, liberty, and the pursuit of happiness. The "rugged individual" in popular imagination is a "self-made" man who sees dependence on the "nanny state" as emasculating, whereas "community" suggests a more stereotypically feminine kind of collaborative spirit. How is this struggle played out and personified in contests for the presidency? How does it affect men's votes, women's votes? To what extent do these sorts of questions have class, racial, and ethnic dimensions, given that "self-reliance" is easier for

CHAPTER 8: 2012 AND BEYOND

people with means and access to resources than it is for the poor and dispossessed, and people of color are more likely to see themselves as members of *communities* than are many whites?

The framework I have introduced in this book also raises questions about whose economic interests are served when "strength" in a president is defined narrowly and conventionally. These questions are perhaps especially relevant when it comes to the areas of military spending and foreign policy, where immensely wealthy and powerful corporations have a vested interest in maintaining a system that depends, to an important degree, on the continued valorization of a very limited, inflexible definition of presidential masculinity. Despite the cultural progress we have made since the 1960s in expanding and deepening our sense of what it means to "be a man," if a potential presidential candidate makes even the mildest suggestion that gigantic military budgets are unsustainable and compromise our ability to address pressing human needs at home, *he* is likely to be met with ridicule by the pundits on TV, radio, and the blogosphere, and declared "unelectable" on account of his soft manhood, while *she* is likely to be judged not ready to play with the big boys. It is telling that Dwight D. Eisenhower, the highly decorated commander of Allied Forces in Europe during World War II and two-term Republican president, delivered his famous warning about the power of the military-industrial complex only three days before he left office in 1961. Few political leaders since have had the standing—or courage—to make similar statements, and the ones who have, like George McGovern in 1972, suffered major electoral defeats. So while the presidency will continue to be the site of an ongoing cultural contest about the ever-changing meanings of manhood, it is necessary to acknowledge that there are significant institutional and financial constraints on a (male) presidential candidate or president's leadership in this domain.

There will, of course, be significant constraints on a woman candidate's leadership, as well. The key difference is that when a woman is elected president she will disrupt the traditional gender order and spark a national dialogue on attitudes and beliefs about womanhood *and* manhood, more than any man possibly could. That might be the ultimate irony. It will be necessary for a woman to win the election and go to work in the Oval Office for us to see just how crucial the presidency has always been in the symbolic architecture of men's cultural dominance.

LEADING MEN

Notes

INTRODUCTION

1. Bashir and Lewis, "Discussing Obama," Media Matters for America online, August 20, 2008, http://mediamatters.org/research/2008/08/20/discussing-obama-limbaugh-suggests-dems-media-b/144493.

2. Brownstein, "Reconcilable Differences," *Atlantic Magazine*, September 2008, http://www.theatlantic.com/magazine/archive/2008/09/reconcilable-differences/306942/?single_page=true.

3. Kuhn, *The Neglected Voter*, 73.

4. Ibid., 141.

5. Matthews, "The Final Word is Hooray!" *FAIR*, March 15, 2006.

6. Wilner, *Washington Post*, September 27–October 3, 2004, 22.

7. Stern, Andy interview by Bill Moyers, *Bill Moyers Journal*, June 15, 2007.

8. Westen, *The Political Brain*, ix.

9. Ibid., 36.

10. Ducat, *The Wimp Factor*, 23.

11. Kuhn, *The Neglected Voter*, 75.

12. Jarding and Saunders, *Foxes in the Henhouse*, 192.

13. Dowd,"Man in the Mirror," *New York Times*, October 4, 2011, A27.

14. Ibid., "Who's Tough Enough?" *New York Times*, February 1, 2012, A27.

CHAPTER I

1. Han and Heldman, *Rethinking Madam President*, 49.

2. Bacevich, *The Limits of Power*, 68.

3. Kahn, in Kahn and Kellner, "Oppositional Politics and the Internet," *Cultural Politics*, vol. 1:1, 2005, 79.

4. Kimmel, *Manhood in America*, 36.

5. Ibid., 38.

6. Ibid., 37.

7. Postman, *Amusing Ourselves to Death*, 7.

8. Kellner, "Presidential Politics: The Movie," 1, http://pages.gseis.ucla.edu/faculty/kellner/2009_essays.html.

9. Deaver, *Behind the Scenes*, 73.

10. Miller, *On Politics and the Art of Acting*, 77.

11. Ibid., 80.

12. *Etymology Dictionary Online*, http://www.etymonline.com/index.php?allowed_in_frame=0&search=campaign&searchmode=none.

13. Sanger, "In Courting West Virginians, Bush Speaks of Military Might," *New York Times*, July 5, 2004, http://www.nytimes.com/2004/07/05/politics/campaign/05campaign.html.

14. Miller, *On Politics and the Art of Acting*, 81 .

15. Abrams, "Gingrich and Reagan," *National Review Online*, January 25, 2012.

16. Griffith, "Where We Went Wrong," The Truman National Security Project, May 2005.

17. Katz, "Advertising and the Construction of Violent White Masculinity," in *Gender, Race, and Class in Media*, 261–269.

18. Enloe, *The Morning After*, 154.

19. Ducat, *The Wimp Factor*, 184.

20. Emery, "It's Not Race, It's Arugula," *Weekly Standard*, June 23, 2008, 013:39.

21. Berke, "A Nation Challenged," *New York Times*, December 9, 2001, http://www.nytimes.com/2001/12/09/us/nation-challenged-president-jokes-remain-but-many-say-bush-showing-signs-war-s.html?pagewanted=all.

22. Hirsh, "Worlds Apart," *Newsweek*, October 6, 2008, 28.

23. Grabe and Bucy, *Image-Bite Politics*, 74.

24. Ibid., 5.

25. Lakoff and Johnson, *Metaphors We Live By*, 6.

26. Lowry, "Buckling His Chin Strap: Sen. George Allen—Likable, Conservative, and Tough—Prepares to Run for President," *National Review*, November 7, 2005, 33.

27. Luntz, *Words That Work*, 41.

28. Howe, "Metaphors in Contemporary American Political Discourse," *Metaphor and Symbolic Activity*, 3:2, 1988, 93–94.

29. Miller and Brownstein, "McCain Delivers Hard Left to Christian Right," *Los Angeles Times*, February 29, 2000, 1.

30. Dyson, "The First Presidential Debate," *The Tavis Smiley Show*, September 30, 2004.

31. Ibid.

32. Barabak, "Defiant Sarah Palin Comes Out Swinging," *Los Angeles Times*, September 4, 2008, http://articles.latimes.com/2008/sep/04/nation/na-ledeall4.

33. Editorial, "Politics of Attack," *New York Times*, October 8, 2008, http://www.nytimes.com/2008/10/08/opinion/08wed1.html?pagewanted=print.

34. Seelye, "A Passionate Persona Forged in a Brutal Defeat," *New York Times*, March 17, 2012, A1.

35. Johnson, "Romney Fires up Conservatives with Spirited Jabs at Obama," *Boston Globe*, June 2, 2012, A5.

36. Schweizer, "Don't Punt On Iran," *USA Today*, June 26, 2007, 13A.

37. Howe, "Metaphors in Contemporary American Political Discourse," 92.

38. Giuliani, CNN.com, August 31, 2004, www.cnn.com/2004/allpolitics/08/30/guiliani.transcript/index.html.

39. Richter, "White House Sees Long-Term Role for U.S. Forces in Iraq," *Los Angeles Times*, May 31, 2007, http://articles.latimes.com/2007/may/31/world/fg-bushiraq31.

40. Lugar, "Beyond Baghdad," *Washington Post*, January 30, 2007, A17.

41. Milbank, "Mixing Politics, Pigskins: When Allen Talks, Football Jargon Flows," *Washington Post*, February 6, 2005, C01.

42. Ibid.

43. Wickham, "With Kagan Nomination, Black Leaders Left on the Sidelines," *USA Today*, May 18, 2010, 11A.

44. Nicholas, "Obama Setting his Sights Lower," *Los Angeles Times*, September 8, 2011, A11.

45. Mehta, "In Iowa, the Campaign Season Is Now," *Los Angeles Times*, September 30, 2012, A8.

46. Leibovich, "Speaking Freely, Biden Finds Influential Role," *New York Times Online*, March 28, 2009, http://www.nytimes.com/2009/03/29/us/politics/29biden.html?_r=1.

47. Hart, "Obama the Snob," *FAIR (Extra!)*, July/August 2008.

CHAPTER 2

1. Cowie, *Stayin' Alive*, 6.

2. Hamill, "The Revolt of the White Lower Middle Class," in *New York Stories*, 55.

3. Ibid., 57.

4. Perlstein, *Nixonland*, 498.

5. Ibid., 498–499.

6. Nunberg, *Talking Right*, 60.

7. Ibid., 60.

8. Rosen, *The World Split Open*, 334.

9. Rich, "Stag Party," *New York Times Magazine*, March 25, 2012, http://nymag.com/news/frank-rich/gop-women-problem-2012-4/.

10. Thompson, *The Great Shark Hunt*, 208–209.

11. Dowd, "Not Feeling Groovy," *New York Times*, *Week in Review*, July 4, 2004, 9.

CHAPTER 3

1. Colbert, "The Colbert Report," August 13, 2008.

2. Morris, "A Celebration of Reagan," *New Yorker*, February 16, 1998, 50.

3. *St. Petersburg Times*, "The Anniversary of a Miracle," *St. Petersburg Times Online*, February 22, 2005, http://www.sptimes.com/2005/02/22/news_pf/Sports/The_anniversary_of_a_.shtml.

4. Kuhn, *The Neglected Voter*, 69.

5. Jeffords, *Hard Bodies*, 10.

6. Greenwald, *Great American Hypocrites*, 107.

7. Jeffords, *Hard Bodies*, 11.

8. Bunch, *Tear Down This Myth*, 32.

9. Wills, *John Wayne's America*, 30.

10. Ibid., 31.

11. Slotkin, *Gunfighter Nation*, 644.

12. Davis, "American Icon," *American Cowboy Magazine*, http:\\www.americancowboy.com/mj07/the_duke/index.shtml.

13. Johnson, *Sleepwalking through History*, 79.

14. Greenwald, *Great American Hypocrites*, 13–15.

15. Miller, *On Politics and the Art of Acting*, 40.

16. Bunch, *Tear Down This Myth*, 38.

17. Johnson, *Sleepwalking*, 45.

18. Deaver, *Behind the Scenes*, 40.

19. Sheehy, *Character: America's Search for Leadership*, 282.

20. Bunch, *Tear Down This Myth*, 106.

21. Sheehy, *Character*, 281.

22. Wills, *John Wayne's America*, 233.

23. Bunch, *Tear Down This Myth*, 7.

24. Basso, McCall, and Garceau, *Across the Great Divide*, 231.

25. Ibid., 16.

26. Price, "Cowboys and Presidents," exhibition text, Autry National Center.

27. Kimmel, *Manhood in America*, 292.

28. Gibson, *Warrior Dreams*, 11.

29. Ibid., 268.

30. Ibid., 269.

31. Edsall, *Building Red America*, 166.

32. Ibid., 168.

33. Wills, *Reagan's America*, 340.

34. Goldberg, "Looking Back, Looking Forward," *The Nation*, December 2, 2004, 8.

35. Hofstadter, *Anti-Intellectualism in American Life*, 171.

36. Ibid., 186.

37. Ibid., 196.

38. Westen, *The Political Brain*, 157.

39. Postman, *Amusing Ourselves to Death*, 108.

40. Ibid., 109.

41. Schieffer and Gates, *The Acting President*, 181.

42. Dickinson, "The Fox News Fear Factory," *Rolling Stone Magazine*, June 9, 2011, 58.

43. Slotkin, *Gunfighter Nation*, 644.

CHAPTER 4

1. Ducat, *The Wimp Factor*, 62.

2. Davey, "Drifting Right, Illinois is Test for Romney," *New York Times*, March 19, 2012, A10.

3. Oshinsky, "What Became of the Democrats?" *New York Times*, October 20, 1991, http://www.nytimes.com/1991/10/20/books/what-became-of-the-democrats.html?pagewanted=all&src=pm.

4. Kuhn, *The Neglected Voter*, 152.

5. Longley and others, *Deconstructing Reagan*, 74.

6. Entman and Rojecki, *The Black Image in the White Mind*, 78.

7. Ducat, *The Wimp Factor*, 46.

8. Jamieson, *Dirty Politics*, 17.

9. Ibid.

10. Ducat, *The Wimp Factor*, 89.

11. Adams, "Five Myths About Defense Spending," Stimson Center, January 18, 2011, http://www.stimson.org/spotlight/five-myths-about-defense-spending/.

CHAPTER 5

1. Nunberg, *Talking Right*, 116.

2. Applebome, "The 1992 Campaign: Death Penalty," *New York Times*, January 25, 1992, http://www.nytimes.com/1992/01/25/us/1992-campaign-death-penalty-arkansas-execution-...

3. Malin, *American Masculinity under Clinton*, 146-147.

4. Johnson, "Texas Standoff," *USA Today*, March 30, 2012, 1A.

5. Wolcott, "I'll Be So Glad When This Summer of Love is Over," *Vanity Fair*, September 4, 2009, http://www.stimson.org/spotlight/five-myths-about-defense-spending/.

6. Frum, "Why Rush is Wrong," *Newsweek*, March 16, 2009, 26–32.

7. Chafets, *Rush Limbaugh: An Army of One*, 81.

8. Chafets, "Late Period Limbaugh," *New York Times Magazine*, July 6, 2008, 3.

9. *Time Magazine*, January 23, 1995, cover.

10. Chafets, "Late Period Limbaugh, 3."

11. Neuharth, "Limbaugh is a Clown so Let's Laugh at Him," *USA Today*, March 8, 2012, http://www.usatoday.com/news/opinion/forum/story/2012-03-09/rush-limbaugh-sandra-fluke-controversy/53421500/1.

12. Chafets, *Rush Limbaugh*, 204.

13. Ducat, *The Wimp Factor*, 17.

14. Greenwald, *Great American Hypocrites*, 110.

15. Al Gore, *The Assault on Reason*, 66.

16. Media Matters, "Limbaugh Describes the 'New Castrati,'" Media Matters for America online, March 8, 2011, http://mediamatters.org/iphone/research/201103080032.

17. Edsall, *Building Red America*, 183.

18. Greenwald, *Great American Hypocrites*, 99.

19. Cohen, *Cable News Confidential*, 67.

20. Ibid.

21. Ducat, *The Wimp Factor*, 238.

22. Limbaugh, Rushlimbaugh.com, http://www.rushlimbaugh.com/home/daily/site_062608/content/01125111.guest.html.

23. Michael Kimmel, *The History of Men*, 20.

24. Ibid.

25. Prager, Dennis, "Libeling the Right: the key to the left's success" www.dennisprager.com, January 18, 2011

26. Gelles, *USA Today*, October 20, 2004, 1D.

27. Deaver, *Behind the Scenes*, 40.

28. Page, "First Lady: Married to the Job," *USA Today*, October 20, 2004, 1D.

29. Gorov, "The Other Running Mates," *Boston Globe*, August 13, 1990, 35.

30. Neuffer, "From Partner to Helpmate," *Boston Globe*, July 20, 1992, 9.

31. Stanley, *The Crusader: The Life and Tumultuous Times of Pat Buchanan*, 3.

32. Carlson, "All Eyes on Hillary," *Time*, September 14, 1992, 28.

33. Ducat, *The Wimp Factor*, 10.

34. Margaret Carlson, "All Eyes on Hillary," *Time,* September 14, 1992, 30.

35. Ducat, *The Wimp Factor*, 11.

36. Ibid., 19.

37. Buckley, "A Convention for Carnivores," *New York Times*, September 5, 2004, 9.

38. Traister, *Big Girls Don't Cry*, 47.

39. Ibid., 48.

40. Ibid., 49.

41. Noonan, "While McCain Watches," *Wall Street Journal*, April 18, 2008, http://www.peggynoonan.com/article.php?article=410.

42. Hogue, "America's First Lady Blues," *The Nation*, February 6, 2012, 5.

43. Ibid.

44. Duerst-Lahti, "Masculinity on the Campaign Trail," in Han and Heldman, eds., *Rethinking Madam President*, 91.

45. Ibid., 96.

46. Han and Heldman, *Rethinking Madam President,* 136.

47. Duerst-Lahti, "Masculinity on the Campaign Trail," in *Rethinking Madam President,* 96.

48. Pollack, *Real Boys: Rescuing Our Sons from the Myths of Boyhood,* xxv.

49. Fridkin and Kenney, "Examining the Gender Gap in Children's Attitudes toward Politics," *Sex Roles*, vol. 56 (3–4), 2007, 133.

50. Tannen, *The Argument Culture*, 284.

51. Kagan, *Of Paradise and Power,* 4–5.

52. Ibid., 3.

53. Levenson, "Rivals Giuliani, Romney Make it a 1-on-1 Fight," *Boston Globe,* October 11, 2007, http://www.boston.com/news/nation/articles/2007/10/11/rivals_giuliani_romney_make_it_a_1_on_1_fight/?page=full.

54. Bruni, "And Now…Professor Gingrich," *New York Times Sunday Review,* December 3, 2011, 3.

55. Hofstadter, *Anti-Intellectualism in American Life*, 19.

56. Brooks, "Combat and Composure," *New York Times*, May 6, 2008, A27.

57. Kuhn, *The Neglected Voter*, 87.

58. Prager, *Still the Best Hope: Why the World Needs American Values to Triumph,* 82–83.

59. Meacham and Thomas, "The Vices of the Virtues," *Newsweek,* October 6, 2008, 23.

60. Palmer, "Symbols Can Mean Everything," *Boston Globe,* August 30, 1992, 64.

CHAPTER 6

1. Cohen, "Ardent Faith Squares Off Against Earnest Reflection," the *New York Times*, *Week in Review*, October 24, 2004, 5.

2. Chomsky, *Interventions*, 98.

3. Ibid.

4. Faludi, *The Terror Dream*, 147.

5. Fineman, "Rove Unleashed," *Newsweek*, December 6, 2004, 23.

6. Glazov, "Symposium: The Return of Manhood," *FrontPageMagazine.com*, August 8, 2003.

7. Ibid.

8. Tomkins, *West of Everything: The Inner Life of Westerns*, 45.

9. Ducat, Stephen, "The Wimp Factor," interview by Lakshmi Chaudry, AlterNet, *www.alternet.org/story/20343/the_wimp_factor*, October 28, 2004.

10. Hochschild, "Let Them Eat War," *TomDispatch.com*, October 2, 2003.

11. Matthews, "The Final Word is Hooray!" *FAIR*, March 15, 2006.

12. Apple, "Despite a Razor-Thin Loss in 2000, GOP Again Forecasts a Victory in Wisconsin," *New York Times*, October 17, 2004, A-11.

13. Rich, Frank "How Kerry became a girlie-man," *New York Times*, Sept. 5, 2004, http://www.nytimes.com/2004/09/05/arts/05RICH.html?pagewanted=print& position=&_r=0p. retrieved 9-27-12 from

14. Lucado, et al., *Seven Promises of a Promise Keeper*, 22.

15. Hedges, "The Christian Right and the Rise of American Fascism." www.theocracywatch.org, November 15, 2004.

16. Pew Research Center, "Religion and the Presidential Vote," December 6, 2004, http://people-press.org/commentary/?analysisid=103.

17. Cohen, "Ardent Faith Squares Off Against Earnest Reflection," *New York Times*, *Week in Review*, October 24, 2004, 5.

18. Ducat, *The Wimp Factor*, vii.

19. Edsall, *Building Red America*, 177.

20. Ducat, *The Wimp Factor*, 159.

21. Ibid., 200.

22. CNN.com, "Cheney Blasts Kerry Over 'Sensitive War' Remark," August 12, 2004, http://articles.cnn.com/2004-08-12/politics/cheney.kerry_1_sensitive-war-lynne-cheney-kerry-spokesman-phil-singer?_s=PM:ALLPOLITICS.

23. Greenwald, *A Tragic Legacy*, 133.

24. Ibid.

25. Dionne, "The Rebirth of McCarthyism," *Seattle Times*, June 28, 2005, http://www.washingtonpost.com/wp-dyn/content/article/2005/06/27/AR2005062701317.html.

26. Cromer, "With Bush at the Helm, I'm Not Afraid," *Boston Globe*, Letters to the Editor, April 11, 2004.

27. Howe, "Metaphors in Contemporary American Political Discourse," *Metaphor and Symbolic Activity*, 3:2, 1988, 89.

28. Ibid., 92.

29. Ibid., 90.

30. Foer, *How Soccer Explains the World*, 239.

31. Ibid.

32. Kakutani, "Is Jon Stewart the Most Trusted Man in America?" *New York Times*, August 17, 2008, AR1.

33. Stewart, Jon "The Rolling Stone Interview," by Eric Bates, *Rolling Stone Magazine*, September 29, 2011, 46.

34. Schorn, "*The Colbert Report*," CBS News *60 Minutes*, February 11, 2009, http://www.cbsnews.com/2100-18560_162-1553506.html.

35. Sternbergh, "Stephen Colbert Has America by the Ballots," *New York Magazine*, October 8, 2006, 2.

36. Ibid., 4.

37. Gutterman and Regan, "Straight Eye for the Straight Guy," in Ferguson and Marso, eds., *W Stands for Women: How the George W. Bush Presidency Shaped a New Politics of Gender*, 81.

38. Colbert, *I Am America (And So Can You!)*, 7.

CHAPTER 7

1. Duffy and Gibbs, "The Long Way Home," *Time*, March 17, 2008, 34.

2. Powell, "Taking Blows from All Sides and Weighing When to Punch Back," *New York Times Online*, February 25, 2008.

3. Hewitt, "The Obama Melt," May 26, 2008, http://hughhewitt.townhall.com/blog/g/e9fa1f90-2f4f-4b0d-a562-080bfe6b2f09.

4. Plouffe, *The Audacity to Win*, 215.

5. *New Republic*, "Obama for President," Editorial. November 5, 2008.

6. Dargis and Scott, "How the Movies Made a President," *New York Times*, January 16, 2009, AR1.

7. Woods, "Bringing Sexy Back: Barack Obama and the 'Triumph' of White-Collar Masculinity," http://jewelwoods.com/node/8, July 18, 2008.

8. Parker, "Obama: Our First Female President," *Washington Post*, June 3, 2010, A17.

9. Blow, "Rise of the Fallen?" *New York Times*, September 10, 2011, A19.

10. Milbank, "Obama Needs to Flex His Political Muscle," *Washington Post*, February 28, 2010, A09.

11. Dowd, "One and Done?" *New York Times*, September 4, 2011, 11.

12. Greider, "Does Obama Have the Guts to Play Hardball?" *The Nation*, November 29, 2010. http://www.alternet.org/story/148850/does_obama_have_the_guts_to_play_hardball.

13. Blow, "Rise of the Fallen?" *New York Times*, September 10, 2011, A19.

14. Beinart, "Bin Laden Killing Erases Democrats' Wimp Factor," *Daily Beast*, May 2, 2011. http://www.thedailybeast.com/articles/2011/05/03/osama-bin-laden-killing-erases-democrats-and-obamas-weakness-stereotype.html.

15. Kristof, "Who gets it? Hillary," *New York Times*, March 16, 2005, A23.

16. Leibovich and Zernike, "Seeing Grit and Ruthlessness in Clinton's Love of the Fight," *New York Times*, May 5, 2008, A1.

17. Ibid.

18. Faludi, "The Fight Stuff," *New York Times Online*, May 9, 2008, http://www.nytimes.com/2008/05/09/opinion/09faludi.html.

19. Ibid.

20. Lerner, "Over the Hillary: Feminists Find It Hard to Stand by Their Woman," *Village Voice*, June 2003, 18–24.

21. Ibid.

22. Robin, *The Reactionary Mind*, 10.

23. Ibid.

24. Traister, *Big Girls Don't Cry*, 166.

25. Sandberg, transcript and video of speech at Barnard College by Sheryl Sandberg, chief operating officer, Facebook, May 11, 2011, http://barnard.edu/headlines/transcript-and-video-speech-sheryl-sandberg-chief-operating-officer-facebook.

26. Healy, "Hillary Clinton Searches for Her Inner Jock," *New York Times Online*, June 10, 2007, http://www.nytimes.com/2007/06/10/weekinreview/10healy.html.

27. Faludi, "They Always Play the Gender Card: But Hillary Shuffles the Deck," TomDispatch.com, November 8, 2007, http://www.tomdispatch.com/post/174860.

28. Freeman, "On Pro Football: Dream Job for Rice," *New York Times*, April 17, 2002, http://www.nytimes.com/2002/04/17/sports/on-pro-football-dream-job-for-rice-nfl-commissioner.html?src=pm.

29. Lowry, "Projecting Through the Screen," *The National Review*, October 3, 2008.

30. Zizek, *Living in the End Times*, 270.

CHAPTER 8

1. Weiner, "The Fix," *Washington Post Online*, July 20, 2012, http://www.washingtonpost.com/blogs/the-fix/post/where-obama-and-romney-stand-on-gun-control/2012/07/20/gJQAwMpNyW_blog.html.

2. Schaller, "So Long White Boy," *Salon.com*, September 17, 2007, http://www.salon.com/2007/09/17/white_man/.

3. Ebadi, "A Warning for Women of the Arab Spring," *Wall Street Journal*, March 14, 2012, A13.

4. Boehlert, "Feburary's Sunday Show Interview Tally: 52 Men, 4 Women," Media Matters for America, February 28, 2012, http://mediamatters.org/print/blog/201202280004.

5. Harding, *Whose Science? Whose Knowledge? Thinking from Women's Lives*, 124.

6. Kellner, "Barack Obama and Celebrity Spectacle," International Journal of Communication, 3 (2009), 715–741.

7. Children's Defense Fund, "Protect Children, Not Guns," March 23, 2012, http://www.childrensdefense.org/child-research-data-publications/data/protect-children-not-guns-2012.pdf.

8. Kim, "Guns, Gays, and Democrats," *The Nation*, May 7, 2012, http://www.thenation.com/article/167464/guns-gays-and-democrats#.

9. Stanley, *The Crusader*, 2.

10. Lyons, "A Cake Knife is Useless in a Gunfight," *Salon.com*, http://www.salon.com/2009/09/03/cake_knife/.

11. Nunberg, *Talking Right*, 103.

12. Lerner, "Overcoming Liberal Arrogance and Contempt for Americans Who Voted for Bush," *Tikkun* online, November 8, 2004.

13. Pynchon, "Brainwashed by Radical Feminists, Working Mothers Claim Happiness," *Forbes.com*, February 20, 2012, http://www.forbes.com/sites/shenegotiates/2012/02/20/brainwashed-by-radical-feminists-working-mothers-claim-happiness/.

14. McCright and Dunlap, "Cool Dudes," in *Global Environmental Change* 21:4 (October 2011): 1168.

Bibliography

Abrams, Elliott. "Gingrich and Reagan." *National Review Online*, January 25, 2012. *www.nationalreview.com/articles/.../gingrich-and-reagan-elliott-abra*

Adams, Gordon. "Five Myths About Defense Spending." Stimson Center, January 18, 2011. http://www.stimson.org/spotlight/five-myths-about-defense-spending/ (accessed March 19, 2012).

Anderson, Nick. "Silence of the Wolves, and Their Ilk, in Swing States." *Los Angeles Times*, November 2, 2004.

Apple, R. W. "Despite a Razor-Thin Loss in 2000, GOP Again Forecasts a Victory in Wisconsin." *New York Times*, October 17, 2004, A11.

Applebome, Peter. "The 1992 Campaign: Death Penalty; Arkansas Execution Raises Questions on Governor's Politics." *New York Times*, January 25, 1992. http://www.nytimes.com/1992/01/25/us/1992-campaign-death-penalty-arkansas-execution-... (accessed March 18, 2012).

Bacevich, Andrew J. *The Limits of Power: The End of American Exceptionalism.* New York: Metropolitan Books, 2008.

Barabak, Mark. "Defiant Sarah Palin Comes Out Swinging." *Los Angeles Times*, September 4, 2008. http://articles.latimes.com/2008/sep/04/nation/na-ledeall4 (accessed July 27, 2012).

Bashir, Asli, and Greg Lewis. "Discussing Obama, Limbaugh Suggests Dems, Media Believe 'You Can't Criticize the Little Black Man-Child.' " Media Matters for America online, August 20, 2008. http://mediamatters.org/research/2008/08/20/discussing-obama-limbaugh-suggests-dems-media-b/144493 (accessed September 1, 2008).

Basso, Matthew, Laura McCall, and Dee Garceau. *Across the Great Divide: Cultures of Manhood in the American West.* New York: Routledge, 2001.

Beinart, Peter. "bin Laden Killing Erases Democrats' Wimp Factor." *The Daily Beast*, May 2, 2011. http://www.thedailybeast.com/articles/2011/05/03/osama-bin-laden-killing-erases-democrats-and-obamas-weakness-stereotype.html.

Berke, Richard L. "A Nation Challenged: The President: Jokes Remain, But Many Say Bush Is Showing Signs of War's Burden." *New York Times*, December 9,

2001. http://www.nytimes.com/2001/12/09/us/nation-challenged-president-jokes-remain-but-many-say-bush-showing-signs-wars.html?pagewanted=all (accessed September 5, 2012).

Berkowitz, Alan. "The Social Norms Approach: Theory, Research, and Annotated Bibliography." August 2004. http://www.alanberkowitz.com/papers.php#1

Black, Earl, and Merle Black. *The Rise of Southern Republicans*. Cambridge: Harvard University Press, 2002.

Blow, Charles M. "Rise of the Fallen?" *New York Times*, September 10, 2011, A19.

Boston Globe, June 2, 2012, A5.

Boehlert, Eric. "Feburary's Sunday Show Interview Tally: 52 Men, 4 Women." Media Matters for America online, February 28, 2012. http://mediamatters.org/print/blog/201202280004 (accessed May 16, 2012).

Brooks, David. "Combat and Composure." *New York Times*, May 6, 2008, A27.

———. "The Ike Phase." *New York Times*, March 15, 2011, A31.

Brownstein, Ronald. "For 2004, Bush Has Strength in the White Male Numbers." *Los Angeles Times*, 2004, 1.

———. "Reconcilable Differences." *Atlantic Magazine*, September 2008. http://www.theatlantic.com/magazine/archive/2008/09/reconcilable-differences/306942/?single_page=true (accessed August 10, 2012).

Bruni, Frank. "And Now… Professor Gingrich." *New York Times, Sunday Review*, December 3, 2011, 3.

Buckley, Christopher. "A Convention for Carnivores." *New York Times*, September 5, 2004, 9.

Bunch, Will. *Tear Down This Myth: How the Reagan Legacy Has Distorted Our Politics and Haunts Our Future*. New York: Free Press, 2009.

Carlson, Margaret. "All Eyes on Hillary." *Time*, September 14, 1992, 28.

Chafets, Zev. "Late Period Limbaugh." *New York Times Magazine*, July 6, 2008. http://www.nytimes.com/2008/07/06/magazine/06Limbaugh-t.html?_r=1&ref=rushlimbaugh (accessed August 10, 2012).

———. *Rush Limbaugh: An Army of One*. New York: Sentinel, 2010.

Children's Defense Fund. "Protect Children, Not Guns." March 23, 2012. http://www.childrensdefense.org/child-research-data-publications/data/protect-children-not-guns-2012.pdf (accessed August 10, 2012).

Chomsky, Noam. *Interventions*. San Francisco: City Light Books, 2007.

CNN.com. "Cheney Blasts Kerry Over 'Sensitive War' Remark." August 12, 2004. http://articles.cnn.com/2004-08-12/politics/cheney.kerry_1_sensitive-war-lynne-cheney-kerry-spokesman-phil-singer?_s=PM:ALLPOLITICS (accessed July 31, 2012).

Cohen, Jeff. *Cable News Confidential: My Misadventures in Corporate Media*. Sausalito, California: PoliPoint Press, 2006.

Cohen, Roger. "Ardent Faith Squares Off Against Earnest Reflection." *New York Times, Week in Review*, October 24, 2004, 5.

Colbert, Stephen, *I Am America (And So Can You!)*. New York: Grand Central Publishing, 2007.

———. *The Colbert Report*, August 13, 2008.

Connell, Raewyn. *Gender and Power*. Stanford: Stanford University Press, 1987.

Cowie, Jefferson. *Stayin' Alive: The Seventies and the Last Days of the Working Class*. New York: The New Press, 2010.

Crenshaw, Kimberle. "Mapping the Margins: Intersectionality, Identity Politics, and Violence Against Women of Color." *Stanford Law Review*, 43:6, July 1991, 1241.

Cromer, Elizabeth. "With Bush at the Helm, I'm Not Afraid." *Boston Globe*, Letters to the Editor, April 11, 2004.

Dargis, Manohla, and A. O. Scott. "How the Movies Made a President." *New York Times*, January 16, 2009, AR1.

Davey, Monica. "Drifting Right, Illinois is Test for Romney." *New York Times*, March 19, 2012, A10.

Davis, Ronald L. "American Icon." *American Cowboy Magazine*, http:\\www.americancowboy.com/mj07/the_duke/index.shtml (accessed February 2, 2009).

Deaver, Michael. *Behind the Scenes*. New York: William Morrow, 1987.

Dickinson, Tom. "The Fox News Fear Factory." *Rolling Stone Magazine*, June 9, 2011.

Dionne, E. J. "The Rebirth of McCarthyism." *Seattle Times*, June 28, 2005. http://www.washingtonpost.com/wp-dyn/content/article/2005/06/27/AR2005062701317.html (accessed July 31, 2012).

Dougherty, Jill, and Catherine Berger. "Cheney Blasts Kerry Over 'Sensitive War' Remark." http://www.cnn.com/2004/ALLPOLITICS/08/12/cheney.kerry/index.html (accessed August 12, 2004).

Dowd, Maureen. "Man in the Mirror." *New York Times*, October 4, 2011.

———. "Not Feeling Groovy." *New York Times, Week in Review*, July 4, 2004, 9.

———. "One and Done." *New York Times*, September 4, 2011, 11.

———. "Who's Tough Enough?" *New York Times*, January 31, 2012.

Ducat, Stephen. *The Wimp Factor: Gender Gaps, Holy Wars, and the Politics of Anxious Masculinity*. Boston: Beacon Press, 2004.

———. "The Wimp Factor," interview with Stephen Ducat by Lakshmi Chaudry. AlterNet, www.alternet.org/story/20343/the_wimp_factor, October 28, 2004 (accessed September 4, 2012).

Duerst-Lahti, Georgia. "Masculinity on the Campaign Trail," in *Rethinking Madam President: Are We Ready for a Woman in the White House?*, edited by Lori Cox Han and Caroline Heldman. Boulder: Lynne Rienner Publishers, 2007.

Duffy, Michael, and Nancy Gibbs. "The Long Way Home." *Time Magazine,* March 17, 2008.

Dyson, Michael Eric. "The First Presidential Debate." *The Tavis Smiley Show,* National Public Radio, September 30, 2004. http://www.npr.org/templates/story/story.php?storyId=4054526.

Ebadi, Shirin. "A Warning for Women of the Arab Spring." *Wall Street Journal,* March 14, 2012, A13.

Edsall, Thomas. *Building Red America: The New Conservative Coalition and the Drive for Permanent Power.* New York: Basic Books, 2006.

Emery, Noemie. "It's Not Race, It's Arugula." *Weekly Standard,* June 23, 2008, 013:39.

Enloe, Cynthia. *The Morning After: Sexual Politics at the End of the Cold War.* Berkeley: University of California Press, 1993.

Entman, Robert M., and Andrew Rojecki. *The Black Image in the White Mind: Media and Race in America.* Chicago: The University of Chicago Press, 2000.

Etymology Dictionary Online. http://www.etymonline.com/index.php?allowed_in_frame=0&search=campaign&searchmode=none (accessed May 21, 2012).

Faludi, Susan. *Stiffed: The Betrayal of the American Man.* New York: William Morrow and Company, 1999.

——. "The Fight Stuff." *New York Times,* May 9, 2008. http://www.nytimes.com/2008/05/09/opinion/09faludi.html (accessed August 10, 2012).

——. *The Terror Dream: Fear and Fantasy in Post-9/11 America.* New York: Metropolitan Books, 2007.

——. "They Always Play the Gender Card: But Hillary Shuffles the Deck," TomDispatch.com, November 8, 2007. http://www.tomdispatch.com/post/174860 (accessed September 4, 2012).

Fineman, Howard. "Rove Unleashed." *Newsweek,* December 6, 2004, 23.

Foer, Franklin. *How Soccer Explains the World.* New York: Harper Perennial, 2004.

Frank, Thomas. *What's the Matter with Kansas?: How Conservatives Won the Heart of America.* New York: Metropolitan Books, 2004.

Freeman, Mike. "On Pro Football: Dream Job for Rice: NFL Commissioner." *New York Times,* April 17, 2002.

Fridkin, Kim L., and Patrick J. Kenney. "Examining the Gender Gap in Children's Attitudes Toward Politics." *Sex Roles,* vol. 56 (3–4), 2007, 133.

Frum, David. "Why Rush Is Wrong." *Newsweek,* March 16, 2009, 26–32.

Gelles, Karl. *USA Today.* October 20, 2004, 1D.

Gibson, James William. *Warrior Dreams: Violence and Manhood in Post-Vietnam America.* New York: Hill and Wang, 1994.

Giuliani, Rudy. CNN.com. August 31, 2004, www.cnn.com/2004/allpolitics/08/30/guiliani.transcript/index.html

Glazov, Jamie. "Symposium: The Return of Manhood." *FrontPageMagazine.com*, August 8, 2003.

Goldberg, Danny. "Looking Back, Looking Forward." *The Nation*, December 2, 2004, 5.

Gore, Al. *The Assault on Reason*. New York: Penguin, 2007.

Gorov, Lynda. "The Other Running Mates: The Perplexing Lives of Political Wives." *Boston Globe*, August 13, 1990, 35.

Grabe, Maria Elizabeth, and Erik Page Bucy. *Image-Bite Politics: News and the Visual Framing of Elections*. New York: Oxford University Press, 2009.

Greenwald, Glenn. *A Tragic Legacy: How a Good vs. Evil Mentality Destroyed the Bush Presidency*. New York: Crown Publishers, 2007.

———. *Great American Hypocrites: Toppling the Big Myths of Republican Politics*. New York: Crown Publishers, 2008.

Greider, William. "Does Obama Have the Guts to Play Hardball?" *The Nation*, November 29, 2010. http://www.alternet.org/story/148850/does_obama_have_the_guts_to_play_hardball.

Griffith, Loren. "Where We Went Wrong: How the Public Lost Faith in Democrats' Ability to Protect Our National Security, and How to Stage a Comeback." The Truman National Security Project, May 2005. http://www.trumanproject.org/trumanpaper3.html.

Gutterman, David, and Danielle Regan. "Straight Eye for the Straight Guy." In *W Stands for Women: How the George W. Bush Presidency Shaped a New Politics of Gender*, edited by Michaele L. Ferguson and Lori Jo Marso. Durham and London: Duke University Press, 2007.

Hamill, Pete. "The Revolt of the White Lower Middle Class." In *New York Stories*, edited by Steve Fishman, John Homans, and Adam Moss. New York: Random House, 2008.

Han, Lori Cox, and Caroline Heldman. *Rethinking Madam President: Are We Ready For a Woman in the White House?* Boulder, Colorado: Lynne Reinner Publishers, 2007.

Harding, Sandra. *Whose Science? Whose Knowledge? Thinking from Women's Lives*. New York: Cornell University Press, 1991.

Hart, Peter. "Obama the Snob." *F.A.I.R./EXTRA*, July/August 2008. http://www.fair.org/index.php?page=3577 (accessed August 10, 2012).

Healy, Patrick. "Hillary Clinton Searches for Her Inner Jock." *New York Times*, June 10, 2007.

Hedges, Chris. "The Christian Right and the Rise of American Fascism." Theocracy Watch, November 15, 2004.

http://www.scribd.com/doc/43550103/Chris-Hedges-The-Christian-Right-and-the-Rise-of-American-Fascism (accessed August 9, 2012).

Hewitt, Hugh. "The Obama Melt." May 26, 2008. http://hughhewitt.townhall.com/blog/g/e9fa1f90-2f4f-4b0d-a562-080bfe6b2f09 (accessed May 26, 2008).

Hirsch, Michael. "Worlds Apart." *Newsweek*, October 6, 2008.

Hochschild, Arlie. "Let Them Eat War." *TomDispatch.com*, October 2, 2003.

Hofstadter, Richard. *Anti-Intellectualism in American Life.* New York: Alfred A. Knopf, 1963.

Hogue, Ilyse. "America's First Lady Blues." *The Nation*, February 6, 2012.

Howe, Nicholas. "Metaphors in Contemporary American Political Discourse." *Metaphor and Symbolic Activity*, 3:2, 1988, 87–104.

Jamieson, Kathleen Hall. *Dirty Politics: Deception, Distraction, and Democracy.* Oxford: Oxford University Press, 1993.

Jarding, Steve, and Dave "Mudcat" Saunders. *Foxes in the Henhouse.* New York: Touchstone, 2006.

Jeffords, Susan. *Hard Bodies: Hollywood Masculinity in the Reagan Era.* New Brunswick, NJ: Rutgers University Press, 1993.

Johnson, Glen. "Romney Fires up Conservatives with Spirited Jabs at Obama." *Boston Globe*, June 2, 2012, A5.

Johnson, Haynes. *Sleepwalking through History: America in the Reagan Years.* New York: Norton, 1991.

Johnson, Kevin. "Texas Standoff is Emblematic of the Nation's Growing Anti-Government Sovereign Movement." *USA Today*, March 30, 2012, 1A.

Kagan, Robert. *Of Paradise and Power: America and Europe in the New World Order.* New York: Knopf, 2003.

Kahn, Richard, and Douglas Kellner. "Oppositional Politics and the Internet: A Critical/Reconstructive Approach." *Cultural Politics*, vol. 1:1, 2005, 79.

Kakutani, Michiko. "Is Jon Stewart the Most Trusted Man in America?" *New York Times*, August 14, 2008, AR1.

Katz, Jackson. "Advertising and the Construction of Violent White Masculinity: From Eminem to Clinique for Men." In *Gender, Race and Class in Media: A Text Reader*, edited by Gail Dines and Jean Humez. Thousand Oaks, CA: Sage Publications, 2003.

Kellner, Douglas. "Presidential Politics: The Movie." http://pages.gseis.ucla.edu/faculty/kellner/2009_essays.html (accessed May 23, 2012).

———. "Barack Obama and Celebrity Spectacle." *International Journal of Communication*, 3 (2009), 715–741.

Kim, Richard. "Guns, Gays, and Democrats." *The Nation*, May 7, 2012.

Kimmel, Michael. *Manhood in America: A Cultural History.* New York: Free Press, 1996.

——. *The History of Men: Essays on the History of American and British Masculinities.* Albany: State University of New York Press, 2005.

Kristof, Nicholas. "Who Gets It? Hillary." *New York Times*, March 16, 2005, A23.

Kuhn, David Paul. *The Neglected Voter: White Men and the Democratic Dilemma.* New York: Palgrave MacMillan, 2007.

Lakoff, George, and Mark Johnson. *Metaphors We Live By.* Chicago: University of Chicago Press, 1980.

Leibovich, Mark. "Speaking Freely, Biden Finds Influential Role." *New York Times Online* March 28, 2009.
http://www.nytimes.com/2009/03/29/us/politics/29biden.html?_r=1

Leibovich, Mark, and Kate Zernike. "Seeing Grit and Ruthlessness in Clinton's Love of the Fight." *New York Times*, May 5, 2008, A1.

Lerner, Michael. "Overcoming Liberal Arrogance and Contempt for Amerricans Who Voted for Bush." *Tikkun* online, November 8, 2004. Accessed via email, November 9, 2004.

Lerner, Sharon. "Over the Hillary: Feminists Find It Hard to Stand by Their Woman." *Village Voice*, June 2003, 18–24.

Levenson, Michael. "Rivals Giuliani, Romney Make it a 1-on-1 Fight." *Boston Globe*, October 11, 2007.
http://www.boston.com/news/nation/articles/2007/10/11/rivals_giuliani_romney_make_it_a_1_on_1_fight/?page=full (accessed September 7, 2012).

Limbaugh, Rush. Rushlimbaugh.com.
http://www.rushlimbaugh.com/home/daily/site_062608/content/01125111.guest.html (accessed June 26, 2008).

Longley, Kyle, Jeremy D. Mayer, Michael Schaller, and John W. Sloan. *Deconstructing Reagan: Conservative Mythology and America's Fortieth President.* New York: M. E. Sharpe, Inc., 2007.

Lowry, Richard. "Buckling His Chin Strap: Sen. George Allen—Likable, Conservative, and Tough—Prepares to Run for President." *National Review*, November 7, 2005.

——. "Projecting Through the Screen." *National Review*, October 3, 2008.

Lucado, Max, Dr. Gary Smalley, Bill Bright, and Charles R. Swindoll. *Seven Promises of a Promise Keeper.* Focus on the Family Publishing, 1999.

Lugar, Richard. "Beyond Baghdad." *The Washington Post*, January 30, 2007, A17.

Luntz, Frank. *Words That Work: It's Not What You Say, It's What People Hear.* New York: Hyperion, 2007.

Lyons, Gene. "A Cake Knife is Useless in a Gunfight." *Salon.com*,
http://www.salon.com/2009/09/03/cake_knife/ (accessed September 3, 2009).

Malin, Brenton J. *American Masculinity under Clinton: Popular Media and the Nineties "Crisis of Masculinity."* New York: Peter Lang, 2005.

Manhola, Dargis, and A. O. Scott. "How the Movies Made a President." *New York Times*, January 16, 2009.

Matthews, Chris. "The Final Word is Hooray!" *FAIR*, March 15, 2006. www.fair.org/index.php?page=2842 (accessed August 10, 2012).

McCain, John, with Mark Salter. *Why Courage Matters: The Way to a Braver Life.* New York: Random House, 2004.

McCright, Aaron, and Riley Dunlap. "Cool Dudes: The Denial of Climate Change among Conservative White Males in the United States." *Global Environmental Change* 21:4 (October 2011): 1163–1172.

Meacham, Jon, and Evan Thomas. "The Vices of the Virtues." *Newsweek,* October 6, 2008, 23.

Media Matters. "Limbaugh Describes the 'New Castrati': You're Like Geishas— You Gesticulate Like You're Effeminate." Media Matters for America online, March 8, 2011. http://mediamatters.org/iphone/research/201103080032 (accessed April 8, 2012).

Mehta, Seema. "In Iowa, the Campaign Season Is Now." *Los Angeles Times,* September 30, 2012, A8.

Memmott, Mark, and Drinkard, Jim. "Election Ad Battle Smashes Record in 2004." *USA Today,* November 25, 2004.

Messerschmidt, James. *Hegemonic Masculinities and Camouflaged Politics: Unmasking the Bush Dynasty and Its War Against Iraq,* Boulder: Paradigm Press, 2010

Milbank, Dana, "Mixing Politics, Pigskins: When Allen Talks, Football Jargon Flows." *Washington Post*, February 6, 2005, C01.

——. "Obama Needs to Flex his Political Muscle." *Washington Post*, February 28, 2010, A09.

Miller, Arthur. *On Politics and the Art of Acting.* New York: Viking, 2001.

Miller, T. Christian, and Ronald Brownstein, "McCain Delivers Hard Left to Christian Right." *Los Angeles Times*, February 29, 2000, 1.

Morris, Edmund. "A Celebration of Reagan." *The New Yorker*, February 16, 1998, 50.

Neuffer, Elizabeth. "From Partner to Helpmate: Hillary Clinton Spurs Debate on Presidential Wives." *Boston Globe,* July 20, 1992, 9.

Neuharth, Al. "Limbaugh is a Clown So Let's Laugh at Him." *USA Today*, March 19, 2012. http://www.usatoday.com/news/opinion/forum/story/2012-03-09/rush-limbaugh-sandra-fluke-controversy/53421500/1 (accessed September 6, 2012).

New Republic, "Obama for President." Editorial., November 5, 2008.

New York Times, "Politics of Attack." Editorial. October 8, 2008. http://www.nytimes.com/2008/10/08/opinion/08wed1.html?pagewanted=print (accessed August 7, 2012).

Newsom, Jennifer Siebel. *Miss Representation*. http://www.MissRepresentation.org.

Nicholas, Peter. "Obama Setting His Sights Lower." *Los Angeles Times*, September 8, 2011, A11.

Noonan, Peggy. "While McCain Watches." *Wall Street Journal*, April 18, 2008. http://www.peggynoonan.com/article.php?article=410 (accessed March 3, 2009).

Nunberg, Geoffrey. *Talking Right*. New York: Public Affairs, 2006.

Oshinsky, David. "What Became of the Democrats?" *New York Times*, October 20, 1991. http://www.nytimes.com/1991/10/20/books/what-became-of-the-democrats.html?pagewanted=all&src=pm (accessed July 30, 2012).

Page, Susan. "First Lady: Married to the Job." *USA Today*, October 20, 2004, 1D.

Palmer, Thomas C. "Symbols Can Mean Everything: More Important than Substance, Image May Make the President." *Boston Globe*, August 30, 1992.

Parker, Kathleen. "Obama: Our First Female President." *Washington Post*, June 3, 2010, A17.

Pawlenty, Tim. *Courage to Stand: An American Story*. Carol Stream, Illinios: Tyndale House Publishers, 2011.

Perlstein, Rick. *Nixonland: The Rise of a President and the Fracturing of America*. New York: Scriber, 2008.

Pew Research Center. "Religion and the Presidential Vote." December 6, 2004, http://people-press.org/commentary/?analysisid=103 (accessed March 12, 2009).

Plouffe, David. *The Audacity to Win*. New York: Penguin, 2009.

Pollack, William. *Real Boys: Rescuing Our Sons from the Myths of Boyhood*. New York: Henry Holt and Company, 1998.

Postman, Neil. *Amusing Ourselves to Death: Public Discourse in the Age of Show Business*. New York: Penguin Books, 1985.

Powell, Michael. "Taking Blows From All Sides and Weighing When to Punch Back." *New York Times*, February 25, 2008.

Prager, Dennis. *Still the Best Hope: Why the World Needs American Values to Triumph*. New York: Broadside Books, 2012.

Price, Byron. "Cowboys and Presidents." Exhibition text, Autry National Center, 2008.

Pynchon, Victoria. "Brainwashed by Radical Feminists, Working Mothers Claim Happiness." *Forbes.com*, February 20, 2012. http://www.forbes.com/sites/shenegotiates/2012/02/20/brainwashed-by-radical-feminists-working-mothers-claim-happiness/ (accessed August 10, 2012).

Rich, Frank. "Stag Party: The GOP's Woman Problem Is That It Has a Serious Problem with Women." *New York Magazine*, March 25, 2012. http://nymag.com/news/frank-rich/gop-women-problem-2012-4/ (accessed July 27, 2012).

——. "How Kerry became a girlie-man," *New York Times*, Sept. 5, 2004, http://www.nytimes.com/2004/09/05/arts/05RICH.html?pagewanted=print&position=&_r=0p. (accessed September 27, 2012)

Richter, Paul. "White House Sees Long-Term Role for U.S. Forces in Iraq." *Los Angeles Times*, May 31, 2007. http://articles.latimes.com/2007/may/31/world/fg-bushiraq31 (accessed July 27, 2012).

Robin, Corey. *The Reactionary Mind: Conservatism from Edmund Burke to Sarah Palin*. New York: Oxford University Press, 2011.

Romney, Mitt. *No Apology: The Case for American Greatness*. New York: Saint Martin's Press, 2010.

Rosen, Ruth. *The World Split Open: How the Modern Women's Movement Changed America*. New York: Penguin, 2000.

Rove, Karl. *Courage and Consequences: My Life as a Conservative in the Fight*. New York: Threshold Editions, 2010.

Sandberg, Sheryl. Transcript and video of speech at Barnard College by Sheryl Sandberg, chief operating officer, Facebook. May 11, 2011.
http://barnard.edu/headlines/transcript-and-video-speech-sheryl-sandberg-chief-operating-officer-facebook (accessed August 2, 2012).

Sanger, David. "In Courting West Virginians, Bush Speaks of Military Might." *New York Times*, July 5, 2004.
http://www.nytimes.com/2004/07/05/politics/campaign/05campaign.html (accessed September 5, 2012).

Schaller, Thomas F. *Whistling Past Dixie: How Democrats Can Win Without the South*. New York: Simon and Schuster, 2006.

——. "So Long White Boy." *Salon.com*, September 17, 2007.
http://www.salon.com/2007/09/17/white_man/(accessed August 10, 2012).

Schieffer, Bob, and Gary Paul Gates. *The Acting President: Ronald Reagan and the Supporting Players Who Helped Him Create the Illusion that Held America Spellbound*. New York: E. P. Dutton, 1989.

Schorn, Daniel. "The Colbert Report." CBS News, *60 Minutes*, February 11, 2009. http://www.cbsnews.com/2100-18560_162-1553506.html (accessed August 10, 2012).

Schouten, Fredreka. "Political Spending Races toward Record $5.3 Billion." *USA Today*, October. 23, 2008, 1.

Schweizer, Peter. "Don't Punt On Iran," *USA Today*, June 26, 2007, 13A.

Seelye, Katharine Q. "A Passionate Persona Forged in a Brutal Defeat," *New York Times*, March 17, 2012, A1.

Sheehy, Gail. *Character: America's Search for Leadership*. New York: William Morrow and Company, 1988.

Shrum, Robert. *No Excuses: Concessions of a Serial Campaigner*. New York: Simon and Schuster, 2007.

Slotkin, Richard. *Gunfighter Nation: The Myth of the Frontier in Twentieth-Century America*. New York: Atheneum, 1992.

St. Petersburg Times. "The Anniversary of a Miracle." *St. Petersburg Times Online*, February 22, 2005.
http://www.sptimes.com/2005/02/22/news_pf/Sports/The_anniversary_of_a_.shtml., (accessed August 19, 2008).

Stanley, Timothy. *The Crusader: The Life and Tumultuous Times of Pat Buchanan*. New York: St. Martin's Press, 2012.

Stern, Andy. Interview by Bill Moyers. *Bill Moyers Journal*, PBS, June 15, 2007.
http://www.pbs.org/moyers/journal/06152007/transcript2.html

Sternbergh, Adam. "Stephen Colbert Has America by the Ballots." *New York Magazine*, October 8, 2006, 2.

Stewart, Jon. "The Rolling Stone Interview," by Eric Bates. *Rolling Stone Magazine*, September 29, 2011.

Tannen, Deborah. *The Argument Culture: Moving from Debate to Dialogue*. New York: Random House, 1998.

Thompson, Hunter S. *The Great Shark Hunt (Gonzo Papers)*. New York: Simon and Schuster, 1979.

Time Magazine, January 23, 1995, cover.
http://www.time.com/time/covers/0,16641,19950123,00.html (accessed August 7, 2012).

Tomkins, Jane. *West of Everything: The Inner Life of Westerns*. New York: Oxford University Press, 1994.

Traister, Rebecca. *Big Girls Don't Cry: The Election that Changed Everything for American Women*. New York: Free Press, 2010.

Trump, Donald, J. *Time to Get Tough: Making America #1 Again*. Washington, DC: Regnery Publishing, 2011.

Weiner, Rachel. "The Fix." *Washington Post Online*, July 20, 2012.
http://www.washingtonpost.com/blogs/the-fix/post/where-obama-and-romney-stand-on-gun-control/2012/07/20/gJQAwMpNyW_blog.html (accessed August 8, 2012).

Westen, Drew. *The Political Brain: The Role of Emotion in Deciding the Fate of the Nation*. New York: PublicAffairs, 2007.

Wickham, DeWayne. "With Kagan Nomination, Black Leaders Left on the Sidelines." *USA Today*, May 18, 2010, 11A.

Wills, Garry. *John Wayne's America*. New York: Touchstone, 1997.

———. *Reagan's America*. New York: Penguin, 1988.

Wilner, Elizabeth. *Washington Post National Weekly Edition.* September 27--October 3, 2004, 22.

Wolcott, James. "I'll Be So Glad When This Summer of Love is Over." *Vanity Fair*, September 4, 2009. http://www.stimson.org/spotlight/five-myths-about-defense-spending/ (accessed August 10, 2012).

Woods, Jewel. "Bringing Sexy Back: Barack Obama and the 'Triumph' of White-Collar Masculinity." July 18, 2008. http://jewelwoods.com/node/8 (accessed March 17, 2009).

Zizek, Slavoj. *Living in the End Times.* London: Verso, 2011.

Index